PENGUIN BOOKS

FOX ON THE RUN

GRAEME FOWLER was born in Accrington and lived there for the first thirty years of his life. After Accrington Grammar School and Bede College, Durham, where he qualified as a teacher, he became a professional cricketer for Lancashire, winning his county cap in his first full season. The first English batsman to score a double century in a Test in India, he has played in twenty-one Tests so far. He now lives in Cheshire.

Having previously collaborated with Peter Reid, Tony Woodcock and Eamon Dunphy (*Only a Game?*, Penguin 1985), Peter Ball is becoming something of a specialist in sporting diaries as well as collections of quotations: he was co-editor of *The Book of Football Quotations* (1984) and *The Book of Cricket Quotations* (1986). He started *Time Out*'s sports section in 1973 as sports editor and remained there for nine years. Following a spell as a freelance covering northern football and cricket for *The Times*, he joined the *London Daily News* as football correspondent during its brief existence. He has now returned to freelancing, writing articles on cricket and football in the north, where he lives with his wife and three sons.

D1638702

GRAEME FOWLER

with Peter Ball

FOX ON THE RUN

PENGUIN BOOKS

PENGUIN BOOKS

Published by the Penguin Group
27 Wrights Lane, London W8 5TZ, England
Viking Penguin Inc., 40 West 23rd Street, New York, New York 10010, USA
Penguin Books Australia Ltd, Ringwood, Victoria, Australia
Penguin Books Canada Ltd, 2801 John Street, Markham, Ontario, Canada L3R 1B4
Penguin Books (NZ) Ltd, 182–190 Wairau Road, Auckland 10, New Zealand

Penguin Books Ltd, Registered Offices: Harmondsworth, Middlesex, England

First published by Viking 1988
Published in Penguin Books 1989
1 3 5 7 9 10 8 6 4 2

Made and printed in Great Britain by
Richard Clay Ltd, Bungay, Suffolk
Filmset in 10/12pt Palatino Lasercomp

For Margaret and Bob

CONTENTS

INTRODUCTION

PETER BALL

In 1987 Lancashire had their most successful season in the county championship since 1960, finishing second, four points behind Nottinghamshire. A major factor in their success was the return to form of Graeme Fowler, who ended the season as the highest English run-scorer with 1,800 runs in first-class cricket, a total surpassed only by the brilliant young Zimbabwean Graeme Hick.

By general consensus among his team-mates, Graeme was playing better than ever, and the only surprise was his failure to recover his England place, his form not even meriting his inclusion among the thirty-five originally approached for their availability for the winter tours. It was the more surprising because until he sustained a neck injury in a car crash in 1978, which surfaced in 1985 with disastrous effects, he was on the point of establishing himself as a major England batsman. In his first 20 Tests he scored 1,238 runs, more than such prolific batsmen as Geoffrey Boycott (1,134) and John Edrich (1,130) as well as the stylistically more comparable Graham Gooch (983). Included in that total were runs acquired during a series of standing up doggedly to the awesome firepower generated by the 1984 West Indians, and he also became the first England player to score a double century in a Test in India. There were not many easy runs in that impressive aggregate, a remarkable achievement by a player who found himself playing Test cricket only a year after being converted to an opening batsman in 1981 and claiming a regular place in his county side.

In spite of scoring 86 in his first Test against Pakistan in

1982, his appearances were initially sporadic. In 1984, however, at the age of twenty-seven, he played in all five Tests against the West Indies, emerging as one of the few Englishmen to enhance their reputation, never flinching in the face of constant battering from the West Indies fast bowlers, and taking the attack to them well enough to become one of the only two England batsmen to score a century in that series. In the absence of Gooch, who was still serving his suspension for the unofficial tour of South Africa, he was unchallenged as the established England opening batsman, and his selection for the tour of India in the winter of 1984–5 and the subsequent one-day series in Australia was automatic.

Which is where this book begins. Originally conceived as the diary of an average year in the life of an average international cricketer, if such an animal exists, it instead became one of the most dramatic and revealing stories an international sportsman can ever have written. The very beginning should have warned us that the extraordinary was to become the norm, the tour starting with the assassination of Indira Gandhi.

Eventually things returned to 'normal' and, as the tour progressed, Graeme continued to build his reputation. Even as England claimed the series, however, the warning signs appeared. A fever which accompanied a stiff neck meant that they were ignored at the time, but subsequently they could not be, as the calcification of the bone on the old injury ravaged him physically and psychologically. A Test player with a growing reputation when the story starts, he returned from India as a pillar of the England team. In the space of two months he went from an international player to his county second eleven, an almost unparalleled decline.

It was a painful fall, both physically and, as his story reveals, if sometimes unconsciously, mentally. A sensitive, thoughtful man behind the happy-go-lucky extrovert public persona, he found it increasingly difficult to put a brave face on things, but rather than admit to his growing fears, pain and frustration, even to his diary, he bottled it up, finding release in adding a sharp, sometimes hurtful edge to his quick wit. As he now admits, he was not at his nicest during that period. Who would have been? Rehabilitation was not easy either. By the time the 1986 season started he had also gone through the trauma of a broken marriage, but at least his neck problem had finally been resolved. His return to physical health was demonstrated immediately as he began the season with 180 against Sussex in his first game, and the book closes with him looking forward to just concentrating on playing cricket.

However, it was not to be quite as simple as that. His physical recovery was marked, but the psychological scars took longer to heal. His separation did not help, and neither did the chaos at Lancashire, where he was one of four players to captain the side during the season – on one occasion with the official captain and vice-captain, Clive Lloyd and Jack Simmons, sharing the twelfth-man duties, a sight which provoked even *The Times* to asperity.

With that background, his instant recall to the international scene for the one-day matches against Australia was, hardly surprisingly, not a success. As he had remarked the previous season, one-day matches are even more pressurized when you are on trial, and a collision with Gatting which led to his run-out just as he was beginning to settle did not help to press his case. He was dropped from the England team again and was a bystander as England desperately permed a series of opening batsmen in the search for a partner for Gooch.

His county performances were no more than satisfactory – he passed 1,000 runs – but even that was largesse after the previous year. He also played his part in helping Lancashire to the NatWest Trophy final. Their defeat at Lord's was followed two days later by the dismissal of the manager and coach,

Jack Bond and Peter Lever, and with the subsequent resignation of the autocratic chairman, Cedric Rhoades, there was a more congenial background awaiting Fowler when he returned from a winter in Australia.

That his rehabilitation was complete was quickly demonstrated as he thrived in the new Lancashire set-up. He had apparently dropped down the list of selectors' priorities, however, and his record of three centuries and twelve 50s still apparently placed him behind Broad, Robinson, Moxon, Gooch and even Metcalfe in the England opening batting stakes, in spite of outscoring all of them. Unlike Gooch, he was not given the opportunity of the MCC Centenary match to remind them of his worth. At thirty he was clearly enjoying his best-ever season, and it seemed only a matter of time before he forced his way back into the test reckoning.

Nineteen eighty-eight was less successful, however. While Mendis scored prolifically from the start of the season, the other Lancashire batsmen struggled for form as Old Trafford again produced some wickets with varying bounce and excessive movement, and Fowler suffered along with the rest − if not, for a long time, even more so. By the end of the season he had battled his way back to some kind of form, scoring his thousand runs and playing a useful part as the team made up for a generally disappointing season by beating the otherwise all-conquering Worcestershire side in the Refuge Assurance Cup Final at Edgbaston.

Clearly, there are still some pages of Fowler's diary yet to be written. A recall to the test arena now looks unlikely, but no one who reads the story in these pages will doubt his ability to emerge triumphant, for to have survived the traumas of the period revealed in his diary speaks volumes for his character.

PREFACE

When I was first asked to write this book, I did not wholly share the opinion voiced by Peter Ball in his introduction that I was the established England opening batsman. I had been picked when I felt I wasn't in form, and on the other hand I had been left out in New Zealand when I was in form. I had already had a taste of how fickle human judgement can appear at times, and also of how cricket can take you to the top and to the depths, all with comparative ease and often with great haste. So I was always a bit suspicious about the way I was regarded. I felt more like a temporary stop-gap until the 'proper openers' were available. I also felt that my small frame, young appearance, agility and boyish sense of humour positioned me as the 'kid' of the side, and too often I played up to that image. Only if people wanted to scratch well beneath the surface did they discover that I thought deeply about the game which I love and which had already taken me round the world three times.

When we set off on tour, I finally felt that my cricketing adolescence was ending and adulthood emerging. The responsibility of being senior opener helped, and I enjoyed the role. But no one could have foreseen the path ahead, its memorable heights and its depths of despair. Re-reading the book now reminds me how starkly contrasting the two sides of my life in this period were. One side I shall never forget, as it has been better than my wildest dreams. The other side I shall always try to forget. The professional and personal despair has left its marks on me, and I am not sure how I feel about having my life down on paper in such detail for all to see, particularly in such subjective terms. What I wrote in my day-to-day account was true as I saw things then. It was how I thought and felt at the time. Time moves on, however, and I know now how subjective my vision was. Sometimes I got lost and really could not see the wood for the trees. But this book tells you how I felt at the time.

Throughout the period of the book, things happened which still leave tainted memories. Professionally, I feel partly responsible for the demise of John Abrahams. He needed senior players not only to perform on the field, but also to back him up off it and, possibly even more important, remain good friends socially. But due to my personal misery with what I now know as a marriage breakdown, my physical problems and a continual failure at cricket and loss of the ability to cope as a normal functioning cricketer, I abandoned John Abrahams. Not only did I stop supplying my bit of his defensive shield, but I also poked 'sticks' at him to compound his situation. When you have been to the top and then plunge to the bottom, you find out things about yourself which you didn't know before, and you find strengths and weaknesses. John felt the full force of one of my weaknesses and for that I am deeply sorry.

My marriage did not develop as I expected it to, and that chapter is now closed. To say more is not necessary, except that that too was an area where at times my thoughts and behaviour left behind scars. Anyone who is divorced will know my meaning. To all those whose expectations I failed to reach and those whom I deeply hurt, I apologize.

At the end of the day it was a hell of a time, and here it is. Peter and I talked for many hours deciding what to leave out and how to put things. In the end we left nothing out and did not change anything. We became close during this book, because it meant so much to both of us. It is a story that at times neither of us liked, but we had to tell it the only way we could — honestly. So read on.

Graeme Fowler
Perth, Western Australia
December 1987

DRAMATIS PERSONAE

Sportsmen's nicknames are a study in themselves. Some are obvious: the diminutive when the name has more than one syllable (e.g., Cow for Cowdrey or Jeffo for Jeffries); others are less so. Some are clearly designed to signify membership of the in-group — the use of second Christian names (e.g., Clive *Hubert* Lloyd or Paul John *Walter* Allott). Others are obscure and, to confuse matters further, constantly changing. Some are either too vulgar to use, or of too vulgar origins to be explained. The following guide is far from complete, but is offered in the hope that it will make the book intelligible.

Aby · John Abrahams

Al · Al Ormrod

Albert · John Abrahams (after Schweitzer)

Arkle · Derek Randall

Bird · Joel Garner

Bolt · Bernard Thomas

Both · Ian Botham

Brick · Stephen Wall

Bumble · David Lloyd

C D · Pete Owen (Lancashire's coach-driver)

Chaddy · Martin Chadwick

Chopper · Tim Robinson

Chump · David Makinson

Cow · Chris Cowdrey

Didge · Roger Watson

Dog · Bruce French

Domino · Mark Chadwick

Ellie · Richard Ellison

Fido · Bruce French

Flash · Norman Cowans

Fow · Graeme Fowler

Foxy · Graeme Fowler

Fozzy · Neil Foster

Frenchy · Bruce French

Froggy · Martyn Moxon

Gatt · Mike Gatting

Giff · Norman Gifford

Goat · Phil Edmonds

Goochie · Graham Gooch

Goose · Bob Willis

The Great Dane · Soren Henriksen

Harry · Harry Pilling

Harvey · Neil Fairbrother

The Headless Chicken · Tony Murphy

Henri (but pronounced the English way) · Phil Edmonds

Herby Derby · Soren Henriksen

Herman · Neil Foster (after Munster)

Hubert · Clive Lloyd

Jabba the Hat · Mike Gatting

Jeffo · Steve Jefferies

Kippy · Christopher Smith

Lamby · Allan Lamb

Legger · Allan Lamb

Little Pig · Roger Watson

Little Ted · Neil Fairbrother

Lubo · David Gower

Marine Boy · Vic Marks

Nellie · Richard Ellison

Nobby · Paul Downton

Norrie · Peter Lever

Onky · Alan Ormrod

Patto · Pat Patterson

Percy · Pat Pocock

Pigs in Space · Roger Watson

Prince · Chris Cowdrey

Pring · Derek Pringle

Robbo · Tim Robinson

Shaggy · David Gower

Shauny · Steve O'Shaughnessy

Simmo · Jack Simmons

Skid · Vic Marks

Slug · Mark Chadwick

Spiro · John Agnew

Stanny · John Stanworth

TC (Turncoat) · David Gower

Thatch · Ian Folley

Tosh · Chris Maynard

Walt, Walter · Paul Allott

Winker · Mike Watkinson

Yosser · David Hughes

PART ONE

TOURING

OCTOBER

30

Today sixteen cricketers travelled from various parts of the country to London – the party for the tour to India and Australia which leaves tomorrow.

I am embarking on it with mixed feelings, to say the least. And I suspect that several others will share those feelings, especially those who spent the summer in the Test team playing the West Indies. By the end we were shell-shocked from the battering. There was just no respite. It finally got to me in the final Test, when I spent two hours at the wicket ducking and weaving, with survival as the only object. Afterwards I went into the dressing-room and said, 'I don't know why they bother to put the stumps up, because none of those buggers are trying to hit them.' I was really angry, fed up with being an aunt sally.

The West Indies' view of cricket is just on a different plane to ours. I remember saying to Michael Holding one day that he had bowled well, and he dismissed it, saying he hadn't felt right. When I said it had seemed pretty quick to me, he replied, 'No, I had no power.' He expects to be able to knock you backwards with the strength of the blow when you play a defensive stroke, and if he isn't doing that he has 'no power'.

Trying to cope with that was a draining task for us, and one we weren't able to do very well. We lost the Test series 5-0, and the last thing we wanted then was that Test with Sri Lanka, which brought us so much criticism.

India at least won't be like playing the West Indies. But I

have some reservations about the trip. It is a long time away from home, and I'm not really looking forward to it. I'd like to spend the winter at home with Stephanie. This is my third tour, so I'm feeling a bit blasé about it. The first one is a novelty; the second, you know the ropes; and the third is 'another bloody tour'.

This, though, will be the first tour I go on as the established England opener. Chris Broad has been left behind, and Tim Robinson and Martyn Moxon, neither of whom have played in a Test yet, are the other openers in the party, so I should start as the established player. That should mean I get a fair amount of cricket, which is vital. In New Zealand last winter I scored 83 and 104 in the penultimate game before the first Test. I was rested for the last game, in which Chris Smith got 138, and so I was left out of the first Test and from then on there was no continuity, which is so important for a batsman. So that will be different, I hope. And there is no Ian Botham, who is taking the winter off, so that probably means this tour will be different too.

We had the normal routine today: went to Lord's to be decked out in our tour gear, had all the usual press and photographers in attendance, signed loads of bats, had a pre-tour dinner and then went to a hotel near the airport. Tomorrow morning we fly to Delhi.

It is good to have Vic 'Skid' Marks on the trip. I really enjoy his wry humour. In fact, with Percy and Henri the spinners will be an interesting group.

31

We had a good flight. Club class, but I spent about four hours in the galley, playing cards while Jabba ate cheese and peanuts, so it was enjoyable. The B A crew were pleasant. I didn't even see the film between the time in the galley and knocking back red wine.

The arrival, though, was unusual. There was no one to meet us, which was a complete mystery to anyone who has been here before. I expected hordes of people clambering everywhere, but not a sign of anyone, not even the usual official party. We did arrive at 5.13 a.m. local time, which might have had something to do with it. At the hotel, however, we were met by three musicians dressed up as Mexicans, who welcomed us with 'Home on the Range'!

We went straight to bed, and when we woke up it was to the news that Indira Gandhi had been shot by Sikhs. The first reaction was one of incredulity, followed by horror, shock, etc. But as the day went on and tales began to come back to the hotel of what was happening in Delhi, we began to wonder where that left us. Everybody is in chaos. The tour is in limbo. Do we carry on or do we fly home?

NOVEMBER

1

The fighting in the streets is getting worse. Our hotel is away from the centre, so we are a little detached from it. The people from the Imperial Hotel, which is right in the city centre, were evacuated out here because they were virtually under siege. Four of the press, including Graeme Morris, were set upon last night – from all accounts their hard journalism was antagonistic to the locals.

Even from our hotel we can see the city burning. It is eerie, because all we can do is sit by the pool, work out in the hotel gym, relax and wait. As Vic Marks put it, 'While Delhi is falling, so far I've played bridge and had a sauna and jacuzzi.' I reminded him we'd also played chess.

Needless to say, there was no question of practising. We did not do so as a mark of respect; had we practised, we might have encountered some ugly scenes.

We had a meeting with the tour management this evening. A twelve-day mourning period has been decreed, so there is no question of any cricket in that time, which means the original tour schedule is already out. So there is no point in our being here, quite apart from the possible danger. How strong that is is difficult to tell. Tony Brown, I thought, was a bit harsh in putting down some people's legitimate fears, directed in the main at Allan Lamb. The news has come in that two hotels have been burnt down, that Sikhs are being killed, and that the road to the airport is blocked, which does not add to one's composure. But everything is in limbo at the moment, and the mood among the players is fragile, to say the least.

2

We left the hotel to go to the High Commission for a practice on coconut matting. It was hardly first-class practice, but it served to relieve the boredom. Vic was struck in the face trying to catch a skyer from Giff during fielding practice. He didn't need stitches, but he ended up with a sore black eye and a small cut. In the evening we went back to the High Commission again to play darts and snooker and to have a drink with the people there. We got back to the hotel after midnight and had a laugh at the NBC news reporter who was stationed outside our hotel. He was useless, and I couldn't stop laughing at him.

3

Today is the state funeral. Mrs Gandhi is being cremated. Millions of people have gathered, and it is being transmitted live on TV. Half of the commentary is in English, half in Hindi. There is some Hindi on at the moment, so I've got Barbra Streisand playing. I'm watching with Vic. From the window I can see a lot of the lads are trying to pass time away round the pool.

The latest news is that we may be going to Sri Lanka, but it isn't official yet. Frantic negotiations are taking place to try and salvage some kind of tour, but nothing can happen here until the official period of mourning is over; so even if the tour can start with a new itinerary then, there is no point our being here in the meantime. The High Commission think the violence could get worse – the death toll has risen to 700 – and many of the press who have been here before are very sceptical about any cricket being played at all.

4

We travelled to Colombo on the President of Sri Lanka's plane. It was pretty short notice, and we had to split our baggage to take essentials with us, but it was a great relief and not a bad trip – there were only forty of us on the Tri-Star, so we had plenty of room. We managed to get some Swan lager, which made for a pleasant journey. The President, who had been at the funeral, introduced himself, and didn't seem a bad bloke.

We arrived mid-evening and it was pouring down. As soon as we got here we found the bar full of New Zealand cricketers on their way to Pakistan. It was good to see them and have a drink and a chat and swap stories.

The Chinese restaurant here is excellent. It has been a while since I've eaten lovely satays like they do in this part of the world, and I really relished them.

5

Bonfire night in England. We had ours early this year, and I don't think we'll be celebrating it again today. I just hope nothing else happens. Tamils, stay indoors!

We practised after lunch in the hot, steamy, tropical sun. It was great. If perfection had been the goal, then the wickets could have been better, but it was just a delight to be on a cricket pitch again. My 'net' was not of the highest standard. I've never been a good net player at the best of times, and at the moment all the pieces of my jigsaw are not quite together yet. Feet, arms and legs are not synchronizing. I'm not worried about that. My concentration was good, and the heat did not bother me, so I was very pleased. As always with Norman Gifford, fielding practice was superb. He is really brilliant at hitting catches to suit individuals, and organizing everything to suit everyone's needs and abilities.

Tourist's tummy has found its first victim. Froggy Moxon couldn't be with us at practice – diarrhoea and possibly flu as well. Jabba the Hat Gatting was also queasy. In my experience stomach upsets and illnesses of one form or another are a fact of life on cricket tours. They aren't a sign of weakness. Everyone gets afflicted at some stage or other. My stomach always feels delicate, so I try to be careful. But it is a case of what to trust, and what not to, and you never win. And out here I find beer never helps the problem either.

I'm rooming with Nellie the Ellison. He was hilarious in the room last night. First of all he couldn't get the key to work. Then he became hysterical while trying to make a morning call. At 4.15 a.m. he was drinking orange soda. At 4.20 a.m. he felt bloated. He was sitting in his vest and pyjamas when he announced he was hot. So he switched the air-conditioning on and went to bed under all the blankets, fully clothed. Southern logic! He is very good fun, but he snores and talks in his sleep.

The lads are, or appear to be, getting on well together. We are at ease here. That unspoken tension was left behind in Delhi, along with half our luggage. I said goodbye to my suitcase, so I won't be disappointed if I never see it again.

Vic didn't get hit in the eye today! Instead he walked into some scaffolding and has a lump on his head – just above his left eye. Cow, on the other hand, just had about 300 volts shoot through him when he stood on a brass plate in front of the pool door. They had wired it up to the circuit by mistake. If he had been wet coming the other way, it could have been serious.

6

We had to practise indoors in the morning after tropical rain and heavy dew made the ground too wet. The indoor school was like a sauna. I didn't play too badly – my arms and legs are a little more in control. Then lunch – soup and an omelette – and twenty minutes' lie-down, followed by an outdoor net. The pitch was seaming and turning, so it wasn't really a good net for practice, but it was better than nothing. It was very hot.

Walt has hurt his groin and is as sick as a chip. He will miss the first game because of it. I have said no words of solace. We have known each other for so long that we only need to look at each other and everything is said. But that doesn't stop me feeling sorry for him, and him feeling really sick, even though he doesn't say so.

I first met Walter when we played against one another in a Lancashire v. Cheshire Under-15s match. He bowled big 'Dear Alf' inswingers to right-handers, while all I could do was smash it through extra cover. It was the perfect contest. He didn't get me out and I didn't get any runs. Later that year we went on a coaching course together, and we shared a room. And we've been room-mates ever since. I've spent more nights with him than I have with my wife.

We get on like a house on fire. We hardly ever argue – our relationship is so good that we can read each other like a book, and if it ever looks as if there is a row brewing the other person will do something else to ensure that it never does.

He is a very good bowler now. When he came on the staff he bowled those big inswingers, and one of the senior players at the time, a Test player, said, 'He'll never be a bowler in a thousand years.' But he went away for the winter and worked at his game. He got close to the stumps, got his fingers behind the ball, got over the top and pushed it through and he is now regarded as one of the best English bowlers in English conditions. He bowls a very good line and length seven days a week.

He is often a victim of himself, which most of us are from time to time. His physique is an asset, but it is also a hindrance because being a big lad he struggles for mobility, which has caused one or two problems for him. But his size also means that he keeps going all day. He is as strong as an ox, and he will run in all day long and give everything he has got.

I'm not going to mention his batting, but I will say he got a Test 50 before I did. And he was hell to live with after that, because every time I said anything at Old Trafford about batting he'd say, 'How would you know? How many Test 50s have you got?' So I kept quiet until I played my first Test match. I got 86, so then he couldn't speak to me. But it was always in fun. And then in the 1982–3 tour of Australia and New Zealand I actually topped the first-class bowling averages. So I started spouting about bowling, and when he asked me what I knew about it, I asked him how many times he had topped the English tour averages. So I'm just about one up at the moment.

He is one of the best-liked players on the circuit – although not for his appearance on the field. He is quite aggressive, and can be a nasty so-and-so there. He is not afraid to scream and bawl and shout and he doesn't mind getting carried away. But that is all part of his make-up, and off the field he is a great bloke. If people ever take time to have a drink with him, especially when he has been screaming and trying to knock their heads off on the field, they find that out. He is very soft-hearted, has a fine sense of humour and is a great joiner-in. And he is not afraid to laugh at himself. In fact, even when he is in a temper because things aren't going right on the field, he can immediately see the funny side. Then he is torn between laughing and carrying on being mad, which invariably produces a funny reaction from everybody – and eventually from him.

*

The social committee met for the first time – Vic, Cow and me. Vic is chairman again. Our main function is to raise funds for, and organize, the fancy-dress party at Christmas and the end-of-tour party. We also arrange regular get-togethers for the team – games, charades, silly fines which help pay for the parties, all that sort of thing. It's all in the cause of building up team spirit and group unity, but it is quite important, especially on trips like this one, where the possibilities for social activities are often fairly limited and time can weigh heavily if you are just sitting around the hotel.

In the evening I went to the Oberoi Hotel for a drink with Walt and Lamby. A pleasant evening was spoilt by a hustling Geordie, so we left and went back to the Meridien for a meal in the coffee shop.

7

Board President's XI v. England XI, first day
President's XI: 285-7 (P. A. de Silva 105)

David Gower (Shaggy, Lubo, etc.) has now been named T C (Turncoat) because he used to hate nets until he became captain, but now he is always organizing nets. He lost the toss and we spent a day in the field. Everyone is a little rusty after not having had a match for eight weeks. It was hot and steamy, and at the end of the day I am red-faced, red-blistered and tired. And it feels lovely. I'm so glad to be playing again.

Early on the wicket took off, but it soon settled down. Looking back it was an easy first day, as neither the temperature nor their batsmen realized their full potential. One chap, P. A. de Silva, scored 105. He played the short ball well, but I think our bowlers would admit we gave him a little help. Henri bowled well, and so did Percy.

We were hot and tired at the end, and the sight of Swan lager greeting us as we came through the dressing-room door was wonderful. What a treat. Giff was sitting there waiting – he said that if the fans and air-conditioning in the dressing-room had broken he'd have been bloody hot. He's brilliant.

Poor Froggy looked more knackered than any of us. He spent the two previous days in bed, but gallantly came to the ground to help with the twelfth-man duties, and spent the morning on the can. Vic was the fielding twelfth-man, which caused some mirth, while Froggy, Fido and Cow shared the fetch-and-carry duties. They soon found out that twelfth-men rarely leave the field dry, Lamb and I ensuring that. Fido soon learnt, though. He came out at the next interval wearing Legger's sweater. He still got soaked.

There is a good spirit in the team, although many are still finding their feet and are not sure of their place yet. I hope I can help them because when I started I needed help and didn't get it.

I'm glad we've got Frenchy with us as second wicket-keeper. Otherwise I might have to don the gloves, and I don't think I would enjoy that on these wickets with our spinners! I don't think they'd enjoy it either.

Nellie's nocturnal habits are interesting to say the least. He wakes me up every night with his snoring and talking in his sleep. Clad in vest, pyjamas and under all the blankets he often gets up at about 4 a.m. to get a drink because he is hot.

I have tried to tape his ramblings, but have lost too much sleep in the process. Besides, I need all the sleep I can get as he keeps me awake so much. But I can remember a few of his utterings viz.:

'They're all on various levels. Lest we forget.'

'It's all naff, anyway.'

'Yessirree.'

'Fifty pence is the going rate for policemen these days.'

This morning he went for a swim at 7.30 a.m. We were due to leave at 8.30. At 8.15 he hadn't reappeared, so I went down to the foyer. On the way I saw Giff and explained that Nellie was missing. He'd been stuck in the lift for forty-five minutes! Everyone killed themselves with laughter. He appears to be the sort of bloke that if anything like that is going to happen, it will happen to him. He is a lovely man, really harmless and good company, and far from stupid, but he does have his moments.

8

*Second day. President's XI 298-9 dec.; England 261-7
(Gatting 97, Gower 86, Lamb 53 not out, Fowler 1)*

I was caught behind. I'm still rusty!

Went to the High Commission in the evening, and played darts.

9

*Third day. President's XI 298-9 dec. and 134-7 (Pocock 4
for 54); England 273-9 dec. (Lamb 53). Match drawn.*

We fielded most of the day. Percy bowled well and took 4 wickets. I hung on to one catch for the Goat.

Social committee meeting. Several fines exacted: Henri, who is doing a lot of journalism, for staying at the team hotel instead of the press hotel; Percy for continually talking about players only Giff and the manager have ever heard of; Gatt for being fat. And more of that ilk.

I went to the Intercontinental for dinner with Jabba, Walt and Lubo, and had an excellent seafood meal.

10

Sri Lanka v. England, one-day international.
Sri Lanka 178-5. Rain.

'Rain' does not tell the story. I've never seen such a deluge. They'd got to 178 with about 8 overs left when it came down. It was overcast when we went back out on to the field after lunch, and we'd managed a handful of overs when it started. Within half an hour the ground was awash. Even the steps down on to the field from the pavilion were nearly a foot under water. I have never seen it rain so hard for so long at a cricket ground. Bumble, my fellow Accringtonian and a great humorist, would have loved it. Twenty years on the circuit have made him a connoisseur of 'rain stopped play', and he would willingly travel miles to see rain like that to add to his collection.

Ellie snored all night, so I didn't sleep well – pre-match training seemed really hard work after a bad night. It was really humid in the morning, which didn't help. Walt said he never thought he was going to make it to the wicket after three overs. People don't realize how physically draining humid heat is.

At lunch I felt queasy, ate very little and actually fell asleep for ten minutes before going back out, which is very rare for me. I felt much better after the snooze, but the rain prevented me seeing how long the feeling lasted.

All the crowds here clap in unison, which is very disconcerting until you get used to it.

Skid dropped a catch today. It always happens to poor Skid. Still, maybe he won't boast about beating me at Kensington.

People's characters are starting to show after the initial period of feeling our way around. Especially the new boys. Having

Lubo as captain helps, because he is very good at making people feel at ease. Bob Willis used to make things so intense. But maybe I'm just a little older and more experienced, so it seems more relaxed to me. Bob always led from the standpoint that if he put in 100 per cent effort, and if he bowled to his full potential and we fielded and batted to our full potential, we would beat any side in the world. Tactics ended at that. It was 'Follow me, men!'

To an extent that worked. Tactically David is not the greatest either, but the thing is that professionally you have such respect for them that you do feel motivated to do your best. But I find it easier under Lubo, because I don't feel I have to justify everything I do. With Goose I did. If I got out in a certain way, I felt I had to explain why I'd done what I did, whereas Lubo just knows. Which is the difference between being a batsman and a fast bowler. Bob couldn't understand why, if a wicket went down, somebody else would get out and possibly a third would go too. Whereas David understands the frailty of batsmen from time to time. You only need one ball to do something, and because David understands that, there is a more relaxed atmosphere under him as far as I am concerned as a batsman.

What it was like from a bowler's point of view under Bob I don't know. But he could never understand why people couldn't bowl to keep it down to three an over, so I don't know how helpful they found him. He is very mechanical in his approach to the game, and he gets so hyped up. One thing which never ceased to amaze me was that he was so methodical in everything he did, so mechanical, and yet he bowled so many no-balls. Why hadn't he overcome that? It even ended up with him taking a tape measure out and measuring 73 feet 6½ inches at one stage. But it didn't make any difference, it didn't matter where he ran from, his foot always landed in the same place. He was on the borderline every delivery. And that is a professional fault. I can understand that if you are putting a bit extra in you might bowl the odd no-ball. But regularly? Walt has bowled two no-balls in his entire career. Nobody says you have to have just your heel behind the line.

Coming through the ranks at Lancashire and then going into Test cricket under Bob Willis, I found myself going from one dictatorial system to another. David is more relaxed and you can be yourself. He believes that you have got to Test level because you play and train and prepare yourself in a certain way, so you should just extend that into the Test arena. If I say to him, 'Look, I don't want to bat today in the nets, I just want to knock up or have some thrown at me,' he'll say, 'Fine.' He understands that if you are having a problem with one part of your technique you can go in and have a net which looks dreadful to everyone else, but serves its purpose for you. But if I said to Goose, 'I don't want a net today,' he couldn't understand it. I always got the impression that he thought I was looking for a day off. When he ran nets, bowlers had to bowl off their full run-ups, and batsmen had to treat it as if they were in the middle in a Test match.

Because Lubo is so relaxed, you do get the odd day off. You did with Bob Willis, but in a different way. You were there physically, but your brain wasn't. Like taking a horse to water. I used to go in at times sick of nets. Especially in New Zealand, where I was in good nick, but wasn't playing – not selected. I'd sometimes have my knock and just stop every ball. Goose likes to see you playing defensively. If you smashed it back over the bowler's head and it would have gone one bounce for four, he was quite likely to shout out, 'Play properly!' He used to go mad at Both, who of course smashed it deliberately. But if Both had been in the middle and did what he did in the nets to the same deliveries, it would be a world-class innings. But Goose didn't see that; he just saw

Both smashing everything. He didn't like it. He preferred Chris Tavaré or Chris Smith to someone like Derek Randall or me. So I would just go in and block every ball or play little games like seeing if I could play every ball straight back down the wicket or tuck every one round the corner.

I remember a fielding practice on that New Zealand tour. A. C. Smith, who was the manager, had the gloves on and Giff was hitting catches. We agreed among the lads that the first four catches had got to go down. 'No matter who it is, they've got to go down.' Luckily I wasn't in the first four, because in fielding practice I never drop any. Nor does Lamby. Norman Cowans and Skid do drop them in practice – they don't try to, it is just the way they are. So the catches went up. I think Lubo got one, Kippy Smith got one, and so did someone else. And they all went down. The fourth went to Lamby. He really had to work to drop it because it was straight in, but he opened his hands and out it came. Giff went mad, and he and AC stormed inside. Goose was in the dressing-room and he came out and screamed at the top of his voice. So we all trooped in and he gave us the biggest rollicking under the sun – the whole team: 'The most unprofessional bunch of morons I've ever met, no wonder we're getting beaten,' and so on. He went absolutely spare.

This made us laugh, but then at the end there is always a little sting when somebody starts really criticizing you. If it had been Lubo, he would probably have said, 'Right, see if you can drop the next four as well,' and that would have been the end of it. Where Goose became intense, Lubo adopts a more relaxing approach. He isn't a dictator. His approach at the start of the tour was: 'Listen, lads, we'll have a nice free-and-easy ride as long as you play your socks off. If you don't, then things will have to change, we'll have to have compulsory nets, extra days' training and a disciplinary system. It's going to be better if we work hard and win than if we mess about and lose.'

It is quite funny watching him, though. Because from being a person who disregarded discipline – he wasn't a rebel, he just ignored it – he has been put in a situation where he has to determine the framework. And that is why we have called him T C, because he has talked of compulsory nets.

He is brilliant with Tony Brown, who looks as if he flies off the handle at the slightest provocation and comes out with some outrageous statements. On our first day in India he asked us what we thought and we said, 'Well, we don't know, let you know tomorrow' – that sort of thing. But we weren't certain about the situation, and he had got it into his head that Lamby was leading the doubters who thought we should call off the tour, and he just tore into him. 'So you're the ringleader? Here's your passport, you can bugger off if you want,' which was a bit much after he had asked us what we thought.

But if he goes berserk, Lubo takes him aside and says, 'On my previous ninety-three tours it has always worked better this way,' and that quietens him down. But I would hate to think what it would be like with Tony Brown and Goose as the manager/captain duo. We would all be writing lines.

Tonight we have a Grindlays Bank cocktail party and a ball of some sort to attend. It isn't something you look forward to, but there is nothing else to do. So you go and make the best of it, try and find some humour from it somehow.

It is not a very good first tour for Froggy so far. He is going home because his father is seriously ill.

11

The evening turned out very well. I met Molly and Desmond Howes again, and some other delightful people, and really enjoyed it.

We flew to Bombay today, ready to resume the tour proper. Needless to say, meeting up with all our equipment which we had left behind in Delhi proved less than straightforward. There is no sign of my Nikon.

We left Colombo at 2.30. It was a three-hour flight, and by the time we had checked in I felt shattered. I investigated the bars for half an hour, then came to bed, hopefully to sleep.

12

A long day. We had nets at 9.30 a.m. at the Test ground. I batted a little better – I've started watching the ball a bit more. I requested a second net because I felt I needed it. It was warm and humid, but cool compared to Sri Lanka.

Then I went for a wander with Vic. On first impressions Bombay has not got much going for it, and that is an understatement. The poverty is staggering. People sleep anywhere. Limbless beggars seem to be everywhere, and there are millions, or so it seems, of people with nothing to do but gawk.

In the space of two hundred yards from the hotel we were offered a taxi, money-changing, marijuana, hashish and cocaine. Unbelievable. I took some photos of The Gateway to India, and then of an eye-catching little girl of about eight. That proved my undoing. We were pursued for about four hundred yards by her, her mother, her brother and sister all demanding rupees. Vic copped most of the pressure and was embarrassed. Neither of us liked it, but I am harder than he is and so I could shake them off better than he could.

Then we flew to Jaipur, where we play the Board President's XI tomorrow. The flight was slow and crowded, but a couple of bottles of red wine, U2 and Big Country alleviated the pain.

13

Board President's XI v. England XI, Jaipur, first day
President's XI 189-5

Lubo put them in and we fielded all day on a flat, easy track.

14

Second day. President's XI 198-5 dec. (Malhotra 102 not
out); England 275-4 (Robinson 81, Gower 78 not out,
Fowler 28)

The jigsaw problem is still with me. I can't find all the pieces, and those that are there aren't fitting together at the moment. I batted until lunch, then got out driving at a wide one from the left-arm spinner. I got a very thin edge to the keeper, and was so disgusted I didn't walk.

Chopper played well. If we both get settled in, we will be an ideal opening partnership: right-handed and steady, and left-handed aggression. Not a bad combination.

I'm not sure whether that is really me, though. It seems I am categorized in that way — someone who gets on with it. When I'm out playing a shot, everyone says, 'That's how Foxy plays, so he must continue to play that way.' But the truth is that I feel pressurized to play that way because everyone expects it. I know I can play defensively. Sometimes, too, I wish I wasn't an opening batsman. Having seen my technique on video, I'm sure I could score many more runs at number three or further down the order. And fielding at cover can take the edge off you if you open the innings. Charging around like I do for seven hours can cause minor mistakes early on. You only need to be two inches out and that is it for the day. Back to the tent for another boring day beset by frustration and doubts about being selected.

The wicket was very flat, especially after playing at Old Trafford, where they are terrible, so the pressure was on to score runs. I'm not a good-wicket player in some ways. One error, just one error, and that's the end of your day, ended in a frustrating manner. I feel I am forever trying to prove to everyone how good I am, and I suppose I'm trying to prove it to myself even more. I've often thought that one day I shall be a good player, and I think that day has arrived. From here on in I must prove it; otherwise I shall end up with 20 Tests and nothing else.

My wrist has been troubling me; now my groin is sore. I am keeping that quiet, though – someone might think it is an excuse. The only person I've told about my wrist is Bolt. I'm twenty-seven years old and becoming a physical wreck. Sport seven days a week really messes you up.

We moved hotels after the second night here, and are now staying at the Rambagh Palace. It used to be someone's third palace, but was taken away to pay his taxes. I'm sharing a marble room with Henri now. He is an interesting fellow, although we are poles apart. I never know if I'm getting through to him or not. He certainly feels that too. He is not used to room-mates, and so not used to the give and take you have to have. It is probably as hard for him as it is for me. It comes down to fundamentals – for instance, he likes to have a light on right through the night, while I want to sleep. I'm sure he is afraid of the dark. He is certainly very insecure in many ways, as well as nervous. He will never acknowledge the fact, though. He merely converts it into another feeling as a matter of course.

There is nothing to do here. Absolutely nothing. No wonder the press write about our night-time activities – they've got nothing to do either. It's times like this when relationships between players and press sour, and ill-feelings occur. We suspect they resent us being in the limelight while they are ferried around in our wake. But we resent the fact that we have all the slog and the heartaches, together with the publicity, while most of them earn more from cricket than most of us. There must be something wrong with that.

15

Third day. England XI 444-8 dec. (Ellison 83 not out,
Gower 82, Marks 66); President's XI 198-5 dec. and
117-3 (Azharuddin 52). Match drawn

A tame draw. Nellie played really well, and so did Skid. It is amazing how getting near to the domestic double in the summer has given him much more confidence. It is lovely to see it happening. It couldn't happen to a better bloke.

My groin was O K today.

16

Rest day/travel day. Sightseeing followed by flying to Ahmedebad. To take the sightseeing first, we went up to the Pink City of Jaipur and the Palace and fort at Amber. We travelled in a convoy of four hire cars, Ambassadors, which are probably 1950s in design. The factory out here still churns them out. It reminded me of the Austin Hereford my father had when I was ten.

At the Pink City we stopped in a crowded main street. Lepers and deformed beggars of all shapes and sizes suddenly materialized from nowhere to swarm around our cars. Frenchy was not impressed at all. Neither was I, but I have seen such human wrecks before, and somehow the second time the impact is less powerful.

Then from Amber palace we rode up to the fort on an

elephant, four to a beast – it was slightly less scary than some of the driving. I had mixed reactions to the fort. The idea of Moguls building it in the seventeenth century was fascinating, and in its day the palace/fort was undoubtedly something to marvel at, but it was less spectacular than I had anticipated.

I'd like to be able to explore many of the places we have been on my own or with a single companion rather than in a group, and take photographs to my heart's content. I see places far better when my camera is by my side. Even if I don't take any snaps, it still means I look at places in a different light.

On the way back we stopped at a carpet factory. The workers huddled together, squatting on their haunches and weaving away on dusty boards to produce beauty in what can only be described as a dusty stone shelter. Fozzy purchased a carpet. I hope to, myself, when Stephanie comes out to see Christmas in India, which should be different.

Afterwards we flew to Ahmedebad, not one of India's beauty spots. As we drove in from the airport I said, 'It's 8.30 on a Friday night, what am I doing in Ahmedebad?' There were some ribald answers, and Vic said it probably wasn't much different to Accrington. Not true. In Accrington I could be having a pint. Ahmedebad is a dry town.

17

India Under-25s v. England XI, first day
England 216 (Gatting 52, Fowler 19)

Getting bowled out for 216 was a terrible performance really. We won the toss and batted. I was playing OK – in fact I was settling in quite well when the opening bowler held one back and I was caught and bowled. With a little more confidence, or even half an hour later, I would have followed through and hit it over long on. Being cautious does not always help me. What I need to be is positive, whether in defence or attack.

Fancy being caught and bowled by the opening bowler's slower one! It is a different game from fending off Malcolm Marshall and Joel Garner. It may take some while to get over that series. I shall have to start playing off the front foot again as I do when I'm playing well. But against the West Indies if you ever got one which was pitched up, you couldn't afford to miss the opportunity. Out here you can afford to be more selective, and be prepared to let a few go.

18

England 216; India Under-25s 304-3 (Azharuddin 103 not out, Srikkanth 92, Madhaven 64 not out)

We fielded all day in temperatures of approximately 30°C. We didn't field well, and looked far from penetrating with the ball. I couldn't understand why Skid bowled so little – six overs. Nellie bowled really well, though. He looks as if he can bowl long, accurate spells.

Fozzy got Viswanath to nick a ball to Nobby, who caught it. After a huge appeal the umpire said, 'Not Out.' Unbelievable.

As I walked past the batsman, I said, 'Well caught, Nobby.'

The batsman replied, 'That's cricket.'

I said, 'That's cheating.'

Mind you, if I nick it I won't be walking. It is the law of the jungle out here.

19

Third day. India Under-25s 392-6 dec. (Azharuddin 151, Madhaven 103 not out); England 216 and 117 (Fowler 9). India Under-25s won by an innings and 59 runs.

It pitched outside leg stump and I hit it, so I was very disappointed to be given out lbw.

A bad decision and some rubbish shots resulted in our defeat. Disgrace again. Here we go losing yet again. I hope it doesn't continue. I'm sick of playing for losing sides. So I suppose I shall have to make a huge effort to raise my game, and hopefully so will everyone else. There is nothing better than playing for a winning side.

When we lost, a silence of expectant doom filled the dressing-room. Lubo consoled us by saying it wasn't the end of the world. It isn't. A glance outside the cricket ground in India soon brings that message home.

Over the three days on our bus rides to and from the ground, we watched an ailing donkey slowly die on the roadside. It took three days. It was still there when we left the ground this afternoon. People just walked round it as if it wasn't there. Someone gave it some straw as a last meal, but nobody killed it. And it was a main road. The poverty is incredible, but everybody rushes to the roadside to wave at a bus full of English cricketers. All smiling. They must just accept their lot and get on with it. You see whole families living in the open with no more than a raggy shelter if they are lucky. Naked kids, dirty and dusty, yet still smiling.

They are forever squatting as if to recognize their lowly status. They are very slender in bone structure and muscle, which makes many of them look like insects when they squat. It also gives rise to angular features, some of great beauty. With all the squalor, many have beautiful teeth – or perhaps white teeth sparkle amidst all the drabness and dreariness.

There are so many contrasts. From beauty and bright clothes to the poor and drab and deformed. The sheer volume of people must cause headaches. They forever stand and stare.

20

Last night was whisky night in the team room. A simple game of Fizz Buzz, soon simplified further to Buzz, and the evening passed quickly for a change. We probably needed that as a relief. Before that we had sat down for dinner, and there was this dull feeling as the same restaurant served the same food to the same faces round the table. In fact the food in Ahmedebad was not all that bad, but chicken tikka is becoming tedious.

This morning we had an early flight to Rajkot. First impressions of the place give me the feeling that India is at last about to fulfil some of its promise. Rajkot is not dissimilar to Faisalabad, Pakistan, the place made famous by Ian Botham!

In our room at least there is air-conditioning of the box variety. There are purple cupboards on green walls, plaster cracking, dirty and peeling. The corridors are marble. Lunch was two fried eggs and bread, salad and chips. I hope it improves, or I shall disappear down the nick.

21

West Zone v. England XI, first day
England 231-2 (Fowler 116, Robinson 92 not out, Gower
57)

I batted for just over four hours. The wicket was incredibly flat. When you got in it was difficult to play shots, as there was no pace and even less bounce, but it was pleasant to be able to play off the front foot for 99 per cent of the time. Eventually I started to find some form, knowing that I only had the field to bother about, and not myself. I have come to the conclusion that I am not a good starter. I know I can play much better than this, but it began to come together. Surprisingly, I only faced 229 balls.

The best news was that I found an important bit of the jigsaw, and in an unexpected place. One of my well-known mannerisms is to check my grip before every ball. But somewhere along the way my grip had changed, resulting in my shots being slightly open-faced. I turned my top hand back round the back of the bat slightly, and the ball started to go where I wanted. Extraordinary. I had wondered whether my balance was off, whether my eyes had gone (which they have), and all along my top hand was askew. It's a funny game.

Chopper and I ran quite well between the wickets. We can feel where the other scores their runs, and towards the end a nod was all that was necessary. It was a little like batting with Bumble.

Obviously the pressure has lifted from me now that I'm 'in form'. Before today I was the only batsman not to score 50. Now I am the first person to 100, for the second year running. Palmerston North and Rajkot – difficult to imagine more dissimilar places, but the feeling is the same. In January I wanted to score ten hundreds in the year. I now have five, plus two in one-day matches. I never expected to play in all six tests in the summer, though – maybe I'm becoming a reasonable player at last.

In the evening we went to the Gymkhana Club to play the press at snooker and table tennis. I beat the world at table tennis – well, actually the *News of the World*. Paul Weaver. I felt tired, however, and left early to come back to the mosquito haven to try to sleep. God, what a place this hotel is. At least Henri is quiet.

Froggy returned. It's good to have him back with us.

22

*Second day. England 458-3 dec. (Gatting 136 not out,
Robinson 103); West Zone 66-1*

We batted until mid-afternoon, Chopper and Jabba making
hay. Legger blocked solidly. They messed around, with
Vengsarkar bringing himself on to bowl lobs, which made the
whole thing pointless, so we declared. When we bowled, Flash
got an lbw which didn't look out, but an earlier appeal, which
was turned down, had been.

The evening was a social committee entertainment: fines,
charades, silly little tasks. I hope the others enjoy it, because
thinking them all up is hard work.

23

*Third day. West Zone 315-4 (Vengsarkar 158 not out,
Rajput 79)*

Fielded all day. Surprise, surprise, we bowled very well
although the scoreboard doesn't show it. We had three
indescribable decisions go against us. So really we took six
wickets, not three. Dilip Vengsarkar, who strikes me as very
arrogant, looked horribly out of form to start with. It seems he
has played himself back into it.

24

*Fourth day. England 458-3 dec. and 138-7 (Fowler 2,
Patel 5-42); West Zone 393-7 dec. (Vengsarkar 200 not
out). Match drawn*

Dilip got 200, then declared, leaving us to go through the
motions for the afternoon. Chopper and I were spared the task

of opening. I hate batting for no purpose, and as a result I'm hopeless at it. I went in five, but it made no difference. I predicted to Giff what would happen, and although I really tried my damnedest the inevitable happened. When I came out Giff said, 'Told you so.' I had to laugh.

We went to the Doc's house, which is only sixty yards from the hotel, for the evening. Entertainment included local dancing, a palmist and the Doc's whisky. All enjoyable.

I'm beginning to get used to whisky, which I never used to like. I think we drank them dry. The last two nights Froggy and I got sloshed on brandy and coke, which I don't like, but it meant we slept well and were oblivious to the mosquitoes. It's the only way to guarantee sleep in places like this. No hangovers, just enough to send you off into a deep sleep. And having brought my own pillow with me is a great help – the hotel pillows are two inches thick and solid. Giff is playing hell about me bringing my own – he is jealous and I have to guard it carefully.

I joined in the local dancing by playing the drums, as did Flash. The palmist was another experience. I'll leave you to judge for yourself how accurate it is, but he did tell Smudge that he had nearly drowned as a kid, which he had when he was three, and he told Walt that he would have heart trouble in later years, so it was not all good news. His conclusions about me were:

Aggressive. I should make my own decisions and stick to them, as taking advice would not work for me.

I will be happy, famous and rich. Success will come, but only if I work very hard.

I am a genius at acting or music. If I follow either of those I shall be famous at that as well.

I shall have two sons and one daughter.

I shall live into my eighties.

I am a kind person who helps people.

I am successful in business, but financial transactions are fatal for me.

Someone close to me will die in the relatively near future.

I am a powerful character. If one woman leaves my life there will always be another one straight away. I shall never be alone.

I shall always be healthy.

25

We left Rajkot and flew to Bombay in the morning. Back to the Meridien. Our meal allowance starts now. At last!

There were little inconveniences, of course. Our room – I'm still with Henri – was being painted, so we couldn't get in it until 6 p.m. and had to wait in another one. There was one letter waiting for me, but my cameras still hadn't arrived. Where they were, I had no idea. And as Govind (who looks after our baggage) was on a 24-hour train, our bags didn't arrive until the evening. Filling the afternoon was a problem.

I solved it by taking a bath. After Rajkot it was a pure delight: a clean bathroom and loads of hot water. I prefer showers generally, but today I took my stereo in and wallowed for ages, and then had a shower.

The coffee shop also had the delights of good food and a milk-shake. When we arrived in Bombay from Colombo, I thought the food was not too good. Now it appears delicious. And there is a bar here. It isn't exactly pub of the year, but it is O K, and having one at all is wonderful. The beer, though, cannot hold a candle to a hand-pulled pint of Thwaites, my local brew in Accrington. Oh, for a pint of bitter now!

I've got a series of large angry spots on one leg. They look like boils. It's crossed my mind that my diet is unbalanced, and that may be the cause. But out here it could be anything. Who knows? I do know that my thigh pad rubs them.

Morning nets. I middled everything. My readjusted grip feels good; everything feels good. My new bats from Duncan Fearnley are magnificent. The only problem is that they are a bit too heavy. I don't find a heavy bat awkward and uncomfortable, but it slows my wrist movement at the end of the swing down — my hands just don't go through quickly enough. Fido planed some wood off one of them in Ahmedabad and that feels perfect now. I can't use them in games until 1 January, though — my sponsorship from Sondico lasts until then.

In the afternoon Bolt and I did a tour of Bombay by taxi. It cost 47 rupees (you get fifteen rupees to the pound) and lasted about three hours. We saw the railway station, a dhobi wallah (a laundry) and the infamous 'cages' — the red-light area. It was mid-afternoon, but there was no way I was going to get out of the cab in the cages. It just doesn't feel safe to me.

Our taxi driver was called Mohammed Ali! A very pleasant chap, whose English was quite fair — especially when describing the cages. 'Dirty people come from all over to fuck. Then you might have to see the doctor!' he said, imitating having an injection in his arm. He gets paid 120 rupees for a ten- or eleven-hour day, and has to pay for his own petrol out of that.

The mutilated figures got to me today — one little boy with a collapsed spine in particular. He touched me on the arm when we were stopped at some traffic lights. It caught me off guard and I filled up. I could so easily have cried. I do feel emotional today, but I think I should try to keep it in and help others in the party who can't suppress it. That way it also helps me. I didn't give him any money!

At times cricket appears to be so futile, and justifying my life-style and position seems hard. But then I have worked hard to get here, and if I did not make full use of my opportunities, that would be criminal. Not only must I do myself justice, but also I feel a duty to do so for everyone who would gladly swap places with me. And I couldn't give the little lad a new spine, so all I can do is my best in every sense, and hope it might make him smile for a while.

In the evening we went to a reception given by the Deputy High Commissioner. Those things can sometimes be a pain and other times be really enjoyable. This one was enjoyable. I met some interesting people and I had a conversation with the Deputy and another chap about Accrington. He was born there − it's a small world. Of course, the moment you mention Accrington in a conversation the immediate response is about Accrington Stanley.

On the way back we stopped at the Oleroi for a drink. They have a bar too! Two different bars in two days − whatever next? We even have a telephone and a TV in our rooms.

27

Percy Norris, the Deputy High Commissioner, was assassinated this morning, less than twelve hours after we'd been at his house for a party. Everyone was stunned, horrified . . . the words just don't come to describe how we felt.

When the news sunk in, we also began to wonder where that left us. I suppose we shall ride out this storm and every other one until one of us gets shot. Then it will be too late. All the press lads reckon it could be home-time. I doubt it. I shall never believe they are letting us go home until I land in London. The Test match is due to start tomorrow, and after a lot of political toing and froing it will unless someone high-ranking pulls the plug. 'They' think it is better to go ahead. No one seems too concerned with what the players think, although I'm sure that a vote would see a large majority for calling it all off now.

Believe it or not, we practised. I was not at my best mentally. I am in the twelve along with Gower, Robinson, Gatting, Lamb, Ellison, Cowdrey, Edmonds, Downton, Pocock, Allott and Cowans.

So Skid has been left out. Poor Skid. I think he is bowling better than Percy at the moment, and he can certainly bat better. But I'm not in charge.

Froggy wasn't in contention – he still hasn't played a game yet. But Cow has only played one. He does look good in the nets, though.

28

First Test, first day
England 190-8 (Fowler 28)

I'm not sure we were all mentally attuned to the day. Even if you give 100 per cent and try like hell, prior events must affect you – you can't eradicate them completely. This is not an excuse, but it doesn't make matters any easier.

The English press with us feel the whole tour should be called off, their own presence here guaranteeing that any 'events' will get instant worldwide press coverage. That is a large carrot to dangle before terrorists' noses. If they are planning any more killings (or bombings or God knows what), they might as well wait until the English cricketers are in town. We shall be taken notice of then.

I would be a liar if I said that the thought of being shot at didn't cross my mind. If anyone decided to make their political statement by shooting at an English cricketer, after Lubo at the toss I was the next Englishman to be involved on the field. And as receiver of the first ball I was a nice stationary target.

But it didn't happen, of course. Not much did. We batted badly – there were all manner of strange dismissals. From the moment I hit a full toss straight back to Siva, we produced a collection you would not expect to see gracing an England score-card.

Chopper was sawn off in his first Test innings. He blatantly missed the ball but was adjudged caught behind while sweeping. Only Goat batted in a positive manner. We lasted the day – just – but the pitch is a good one, and not to have taken advantage of it means we could be in serious trouble.

Walt was left out from the twelve. I have a sneaking feeling that he is not fully fit anyway, but only he knows the truth of that.

29

First Test, second day
England 195; India 268-6 (Shastri 45 not out,
Kirmani 20 not out)

Anything less than 300 in the first innings of a Test match and you are up against it. So we are struggling. But if we play well enough we can save the game, which is our first target, and even with a bit of luck we could win it. Until Shastri came in and had stands with Kapil Dev and Kirmani, we were well on target. Now they have a good lead, but if Saturday is fruitful for us, we are in with a shout.

I couldn't believe the way their innings started. After 4 overs they were 33-0. I was standing out there thinking, 'What the hell's going on?' It was like the last 10 overs in a John Player League match, rather than a side's first innings in a Test series. And when you've only scored 195, 33 is a lot to give away immediately. In the end 38 of their first 100 runs went through third man. I'd rather defend a little earlier, but I don't have a say in steering this ship, I only scrub the decks.

Our bowlers' inexperience cost us at times. It crossed my

mind that the senior players haven't been passing on their knowledge as much as we might have done – I include myself in that. One or two of the newer players aren't exactly floundering, but I am sure that they are unsure of their own part and how to play it. I don't think even Flash always knows his role, and he is our strike bowler. Nellie the Ellison got caught up in the 'England player syndrome', trying to bowl as he thinks an England bowler is expected to. I've fallen into that trap myself, so I recognized it, and told him to bowl normally. That was why he was selected.

30

Rest day

As a relatively experienced tourist I should have known better than to build my hopes up. The first rule is to keep an open mind (and disengaged emotions) and then in the event of a disaster you are not upset. On tour everything is heightened, and if you build up your hopes and then the outcome is not favourable it can often leave you depressed and distraught. Which was what happened today. I wasted it on a wild camera chase to the Centaur Hotel, which is where some of our mail has been sent. A telephone call elicited the information that there were a couple of letters and a 'parcel' waiting for me. From the description it sounded as if it could be my cameras. I spent one and a half hours in a dusty cab and ninety-five rupees to discover that the 'parcel' was the *Cricketer* magazine. I was very disappointed.

In the evening there was a cocktail party at the Oberoi for Johnny Walker. They have kindly supplied us with whisky. I used to hate the stuff, but now I drink it almost every night. After Indian beer, even soap and water tastes good. Walt and I recognized the Johnny Walker man. We had met at Lord's at the Benson & Hedges final. He had actually made a real pest of himself, and finally we told him to get lost. Now we are eating out of his hand. We were polite, and he greeted us like long-lost friends, although he obviously remembers us as we do him. Touring can be a strange environment. I smile and drink his whisky, although I still think he is a pest, which makes me a two-faced so-and-so. But maybe he thinks I'm a prick – who knows?

DECEMBER

1

First Test, third day
India 465-8 dec. (Shastri 142, Kirmani 102); England
second innings 19-1 (Fowler 19 not out)

'Nip and a punch for the first of the month.'

'Rabbits.'

I always think of Stephanie on the first of the month. She always greets me with the above, and her bony little fists are like needles, particularly at 8 a.m. I thought longingly of Accrington for another reason today as well. My friends Noel and Dave have their birthdays today and tomorrow. Noel was named Noel because he was born on 1 December. He will be out tonight with our gang drinking some lovely Thwaites beer – the lucky so-and-so.

Cricket. Ah yes!

'We never got a sniff until tea-time' – Chopper.

That summed it up. We really hit the depths as Shastri and Kirmani put together a new Indian seventh-wicket record stand of 235. Then Percy took two wickets in two balls, both caught (the second brilliantly) by Legger at deep mid-wicket as they slogged. He received a standing ovation for his second catch and about a hundredweight of fruit from the crowd.

Then we went into bat, and Chopper was sawn off again. This time he did hit the ball, so he was given lbw. He has had a good début! They have this habit of appealing incredibly well. If the decision goes against them, they all appeal again instantly. Chopper has been given out on the second appeal twice in the match. That pressurizes umpires at the best of times, and the Indian umpires don't fill you with confidence, to say the least. On two occasions the ball ricocheted off my thigh pad through the clutching hands of close fielders for a single. On both occasions when I got to the other end I was asked if I had played it before he signalled leg byes. If he can't tell that, what chance have I when one goes to hand and they all go up for a bat-and-pad decision?

That was at one end. The bloke at the other end gave byes when it hit my leg. Help! But Jabba and I survived. Tomorrow is going to be a long day.

<u>2</u>

First Test, fourth day
England second innings 228-7 (Gatting 136; Fowler 55)

Dave's birthday. Two piss-ups in two days, and here I am stuck in this place. Enough said.

Batting: I was batting well enough to bat all day, but the umpire had other ideas. We saw the openers off, and then the work began. After the West Indies, the pace of Kapil and Sharma is hardly heart-stopping. They are good bowlers. Kapil's record proves it, and in a Test match no one is a fool. Besides, even a fool can bowl a good knacker every now and then, and you only need one! But the real test was against the spin. They have Siva, the leg-spinner, Shastri bowls slow left arm, and Yadav off-ers, so they have the whole range.

It was turning slightly for Shastri and Yadav, more for Siva, who was going round the wicket into the rough. We didn't need to score runs as much as just to occupy the crease. I'm always associated with being free and going for my shots, but I can block as well as anyone else. At heart I'm a professional, and I was saying to myself, 'Organize yourself, keep it ticking along if possible, but don't get tempted into anything risky. Bat all day if you can.'

The whole day I never looked to drive once, as they had four round the bat the whole time. If you move all your weight forwards on the point of impact and it catches the edge, then it will carry to one of the catchers. If you play dead-bat with a loose grip the ball spins off, but even if you edge it it won't carry to them because there is no strength from you behind it. Whereas even a half-volley slightly mishit can get you into trouble if it is turning, however slightly. Off Siva a normal defensive shot ended up at leg gully, which made it look to onlookers as though he was on top. In fact the ball was going where I wanted it to. So driving is out unless you are absolutely sure — why give yourself an 80 per cent chance of scoring a run and a 20 percent chance of getting out when you can defend with 100 per cent security?

Normally when a bowler goes round the wicket, I close my stance slightly to make it appear as if he is still coming at me from the same angle. But against Siva, as it was turning quite sharply on occasions, closing my stance would only have served to tuck me up. Hands and arms have nowhere to go, except into my stomach. By opening up my stance they could pass freely in front of my stomach, giving me the option of playing it or not, and even of pivoting round the ball as it passed by. It might look ungainly at times, but it works!

Sometimes batsmen move quickly if a quick bowler is on, and slowly if a slow bowler is on. I find I play better if I use my speed to my advantage. I can get into position quickly and then play the ball as late as possible, or adjust my position if my first step was wrong, by moving quickly. In doing so I can leave my choice of shot to the last second, let the ball come to me, and so play more safely. I'd also decided to play off the back foot where possible. That meant I could watch the turn and play it or not as I wanted to without being committed to the front foot on that 'in-between' length, when lunging at a ball not quite up to you adds strength to the shot, so that if you edge it it might carry to one of the vultures waiting for a slight error. I find it is easier to adjust from back foot to front than the other way round.

It was all going along quite nicely, and then I was sawn off. In my professional career it was the worst decision I have ever had. I was given out lbw to a ball bowled round the wicket which pitched well outside off stump. I played a shot and it hit me outside the line of the off stump. The reason the umpire gave the decision was that the over before they had had a better appeal turned down. That wasn't out either, but it was closer, and Siva, the bowler, wept. Gavaskar consoled him, and so did the umpire next over. It seems like losing your driving licence: a totting up of points and then bang – 'You're out.'

Out of our first six batsmen, five of the decisions were diabolical, mostly by Swaroop. It is a shame. After all the pre-match drama and then batting badly in the first innings, we still had a chance to salvage the game, but they have almost certainly stopped any chance of our doing so now.

3

First Test, fifth day
England second innings 317 (Downton 62); India second
innings 51-2. India won by 8 wickets

It's a cruel world. We bowled very well, but 48 is no total to bowl at. We did salvage some pride, though, because Norman put the shits up their batsmen. I wish he had more confidence in himself. Because of the way Percy and Downton batted and then the bowling, we came out of it with more optimism than the scores might suggest. In the end we felt the umpires swung it. We have asked for Swaroop not to umpire another test.

Even our press men could not tell if the decisions were dicey. Only we know how bad they were. But if we tell the truth no one will believe us, because it sounds as if we are complaining and making excuses. Well, we are complaining, but we aren't making excuses. The decisions were awful, and they did deny us any chance of saving the game.

Now we are one down. And in a few weeks no one will remember the circumstances, just the result.

4

International sportsmen bundled on to a corporation bus for what promised to be a bus ride of over three and a half hours to Poona. Walt had to stay behind — he isn't fit. He is still having trouble with his back. Percy was also left behind, because Skid will play in the one-day internationals as a better batsman. So too was Froggy, who still hasn't had a game, and French.

They might have been the lucky ones. We were led to believe it was a scenic route. I missed the scenery because I fell asleep. Halfway we stopped at a place called Stud: the middle of India and there was this Mexican ranch with gaucho cowboys as waiters. They can't be serious! We still ate our usual: omelette, baked beans, mineral water, tea and toast — the standard safety foods. It seems strange given the huge role curry has in the county cricketer's diet, but none of us trust the food, and we have good reason not to.

At this point of the journey the air-conditioning in the bus broke down. Brilliant!

I took a bit of stick when I got on the bus for bringing my own pillow with me. After two hours, more than one or two were trying to borrow it or wishing they had had the foresight to do the same. Fortunately, Bisheri Water (we are sponsored by Thums-Up), Gold Spot and Limca were in plentiful supply in a cold box at the front of the bus. Govind, the gopher for the world, was bus-wallah today.

After the journey we had more nets. I can't say I wanted a net, nor can I say for sure that it did me any good, though it did me no harm. And if it did someone some good, it was all worthwhile. It is a team game.

We need to win tomorrow and, boy, do we know it. Criticism flows too easily out of some pens and mouths, and a win would help to stem the tide. Besides, we know we can beat this lot, but we need to prove it to ourselves as well.

<u>5</u>

First one-day international
India 214-6 (45 overs); England 215-6 (Gatting 115,
Fowler 5)

The wicket looked painfully flat. The outfield was very barren, with odd tufts of grass here and there, and from the edge it too looked flat, but when you ran across it, or watched the ball skidding over it, it quickly became obvious that it was not. No one-handed pick-ups on that; it was a case of 'two hands and bollocks behind it', to use the old phrase.

We won the toss and inserted. By so doing we opted for three and a half hours in the field, which is incredibly long for a game of this type. The nervous energy you expend just being on the field is incredible, even before you move for a ball. But under the conditions we were quite happy to restrict them to such a total. I felt Dilip Vengsarkar batted for himself to get a century, and that didn't hurt us.

This game forever baffles me. Some days even just taking

guard feels right. The stance is comfortable. You instinctively feel where the fielders are. The ball looks larger, and 'picking it up' from the bowler's hand poses no problems. Today was such a day. And what happens? I got into position too quickly for a full-length ball on leg stump and hit it gently to mid-on for a catch. Shit! Other days I can feel horrible at the crease and get runs. It doesn't make sense. It seems there are no rules to be obeyed.

As soon as I took my pads off I felt ill and watched no more of the game. I lay down on a bench in the dressing-room. Only the roars of different kinds indicated runs or wickets outside until I fell asleep, hot, wet and weak. The bus journey was a nightmare for me. I awoke in Bombay wringing wet through and still feeling an uneasy sort of tiredness. A very scenic journey in the dark! I can't imagine many international sportsmen putting up with it, but then cricket is a unique sport, played in a unique fashion. But I never dreamt it would be like this when I left college and started with Lancashire 2nd XI in 1978.

The ever-exuberant Jabba was jubilant throughout the trip back, however. Understandably. He'd scored his second international 100 in forty-eight hours. A great effort, and I'm thrilled for him. The press say he has 'arrived'. He's been here for years, and their pressure has been partly responsible for the delay in getting the evidence of how good he is. It is a good job he comes from Middlesex and not elsewhere, though, or he might not have been persevered with! But I think we might still not have seen the best of him.

6

Nets, then the team for the three-day game against North and Central Zones is announced. Froggy makes his début — a record thirty-eight days into the tour. No wonder he said he seems to have had a million nets. Poor Fido also gets a game at last. The lot of the second wicket-keeper is awful. He thinks he is just a paid skivvy. It is a terrible test of your mental resilience, because if you can't keep mental stability you could flip completely.

I'm having a game off. Thank goodness. I need a rest.

7 · 8 · 9

North and Central Zones 186 and 176-3; England 377
(Robinson 138, Cowdrey 70, Moxon 42). Match drawn

One trouble with not playing is it means perpetual nets. We have to be seen to be doing the right thing. I'm lucky in that I am a great 'net' person anyway. I always have a net whenever possible, because I feel they do me good. Not everyone is the same. Some people positively hate them.

The other trouble is that it gives you more time to be introspective. Very often sportsmen become blasé about their life-style, their surroundings and the places they visit. But that can be a necessary response. If you reflect too hard on where you are and what you are doing, the pain might strike the back of your eyes as you realize you'd rather be elsewhere with someone else.

When I married Stephanie, our prospects were of a Lancashire first-team player and a biology teacher. Within twelve months I was waving goodbye wearing my England touring blazer. Now after over three years of marriage I am on my third consecutive tour, and she is a college lecturer. Our lives have changed utterly. This year I have spent over seven months in hotel rooms; she has had over seven months on her own. In the remaining five months, I have probably spent two months seeing her night and day, and the rest of the time at home consisted of leaving one another at 8.15 a.m. and not meeting again until 8.30 or 9 p.m. Not exactly what we envisaged when we got married, expecting a fairly normal existence and the constant companionship of someone we loved. Is it any wonder that sports marriages are always under pressure?

I do miss her. I try to keep my feelings repressed, which is the way to cope through tours anyway. I never allow myself to look forward to anything, because that means you can never be disappointed. Taking everything at face value means relative safety, and so does just doing the everyday things. Eat, sleep, drink, watch and play, and no more. It is a strange existence, strange to have to catch your emotions, bottle them and throw away the bottle, but it helps you to cope. For me it is essential. But at the back of the mind there is always the nagging knowledge that I am missing her and my home life.

And little things catch you off guard. Out here the day's fielding can be brightened for me by a passing butterfly. There are some beautiful species flying around, the type you see adorning lounge and hallway walls in England. But every time I see one I think of Stephanie, because she adores flora and fauna. She is annoyingly well informed on the subject, but her love of nature instantly comes to me when I spy anything. She would love to see the butterflies, and I would love her to see them and share her excitement. But these little subliminal reminders catch you off guard and leave you with a lump in your throat or a smile trying to hide over-full eyes.

When I was a kid I would never have thought that an England cricketer could cry for any reason. This one can when the stream builds up and gets too powerful. Some day I might know if I am soft, or whether I have taken matters in my stride and coped. Out here I am Foxy the England star, not Graeme the husband. The latter is stored away, because letting him out of the bottle is too painful. But this England cricketer is not superhuman. He is an Accrington lad who has achieved the top level in cricket. I am still just an Accrington lad, though. Thank God!

10

After the flight was delayed for two hours, we flew to Delhi. I still felt a little ill, so didn't practise. As it turned out the team only did training exercises because there was no time for a proper net after the flight delay, so I didn't miss anything.

11

Nets again. They were rubbish as well. The actual practice surface was not very good. But still, looking at the test wicket, that might be the right preparation. It looks like a loose mosaic which might not last five days. You can never be sure, though, and if you start thinking that way you can often psych yourself out of the match before you start.

The theme in the team meeting was a positive approach: if it is a bad wicket, that will be in our favour because we are prepared for it. Also, we aren't a bunch of prima donnas like them, and we will buckle down and battle through.

12

Second Test, first day
India 208-6

Skid was left out of the twelve, so it was the same team as for the first test. We lost the toss, which didn't seem too clever in view of our suspicions about the wicket, but we did well. Ellie got Gavaskar in his first over, and although we should perhaps have restricted them a bit more to start with, our performance was quite professional. I had very little to do in the outfield, which was just as well as I still don't feel exactly tip-top.

There was one funny incident. Shastri lapped Percy for two behind square. I chased it to deep square leg, threw the ball back and was returning to straight mid-wicket when Percy bowled the next ball. I was still ten yards out of position when Shastri took a swipe and slotted it straight to me for a simple catch. Had I been correctly placed it would have gone for four!

They were six down at the close. A sharp burst in the morning could do us a lot of good.

13

Second Test, second day
India 307 (Ellison 4-66, Pocock 3-70); England 107-2
(Robinson 53 not out, Fowler 5)

The short sharp burst lasted until after lunch, even though Ellie got Kapil Dev, their best remaining batsman, with his second ball of the morning. Yadav and Siva put on 49 for the last wicket, which we could have done without.

I think I could be trying too hard, too eager to do well. I played at a wide ball and was caught low down at second slip. It swung away at the last minute, but my shot was a little too loose. That left us at 15-1, and then Jabba, after appearing to be all set for another century, was out just before tea, pushing forward, the ball rolling back on to his stumps. So at 60-2 we hadn't had the brightest of starts. But Chopper has perfect patience and played well. He looks really at home out here.

When I got back into the dressing-room I felt ill again. I spent the evening alone in my room, watching *Flashdance* and *Rough Cut*. My college stomach is back with me, I didn't feel well at all, and I fear I've lost about half a stone in weight, which I can't afford.

14

Rest day

I felt better – O K, but not great.

Spent the day with Percy, Lubo and Walt.

We went to the zoo. It was shut.

We went to the Old Fort. It was boring.

We went to the Red Fort. It is now just a glorified shopping arcade.

Oh, well.

Walt's back is very sore. Knowing him as I do – we have roomed together for twelve years now – I can tell it is bad. He isn't a malingerer. It could be the iron bird for him, poor sod, but at least he'll be home for Christmas.

15

Second Test, third day
England 337-5 (Robinson 157 not out, Lamb 52)

The day's events virtually passed me by. I felt bloody awful. I survived through our morning training exercises and then the morning session – long enough to see Legger and Lubo get sawn off. Legger was picked up in the leg trap off his pad, with his bat miles away from it. Lubo was lbw. Ha! But at lunch I ate something which caused my stomach to flare up again. I slept through Chopper getting his hundred. I even slept through everyone clattering in and out at tea-time. I woke up shortly afterwards, wet, hot, dizzy and my stomach very sore. Here we go again.

Walt was under the weather too. He was due to take a fitness test on his back, but stayed in bed with a heavy cold or flu. It gets you all ways out here.

I was delighted for Chopper though. He deserves every run and all the praise he gets.

16

Second Test, fourth day
England 418 (Robinson 160, Downton 74); India second
innings 128-2 (Amarnath 57 not out, Gavaskar 51
not out)

I didn't go to the ground until after lunch, when we were due
to field. It was obvious, though, that I was in no condition to
play, and I was bundled off to the High Commission Hospital
along with Walter. He had failed a fitness test on his back in
the morning, so it was decision day for him. I didn't think
there was any doubt about what the outcome would be. It
was only a matter of time before the medics confirmed his
inward fears and my reading of his face. I got some pills, he
got a ticket home. I went to bed, he fell into a bottle of
whisky. Poor Fox, poor Walt.

Meanwhile Chopper had got 160. Great, brilliant, well
played. Thanks to him we can beat this lot. Come on, lads.
Even through the fever I get an adrenalin surge thinking about
it.

Touring is a peculiar life. One of us is totally depressed.
One is ill. One is totally elated. And a few are bored rigid.
Such a funny way to live.

17

Second Test, fifth day
India second innings 235 (Gavaskar 65, Amarnath 64);
England second innings 127-2 (Fowler 29). England won
by 8 wickets

I'm spending the morning in bed. My stomach is still bad. I
haven't told them how bad, because if I do they might think
I'm weak, so I've kept quiet about it. If we have to bat, I shall

go down to the ground, depending on the situation. I watched the early stages on TV, but then the transmission went off, and I've been trying to follow it on the radio. Not very successfully — the commentary is in Hindi. But Percy and Henri have been bowling well.

In the afternoon the phone call came out of the blue from Bolt. 'Get down to the ground, they are eight down.' Brilliant.

I caught a taxi down there. It cost me twenty-two rupees and Bolt eight — I didn't have enough change and had to rush into the ground and borrow some. By the time I got there they were nine down. Walt made his last cricketing contribution to the tour by coming out with me to the nets. He was to throw a few at me to waken me up fully and to loosen me up as well. He took the job too seriously. His second throw hit me full on the shin. 'Not so —ing fast, you —!' Three throws later they were all out! Christ, here goes, I've got to bat!

We needed 125 to win and I felt like death warmed up. Lubo was ready to open and let me bat down the order. But in these circumstances I thought that if I am fit to bat at all, I was fit to open. Besides, when I sat down the only effect was to make me realize I was ill, so I thought that maybe for a while the adrenalin would take over. And we needed a quickish start, because they were only going to have to bowl around 32 overs, so we needed four an over.

In the event we cruised it. Chopper and I put on 41 in good time. By the time the final twenty overs started we only needed 67. The job was almost done. I was out immediately, caught off bat and pad on the offside, but Jabba and Legger put on 30 not out apiece to give us a brilliant win. It was made by Chopper, Percy and Henri, who returned great figures. They were truly match-winning performances.

I had never felt so ill on a field in my life before. Adrian Murrell said he took a photo of me looking like the most ill man in the world when I was walking off after getting out. I was too sick to join in the liquid celebrations afterwards, but my Tagamet pills seem to be working and I felt better as the evening went on. Later on I had a glass of beer at the High Commission and a Mars bar, which tasted like the most wonderful delicacy ever to pass my lips.

Walt flew home at 2 a.m. It sums up the nature of touring that I, and I'm sure several of the others, had mixed feelings about it, feeling sad for him and envying him at the same time. It is awful not to be able to see the job through; but at the same time the idea of going home, especially at Christmas, is really appealing. I shall miss him. We all will. And he will miss us. I hope he gets right quickly. He is too good a player to be kept out of the game with a back injury.

He gave me his Bovril, his two Walkman extension speakers, and 400 rupees. Merry Christmas, Walt!

18

8 a.m. flight to Gauhati. It is the most scenic place we've visited so far, very lush and green. Gauhati is in Assam, where the tea comes from, and, we quickly discovered, now a place of high security because of its position right in the north on four borders. We set out for a peaceful walk, only to be picked up by the police for security reasons. In spite of it being a day off, they dumped us at the ground — where the crowds mobbed us. The police have a perverse sense of security.

The electricity failed twice, which can be awkward as it gets dark at 4.30. Overall, the hotel is only marginally better than in Rajkot, but the food is good. I am eating a lot in an endeavour to put back my lost weight, so that my clothes might start fitting again.

I roomed with Percy right though Delhi. He is brilliant. The toothpaste was always on my brush and my bed turned down waiting for me. He empties the laundry bags for me. He puts his own laundry in the bin, whereas I always throw mine on the floor, and the sight of it on the carpet annoys him, so he picks mine up too. He fills in the breakfast card at 6 p.m.

Which all sounds a bit prissy, but he isn't at all. He is a terrible practical joker, fruit-throwing escapades and plastic dog turds on omelettes abounding. He makes me laugh even when I'm ill. He has an exuberant, almost naïve enthusiasm for life and for cricket. A very lovely man.

Now I'm rooming with Nobby, who is also good company although completely different to Percy. At least our musical tastes are more compatible. Percy only listens to Barbra Streisand, and thinks that Frankie Goes To Hollywood should stay there.

Only six days until Steph arrives.

<u>19</u>

East Zone v. England XI, first day
England 277-8 (Fowler 114)

Lubo and Robbo took a week off to go tiger hunting in Rajasthan, so Gatt took over and did the right thing – he won the toss. The wicket was river-bed silt – low and slow. It was wet in patches too. It turned from the first ball, but slowly.

Robbo's absence meant that we had a Lancashire–Yorkshire opening partnership, and a successful one. We put on 84 before Froggy was given out caught off bat and pad off Dilip Doshi on the stroke of lunch. I didn't think he'd hit it.

I carried on. I batted for just over four hours. It wasn't a wicket which was conducive to playing shots at all – if it had bounced it would have been hard to play as well as we did. But somehow I felt at ease mentally, and prepared to bat all day. Some days you know after twenty minutes or so that you are set for a long knock. Today was one of them, and I had the pleasure of batting with Froggy, Legger, Gatt, Prince, Henri, Skid and Nobby.

I ran Henri out. My call, but it was not wide enough of mid-wicket, and he made a direct hit. As we crossed Henri saw he was struggling and shouted, 'Oh, you bastard!' I apologized twice – once personally, and once on the air when I was being interviewed by Peter Baxter of the BBC. I like being interviewed, because it means they know you had a good day. It also means that family and friends at home know you are still alive and doing well. They say they find something soothing in hearing a voice, even if it is only on the radio.

Medical report: my ankle is still sore where Walt hit me throwing the ball at Delhi. My stomach has stabilized thanks to Tagamet. But my hands have gone prickly and peeled. They did that in Australia too.

It is either the water or nervous eczema. Bolt says it is the water. Does he know?

I broke another bat at Delhi due to the persistent low bounce. I hope Walt remembers to communicate with Duncan Fearnley for me. The last thing I want to have to worry about are my bats. Mind you, Walt will be getting merry in Bakers restaurant/wine bar now, so he might not be thinking about my bats at all. Lucky so-and-so.

Five days until Stephanie arrives. I wonder how big Smithy, our puppy, is now.

20

Second day. England 290; East Zone 117 (Marks 4-48, Edmonds 2-25) and 3-0

They looked a poor side. Henri bowled well, Skid took 3 wickets in 9 balls, and the middle order collapsed.

21

Third day. East Zone second innings 52 (Edmonds 4-13).
England XI won by an innings and 121 runs

Gatt's inspired field placings helped Herman get 2 wickets in 2 balls. At one stage they were 12-3 and three catches had been put down. I dropped a diving chance at gully, Jabba put one down at first slip and Lamby dropped a chap first ball at third slip. He was on a golden pair as well, but ended up top-scoring with 30. Fozzy and Flash started the decline and East Zone had no will to fight it out for two days, especially after being 12-3 and 17-5. We bowled them out on the stroke of lunch.

Their captain, Dilip Doshi, was as gracious in defeat as he would have been in victory. He is a good bowler and a gentleman. He has an undying love for cricket and I have a lot of time for him. At one stage he bowled a short ball and I tried to force it through mid-wicket. It kept low and a single through square leg resulted. As I got to the other end I said, 'You want it to bounce, I'd like it to bounce. This wicket is no good to anyone really.'

'I know,' he said, 'but I love to bowl on anything. I just love bowling.'

I was named man of the match, and 3,001 rupees went into the team pool. When I was presented with the cheque, I was told the one extra rupee was for luck. It is deemed unlucky to end a figure with a zero – a delightful local custom. But they mean it when they say 'good luck', it isn't an empty phrase here.

The umpires in this game were very good. I had complete faith in them. But pressure is a funny thing, and I would like to see them in an important session during a Test match.

I'm not normally a betting man, but when Henri wagered

100 rupees that Kapil would play in the next Test, I took the bet. Partly for a laugh, but also because it would be good for our morale if Kapil is dropped. The background to that is that the newspapers have reported that he has been dropped, solely on cricketing grounds. I didn't see it because I was in my darkened hotel room at the time, but his performance in the second innings at Delhi was totally irresponsible according to everyone who was there.

Certainly the Indian team are already arguing among themselves, and a conflict between Gavaskar and Kapil is widely rumoured. Power and being put on a pedestal can do strange things to many men. Some believe that they are bigger than the establishment which has bestowed a certain status on them. The truth behind the rumours will undoubtedly prove even stranger. But if Kapil is left out the consequences are potentially stormy. We have already heard that there will be demonstrations at the match in Calcutta if Kapil is not included.

The win gave us a free afternoon. I spent it on the river-bank and also being peddled around the town on a bicycle rickshaw. At one point I had to disembark as the slight gradient proved too much for our spindly driver.

22

We flew to Calcutta one day early, a result of winning a four-day game inside three days. Our reward for that was to be offered an extra day's nets. That seems to me ridiculous when we have only had two days not either travelling or playing. If the captain had been here, I'm sure that would not have happened. But the manager apparently cannot comprehend what touring is like as a player, and doesn't realize that an extra day off will do us more good than nets.

Spiro arrived as Walt's replacement. He brought me a

Duncan Fearnley bat with him. Hooray! Well done, Walt! Spiro was my room-mate for the night.

23

I went for a voluntary net today, so as to be able to pick Steph up tomorrow. The nets were a complete waste of time. They were too wet, and the only people ordered to net were those not playing in the last game, plus the tiger expedition.

The social committee finalized the entertainment for the Christmas Dinner – or at least tried to. Mrs Pocock and family and Mrs Fowler will be present at the fancy-dress lunch, so pre-meal entertainment and the meal 'bits' had to be made suitable for a family show. The fancy dress and the beauty contest will be judged by the ladies and kids, although we will help on the beauty contest.

Had Gatt as room-mate for the night.

24

Picked Steph up at the airport in the ubiquitous Ambassador car. We spent all day and night doing nothing but relaxing and talking about home – how big Smithy (the dog) is now, and all that relevant chit-chat. Steph brought all sorts of presents out, including chocolate. Mmm.

We ate in the Polynesian restaurant. Not a bad meal.

25

Slept very well after the Polynesian meal.

Christmas Day. Drinks with the press – Crash (Lander) and Morrow (Morris) were waiters.

Fancy-dress competition winners: Fozzy as an Indian woman; Legger as an Indian peasant.

Prizes: Herman got a bottle of Henri's Black Label Scotch – the only thing was that it was filled with cold tea. Legger got talcum powder, which he promptly poured over Flash.

Beauty contest: won by Henri. His prize was a plastic telephone. Quite apt.

Christmas lunch: Soup (oxtail?); turkey, roast potatoes, sprouts, peas and carrots; mince pies and Christmas pudding; red and white wine.

Quite tasty, but all very cold. Damn.

Toasts: the Queen, cricket, absent friends (loved ones and Walter).

26

Morning nets and then a flight to Bhubaneswar, where we were given a fairy-light welcome. Millions of locals turned out just to see us arrive. The hotel put on a cocktail party and buffet for us. The room only cost me 221 rupees for Steph. It has a huge bed.

I'm sure when I return home I shall treat every waiter and bartender as an absolute imbecile. But when you order an omelette and baked beans on toast and it arrives on two separate plates, what can you do but laugh or cry? That isn't the worst. In Delhi Lubo ordered four fried eggs and bacon. Result: four plates, each containing two fried eggs and bacon.

27

India v. England, second one-day international
India 252-5, 49 overs (Shastri 102, Srikkanth 99);
England 241-6, 46 overs (Gatting 59, Downton 44
not out, Marks 44, Fowler 15). England won
on faster scoring rate

A really long day. We left the hotel by 7.45 a.m. for the hour's drive to Cuttack. It is hard to prepare yourself mentally for a one-day international, or any other game of cricket for that matter, when you sit in a coach staring out at cultivated fields full of workers. A new culture in front of your eyes is hardly conducive to single-minded thoughts on cricket.

All along the route we were greeted with big, white, cheesy grins and waves of excitement. A lot of the waves were formal salutes familiar to us from programmes like *It Ain't 'Alf Hot, Mum*. At times they do look completely foolish to our eyes, head-wagging, saluting and shouting, 'Hello, Sah'b'. You do wonder though who is taking the mickey out of whom. So comical is their English that, without knowing it, many of us slip into similar speech patterns.

Lubo won the toss and put them in. After 30 overs they were approaching 180-0. Catches eluded us. One six went just over my head at deep mid-wicket, and another I could only tip over the bar, both off Skid. So close, yet not close enough.

But in front of a packed, capacity crowd we plugged away like true professionals, and finally Jabba made the breakthrough when he had Srikkanth given out lbw for 99. Srikkanth had played really well up to 60, but from then on he seemed too aware of his hundred, as did Shastri. It was incredible to watch. At 180-0 we were facing the possibility of chasing 300. They had the ideal platform to wreak havoc playing their shots, having so many wickets in hand. But if anything, they decelerated for the last 20 overs, which only produced about 70 or 80 runs, and Skid nipped in with 3 for 50 at the death.

I had always thought Shastri was a team man, but he didn't look like it today. He gently cruised to his three figures, and then had a huge slog at the next ball. If a player at Lancashire had played like that, he would have been severely reprimanded and probably dropped. If I were Gavaskar, I would have bollocked the lot of them. Mind you, he slid down the order.

Is he frightened of Flash, or is he too playing for his average now? He has hardly led by example. They do not look like a team, but merely eleven individuals.

The rules meant that we had to score 253 in 49 overs, or be ahead on run rate when it got dark. Night falls very quickly here. We didn't make a great start. Chopper was bowled off his pads for 1. I was caught at mid-wicket – it should have been a simple flick over square leg for four, but the ball stopped a little, I was already through with the shot, and I gave a leading edge to Dilip Vengsarkar. Oh for a little more pace in the wicket; it was pleasant to field in spikes on a lush, almost English outfield, instead of the usual concrete, but the wicket as usual was boringly slow.

Gatt played well to put us on our way, aided by Shaggy, but Skid and Nobby were the saviours. They played sensibly with a blend of aggression and working ones and twos as only English one-day cricketers can. They were completely efficient, and it was a joy to watch. Meanwhile the gloom was setting in. Steph, calculator in hand, worked out our run rate every over and related the message to all and sundry. Skid was run out, but finally, as it got darker and darker, Nobby and Nelly edged marginally in front, and Prince was sent out to tell them to appeal against the light, carrying the usual twelfth-man's excuse, new batting gloves which no one wants.

At that stage none of us could see the ball from the boundary. You could only judge its whereabouts by the movement of the fielders. The scoreboard lights were blinding, and when you looked back at the square after looking at the board, your vision was affected by gazing at the light, that was how dark it was. Unbelievably, the umpires after consultation said, 'We shall play one more over and see how it goes.' They must have thought the sun was going to pop back over the horizon for a last curtain call. Either that or they knew we were about 0·2 of a run in front, and that if we played the next over and only scored 3 we would have been behind again; and if they came off then, India would have won. That became academic as we took 9 off the over, and the umpires brought the game to an end. We won!

The crowd, trying to cause disruptions, lit fires in the stands. There were nearly thirty fires flickering. They left silently, like ghosts, when we won, leaving small fires everywhere. They are so incredibly partisan.

I thought it served the Indians right after time-wasting earlier in the innings when it seemed to their advantage. The tables were turned and they fell foul of their own methods. A more dejected bunch I have never seen at the end. They did not come down for the presentation until we had finished. Even Steph was presented with a filigree silver medal — her first international cricket medal, I think. Their misery only made our delight all the stronger. It is amazing how winning affects even the air your breathe. I had a cold shower, by necessity rather than choice, and it felt warm in the glow of victory. The local beer tasted like Thwaites. The long coach journey back was bearable.

Win or lose, the Hotel Konark in Bhubaneswar had promised to lay on free food and champagne for us on the way back, so we stopped off on our way to the airport to refuel. The food was excellent. The champagne was cheap Russian. 'It's like fizzy Sauterne,' said Percy. The flight was delayed and we didn't get back to Calcutta until 11 p.m. — a long and tiring day after getting up at 6.45 a.m. Steph was knackered from the excitement of just watching, so you can imagine how we feel.

Rumours are rife over Kapil. At Eden Gardens there are posters saying: 'NO KAPIL NO TEST'. The selectors seem adamant that it is 'No Kapil', but as yet my 100 rupees are far from safe.

28

The luxury of a day off. We found the Rat Corner in the park, went carpet shopping with Dilip and Kalindy Doshi, and ate in a restaurant with Vic and Anna Marks, who came out today. It was lovely to see her again.

The Rat Corner was quite incredible. As you walked out of the hotel you go through a bus station and come to this park, right in the middle of Calcutta. Going across it there were two pathways bisecting each other, and against the low fencing around a little iron bridge there was a man with a mangle selling sugar-cane, which they grind to turn into a drink, and a man selling corn. We wondered why they should be selling corn, and then we saw. There was this huge open space, almost an arena, a large dusty expanse criss-crossed with holes in the ground. And on it were all these rats. You could literally see a hundred at any time you looked. And people were buying the corn and throwing it to the rats – just like you would feed the pigeons in Trafalgar Square.

There was this one man lying down sleeping, and around him all these mangy rats were fighting, scrabbling for corn and running all over him. It was just unbelievable, but the Indians regarded it as perfectly normal.

The selectors and Board of Control met to discuss the Kapil situation. Result: No Kapil! I collected my 100 rupees from Henri.

29

Nets in the morning. The wickets were very slow, like everything else out here. I bowled Skid, which made my day. Some days I would love to be a fast bowler. That might sound unlikely, but Malcolm Marshall is the same size as me, believe it or not, except that his inside leg is one and half inches longer – I know these intimate details because I had to borrow his clothes once in Tasmania. He is more muscular than me now, admittedly, but he wasn't four years ago.

'Fingers' was present at the nets. He is a masseur – a very good one, with fingers which almost vibrate. At Cuttack while bidding farewell he kissed all of us. He is very demonstrative.

My hand eczema is getting worse.

Tonight for a change we are going to the Polynesian restaurant with Vic and Anna.

30

Skid is not playing again, which I assume means that Chris Cowdrey is. I hope he gets a bowl.

31

India v. England, Third Test, first day
India 170-4

95,000 spectators came to Eden Gardens. It is hard to believe how lush the outfield is, almost English, but the cricket was unmistakably Indian. We lost the toss and fielded all day. They were very slow. Ellie bowled well without luck. It was real Test-match bowling. If he had another two yards of pace, he would not be dissimilar to I. T. Botham in his youth.

The Indians had one or two hiccoughs, but Azharuddin and Shastri were there at the close. Azharuddin is only nineteen, but already looks a good player. He is very wristy, almost Zaheer-like.

JANUARY

1

Third Test, second day
India 176-4. Rain and bad light stopped play

I didn't see the New Year in, but I might just as well have done. Percy and Diane Pocock, Skid and Anna, and Steph and I ate in the Polynesian restaurant, but even with a supply of funny hats it didn't feel like New Year's Eve. We went to bed at 11 p.m., as we were both tired, and I wanted to sleep well as I thought I could be batting today.

No chance. We did not start at 9.45 a.m. because of 'bad light'. The light meter in my camera read 1/500th second at F2·8, which is hardly dark.

We eventually started over an hour later. Shastri played and missed three times, so we came off again for bad light. Then the weather closed in, and Calcutta had rain on New Year's Day — almost unheard of — and that was that for the day.

The boys sat playing cards and reminiscing. Steph said she was bored stiff, and so were most of the rest of the spectators. At one stage they became a little too restless. I tried to throw a bucket of paper on the crowd, and then on to Mike Gatting, but I was stopped by the security guards and the police — they thought it might provoke a riot. As it was, they threw fruit — the ubiquitous missile here — into the pavilion, and a baton charge into the crowd was needed to calm them down.

We get fruit, especially oranges, thrown at us while we are

fielding. Considering they are supposed to like cricketers, they have some strange ways of showing their affection.

2

Rest day

Percy and family — Toby and Sam — Skid and Anna and the Fowlers went on a river trip up the Ganges. That is not quite the same as setting out for a boat trip on the Thames, but Amal Roy Chowdray, our local manager, organized it within half an hour of Steph asking if it was possible to have a river cruise. He contacted the chief of police and the admiral of the port. The Calcutta chief of police also had to contact the colonel in the neighbouring area to ensure that security and hospitality were maintained throughout the day. And on board the tub was a gentleman who had possessed a master's certificate for twenty-one years. Having sailed into Boston, San Francisco and Liverpool, and navigated the Suez Canal, he was brought in especially to oversee our small river trip!

We set off in thick early-morning mist on the dirty waters of the Hoogly, which runs into the Ganges. Our visibility was restricted — all we could see were the vague outlines of passing fishing-boats, and the flotsam and jetsam floating by, rubbish and dead animals: five dead dogs, one goat and something which was so dead we couldn't identify it. Toby, who is eleven, found it hard to believe. Percy just smiled, as if he enjoyed seeing his son educated before his eyes. As we cruised on, the mist lifted to reveal Indians having their daily wash in the polluted waters in front of their meagre dwellings of sack, straw and mud. I've never sailed through someone's bathroom before.

It is a land of strange contradictions. The women always fully covered up, the men never naked, yet they wash, bathe and defecate in the same water, and they will openly urinate anywhere.

We sailed on past the famous jute mills. Calcutta is the most prolific producer of jute in the world. Until early in the century it was the Indian capital, which was moved to Delhi, and all along the banks you can see once-luxurious dwellings decaying. Calcutta is still paying the price for the transfer of the capital to Delhi, the dwellings decaying because the wealth necessary to keep them up has moved on.

As we went past Howrah, our police escort in a motor launch was left behind to be replaced by another in a motorized canoe. We disembarked to see Mahatma Gandhi's monument – an off-white marble obelisk of little grandeur. Its dark wall-plaques were explained and the Mahatma's life was unfolded in pidgin English.

Anna and Stephanie dipped their feet in the holy waters of the river, unaware, or unconcerned, that twenty yards away another bloated, dead mongrel was floating. The locals were pleased by their gesture, and they too seemed happy to have done it. India's contradictions can infect visitors too – we only drink bottled water, yet we dip our feet in pollution. We have a mouse in our hotel room, and we have seen rats in the pool area and in the corridor. In England we would abandon the hotel immediately. Here it is just a way of life. All standards are relative.

We returned to the jetty for a ferry to take us back to our launch. The police held back the locals to ensure that cries of 'Pocock', 'Gatting' and 'Fowler' were not followed up by stronger cries of 'Autograph!' They called out 'Gatting' because my beard has confused Indians. They are now not sure if I am Mike Gatting or Graeme Fowler. I just sign whichever name they shout – it is far simpler to be who they want you to be!

On board lunch was served. Weeks of conditioning had

made us sceptical, but manners and the wish not to offend made us eat, then exclaim our thanks, though the thanks were mainly at finishing it without feeling sick. The Indians looked after us very well — beer, whisky, rum, gin and sherry were available in abundance, but our consumption was small. The air you breathe in Calcutta takes away some of your appetite. You are forever wondering if it will make its presence felt in your stomach, head or bowels. Unless your name is Gatting, that is. He seems able to digest copious quantities of anything with no apparent ill effects.

Having spent the two-hour up journey sightseeing intensely, we spent the return playing logic games. Toby, my little friend, joined in with four ex-university students and held his own. A good father like Percy is far better than all the universities. We got back at 3.15 p.m., tired but pleased that some corner of India now bore our footprints.

<u>3</u>

Third Test, third day
India 348-5 (Azharuddin 110, Shastri 108 not out)

I never thought I would be fielding on the fourth day, but I will be. Boring Shastri, boring Azharuddin. Both got centuries, which seemed their main concern, but on the flattest, most placid wicket imaginable.

Again Nellie bowled bloody well with no luck. Our figures, as you would expect, were tight. Our outfielding was very good indeed. We looked like an organized professional unit whom the Indians were scared of. Certainly, if Sunil Gavaskar wants results, as he claims, his tactics for victory are beyond me. Had they scored quickly, it would have put the pressure on us; as it is, they took a weak-witted option. 90,000 fruit-throwing spectators are surely not pleased. Frenchy, who is an enthusiastic mountaineer, went to Katmandu on New Year's Day to see Mount Everest and have a few days' break. He is turning out to be a good judge. I think everyone would rather be there than play or watch such negative cricket.

We kept ourselves amused by fooling around. Our entertainments ranged from fielding in police hats, acrobatics, conducting the crowd's cries of 'We want Kapil' to throwing in rubber balls. Anything to make a dull day pass more quickly, but also to give ourselves something to wake us up and make us concentrate even more. If you are fooling around, you have to concentrate even harder, because you daren't make a mistake.

151 overs into the match, our all-rounder, C. S. Cowdrey, came on to bowl! He also provided the highlight of the day. After tea he had Gatt at first slip. Lubo said, 'Do you want Gatt a foot wider?'

'No,' said Prince, 'he'd burst.'

I thought being able to find some humour at that stage was a gem in Prince's crown. It is typical of a successful player's ability to find reserves of humour in adversity, Gatt, as always, laughed at himself.

4

Third Test, fourth day
India 437-7 dec.; England 99-2 (Fowler 49)

Gavaskar finally declared in mid-afternoon as the boos and catcalls and barrage of fruit reached epic proportions. He has not made himself very popular here, and he didn't get much sympathy from us. Lubo finally put himself on to bowl in protest. I have never fielded for four consecutive days before.

They didn't endear themselves to us in the field either. Their antics were a disgrace. They went up for a close catch against Lubo, which was clearly just off the pad, and when it was turned down they all went mad, including a 'Jesus Christ Almighty' from Gavaskar. Two overs later the same thing happened to me. Again Vengsarkar was the worst culprit – he indulges in gamesmanship, pushing things to the limit and, indeed, further than any other player I have ever played against. When the appeal was turned down, Siva almost broke down and wept. He was comforted by the fatherly Gavaskar. They could win Oscars.

And all the time it is putting more pressure on the umpires, who have been pretty good in this game. If they had been kids in a school class, I would have sent them packing. Such antics do nothing for the game.

Fancy me getting out on 49 just minutes before the close. I didn't middle a ball from Siva and was caught one-handed by Vengsarkar at full stretch in the 'box' on the legside. Once again I'd done the hard work and then failed to cash in. The runs were enough to take me past the 1,000 mark in Tests, the sixty-fifth Englishman to do so. I've done it in 19 Tests, averaging about 30, which is far from special. But after a summer against the West Indies, my technique is not as I would wish it to be for playing against medium-quicks. I don't get forward enough. I should start wearing my glasses, but I'm afraid to make the transition to playing in them because it can take quite a while and, in a game where such minute fractions affect your timing, it seems risky.

5

Third Test, fifth day
*India 437-7 and 29-1; England 276 (Lamb 67, Gatting
48). Match drawn*

I bowled an over to Prabhakar at my mean medium pace. I have now bowled four overs in Test cricket, and I loved every ball. I should be able to bowl but have never worked at it, and it is getting a bit late to do so now. But I really do enjoy it.

So does Lamby, who took his first Test wicket, getting Prabhakar two overs after I'd softened him up. Lamby had been in histrionic mood all afternoon, borrowing a policeman's helmet and finding a pole and pretending to be a copper, and also throwing oranges around. We weren't taking the final session too seriously. When he came on to bowl, he ran in seventy yards and bowled a no-ball by a good yard. When he got Prabhakar lbw, he proceeded to leap around like a spring lamb. His only comment was, 'Nowhere near as plumb as Allan Border at Perth' — a wicket which had been denied him to his chagrin. Prabhakar was certainly plumb.

That was about all the pleasure we could extract from the match. Considering the crowds here were over 80,000 per day, the Indians played the game from a very defensive position. You would have thought they were one up in the series rather than it being level.

Govind set off with our baggage on a thirty-hour rail trip to Hyderabad. I've almost got packing off to a fine art now — the only thing I take with me as hand luggage is my camera bag.

<u>6</u>

Our flight to Hyderabad was delayed. We were meant to leave the hotel at 1.30 p.m., but we were there until 4.30. It wasn't too bad for me, but a few of the lads had wives and girlfriends to meet in Hyderabad, and every hour must have felt like four to them. We eventually arrived in the Barjara Hotel at 10.45 p.m. Percy and I have said our farewells to Diane, Steph, Toby and Sam and are rooming together again. We consoled one another in the bar.

During the day I had taken him to the Rat Corner. He was

amazed as I was first time round. On the way we stopped to view a small stall set out on a rug. It was selling hardware. A crowd gathered, and we were fascinated by the array of flick knives and other lethal blades of all shapes and sizes. Needless to say, we didn't buy anything.

I also had a shoe-shine from a small boy. They looked like glass when he had finished, so I gave him double what he asked for. He also wanted to clean Percy's nylon and suede running shoes, and what they would have turned out like I can't imagine, but there was no chance to discover because Percy declined the offer.

Gulliver's Travels (a party of English cricket fans) have arrived, including one or two familiar faces. Two doors down from my room is John Heaton, who taught not only me at Junior School, but also my sister Gillian, who is six years older than me. He turned up in Calcutta, and Stephanie failed to recognize him and felt awful. But sometimes faces do go with certain places and environments, and if you see them in unusual surroundings it can throw you completely. I like him because he has always been good to me, but seeing him here makes me feel slightly homesick.

7

I was supposed to be playing in the game against South Zone which started today, and I was looking forward to a good long bat, trying to get one or two parts of my technique sorted out. But it was not to be. The wicket looked grassy and hard, so they asked Flash to play instead, even though he said he had backache. Flash broke down, and I ended up fielding. Lubo won the toss and put them in, Percy and I did the first day's twelfth-man duties between us so that Nobby and Nellie could go back to the hotel to have the day with their loved ones. Needless to say, I was angry.

8

A better day, a very relaxing one. Anna Marks, Fiona Ellison, Ali Downton, Percy and I went sightseeing and had a marvellous day, seeing a fort, the Cherminar, the tombs and a marble temple. We had an excellent lunch accompanied by a couple of beers and it was all very relaxed. In the evening we paddled on the lake which borders the hotel and threw oranges at one another, and Percy and I hatched our plan for tomorrow night's race between press and players.

9

Anna Marks bought sixty rupees' worth of oranges, and our plans were under way. We spent all day in a state of anticipation waiting for the evening. There were to be four teams — two press and two players. Each participant put in 250 rupees, with the winners taking all. The rules we laid down were twice round the island and back to the landing jetty. The first to put their feet back on the mat at the jetty would be the winner. Nellie was judge and adjudicator. The press were represented by Crash and Bopal (Chris Lander and Colin Bateman), and Baxter and Ottway; the players by Lubo and Frenchy, and Cowdrey and Gatting.

After a practice paddle the race was ready to start. By then Percy and I were on our eighth-floor bedroom balcony hiding under cover of darkness with three huge baskets full of oranges and a bucket full of water along with several plastic bags to make water bombs. The fusillade began. We laughed so much pounding the press boats that we could hardly breathe, let alone throw. I laughed so much I nearly fell off the balcony — Percy had to grab me as I toppled over. Water splashes and the sound of splattering oranges accompanied by startled screams filled the air. All the watchers on the first-floor coffee shop patio were shouting — encouragement or abuse – and laughing. To aid our efforts, the island had an illuminated fountain, which drenched anyone who went too close. Prince was soaked as Crash held their boat against Cowdrey's, rendering them helpless under streams of water, to further hilarity. Meanwhile oranges rained down. Prince fell in the lake, but his craft came in a valiant second, Lubo and Frenchy winning by minutes. The press, somewhat unco-ordinated, floundered and came in third and fourth. They had the consolation of having acquired more fruit than anyone else.

Lubo and Frenchy did not pick up the winnings, however. Lubo's boat had broadsided Ottway's and damaged the gunwales, and Ottway was told he had to pay 2,000 rupees for repairs. Ottway, who can be stroppy, said, 'Get stuffed', but the winnings went to repair the loser's craft.

There were also some delicate matters to be dealt with in the aftermath of the expedition. Almost everyone thought it was fun, but one or two of the other guests in the hotel were less amused. A Finn, a guest of the Indian government, accused Percy of throwing ice – in fact it was a shower cap filled with water. Another bloke, who had been going to book a dinner for 500, stormed out, cancelling the dinner. And the sight of Lubo, his beard streaked with orange, had us in further paroxysms as he negotiated delicately with the hotel manager. Percy was in the thick of things, and ended the evening writing a letter of apology. He hadn't meant any harm, he'd just got a bit carried away with the excitement. To cap it all, as he was packing his bags after midnight, we had a power failure. It will all be hilarious in a day or two – in fact it is hilarious now.

10

Oh, the cricket. Flash didn't field again, so it has scarcely been a game off for the twelfth men. We were given garnet necklaces – hardly beautiful, but a lovely gesture.

And the self-congratulation on my packing ability in Calcutta proved to be tempting fate. I forgot to pack the Christmas cake which my cousin's wife, Val, had baked and Stephanie had brought out with her.

12

Two days of nets preparing for the fourth test — which Lubo said in the team meeting could be our opportunity, because the wicket is expected to have a bit of pace and bounce, while the one for the fifth Test in Kanpur will probably be another dead one.

I've been spending a lot of time talking to Percy, who says my bottom hand has crept round the back of my bat again and so I am playing slightly round-arm and also with the face of the bat slightly closed. He has spent two days throwing balls for me to drive using my old grip. It is such a simple thing, but I hadn't noticed it because my hand was moving during the backlift, that is, after I'd checked my grip. The bottom hand nearly always loosens somewhat during the later stages of a shot, but keeping it still until impact is crucial. Percy really is one of the most unselfish professionals I have ever met.

Preparations have been good, except Nellie is unfit, so Fozzy will play.

13

Fourth Test, first day
India 272 (Amarnath 78, Kapil 53, Foster 6-104);
England 32-0 (Fowler 10 not out)

Incredibly, they came out and gave it the charge. Gavaskar took 10 off Fozzy's first over and got out in his third after scoring all 17 of India's runs. Srikkanth then got out, Vengsarkar soon followed, and they were 45-3 in no time at all. Amarnath and Azharuddin then steadied things, so Prince had a go for the breakthrough but then it all went haywire again, with Kapil coming in and smashing it all over the place. It was more like a 60-over match than a Test. But Fozzy bowled really well.

I ended the day injured. The second ball of the game I chased to the extra cover boundary, dived, saved the four, ripped my trouser knee and took a chunk out of my leg. An hour later I did the same thing to the other knee. Result – two septic knees.

The crowd now expects me to perform gymnastic feats after the handstands and handsprings with which I whiled away the time in Calcutta. I sometimes think they enjoy my fielding more than my batting. I could even say they at least recognize me for something, except that everywhere I go I am called Gatting. We do both have beards, but we are hardly the same stature. He also gets called Fowler, but I suspect not as much. All we can do is laugh and play on the situation. Countless times I have been asked to sign Mike Gatting's picture in the little souvenir books of the tour. If I turn the page they will often turn it back, shouting, 'Gatting, Gatting.' And if I do manage to find my own photograph, often Gatt has already signed it. One person will ask, 'Your good name, please?' Before you can answer someone else will shout, 'Gatting.' I will then shout, 'Fowler,' everyone laughs and then says, 'No, no, Uncle, you Gatting!' What can you do?

Prince was told not to run on the wicket by the umpire. He said he was sorry and would try to keep off, using his apologetic face for two seconds, and then forgot all about it. He was never officially warned. When I went out to bat for the last ten or twelve overs of the day, I couldn't believe the damage he had done. The rough was really incredible – two huge patches, one directly in line with my off stump, a perfect target for Sivaramakrishan. In England Prince would have been removed from the attack long before he had done anywhere near the damage he had done. When I said something to the umpire he said, 'With so many people in the crowd, what can I do?'

In the last over Siva hit the rough twice. One went for four byes. The other I inside-edged – a urinating dog shot – to fine leg for a single. 'Good, double figures,' I thought as I trotted up the other end. The umpire gave a leg bye. If in his opinion it hit my leg, I'm glad they didn't appeal; otherwise I could have been given out. Apart from the rough, which is worrying, the wicket has a bit of bounce. So not only are the bowlers pleased, but so am I. If the ball bounces, both good deliveries and good shots are rewarded.

They tested Chopper repeatedly with bouncers after he had mishit the first one he had a go at. They didn't bother trying it with me because I left the first one alone.

It was very hot today, and I'm sure it will be hot tomorrow. After the way they batted we have an opening if we can bat for two days and get a big score – provided Prince hasn't scuttled us with that rough.

14

Fourth Test, second day
England 293-1 (Fowler 149 not out, Robinson 74,
Gatting 50 not out)

Knackered but elated! It was bloody hot, but in some ways that helped as I didn't have enough energy to have a slog. I think I played a very controlled, patient innings – very patient for me. I wish it was always so.

The heat really did take its toll, though. I had to abandon my helmet — it was too hot and sticky, sweat pouring into my eyes — and wore a cap, which gives you a better peak and sighting than a floppy hat. Even so the sweat stung my eyes, and I had to have eye drops administered by Spiro. I had a shower and a complete change of clothes at lunch, and another complete change of clothes and my head stuck in the sink at tea. By then I'd gone through my long-sleeve shirts and had to borrow one of Prince's — which was about twenty sizes too big.

By the last hour I was too knackered to score runs. All I wanted to do was ensure that I will be at the crease tomorrow by batting through a full day for the first time in my career. Fortunately, by then they too were weary. The second new ball did not make me jump about as it should have done, and almost immediately they reverted to a negative line and length. That suited me perfectly. I was happy to block and watch it go past the off stump — without, I hasten to add, playing at it. In the last over Gatt refused a single to keep the weary Fowler from the strike. When I said thanks he just smiled and said, 'Anytime, Fox,' a really unselfish act.

Gatt's endless energy, chatter and mischievously happy grin had helped me keep going when I was really tired during the final stages. Earlier Nellie had been a source of humour and inspiration at drinks intervals. Chopper likes to keep himself to himself while he is at the crease, so I respect that, although I love to natter and help gee one another up. That's my way of keeping my concentration topped up.

When Chopper was out we had put on 178 — a pity it wasn't 200. By that stage we had both been dropped once. I wasn't dropped in the first over of the day, however, although they appealed. The ball then bounced out of Kirmani's gloves, but if he had held on, who knows what the decision would have been? Chopper actually got the best ball of the day — it turned and bounced, and he got a thin edge.

At first I was worried about the rough, but when I had got to 20 or 30 I took a conscious decision to forget about it, and I succeeded. Incredibly, the rough didn't help Siva. In fact I think it mucked him up. Because he was so aware of it, it put pressure on him. He didn't have to bowl any differently to hit it, so what he should have done was just bowl normally. But he saw the rough as clearly as I did, and I think he thought he had to make the ball do strange things. He was showing his inexperience and being impetuous and bowling every ball to get a wicket. And so he was disappointed after every over if he hadn't beaten the bat, so he kept trying harder and it became a vicious circle for him.

I ended up cutting him a lot because he dropped short while trying to make things happen. I didn't drive. I'd got out in Calcutta flicking him away, and I decided not to play that shot because there was no way I would get a run there anyway because of his field placings. So rather than hit it into the fielders, I'd dead-bat it and let it trickle round the corner to leg gully. He might have thought I was inside-edging it, but it was going exactly where I wanted it to, and we were picking up ones and twos.

Apart from Siva, Ravi Shastri should have posed the most threat bowling over the wicket, but he didn't bowl over the wicket much. And they helped us by taking away the close catchers quite early. We were never looking to force the pace, and once the close catchers were banished to the outfield we were able to take a more relaxed defensive approach, because mistakes did not mean dismissals. If I gave a bat-pad when someone hit the rough, there was no one there to catch it. And the absence of the threat meant that there weren't any mistakes.

They are too content to put the field back and let you make a mistake. But once we refused to take the attack to them and were content to just bat on, taking our runs when they came, it meant they couldn't get us out. I thought Gavaskar should have attacked in little bursts and put the fielders in at times. It might have meant 20 runs coming off 3 overs, but it also would have put pressure on us because if we edged there was the chance of a catch. And with the bounce in the wicket, they should have exploited it more than they did.

I only hit one ball in the air all day — I hit Yadav for a straight six. My hands and grip worked well and it went exactly where I wanted it to. It hit Graham Morris's camera lens, which is worth £2,500. Fortunately there was no damage — except to Yadav!

Vic Marks said that that shot is a sign of my change as a batsman. I used to have a shot which he christened the 'Fowler flail', which he said could end up anywhere between cover and square leg. Now he says it is easier to predict where the shot is going to go. I'm sure that I have become more patient. A while ago I would reach a point in the innings where I wanted to lift the ball, just for the sake of doing so. I always believe I'm scoring slowly whatever pace I'm going at, and think maybe I should accelerate a bit. But that didn't cross my mind today — perhaps because it was so hot. I didn't even consider just hitting it in the air. I hit that six because the right ball came along; it wasn't something I'd tried to manufacture. And I had scored about 70 at the time, so I was fairly set.

The hundred came from a Siva overthrow. I must admit I burst out laughing and skipped for joy. It is my third century in 20 Tests. If I am ever going to get a big score, this is the time. 149 not out. I'd like to score a double century tomorrow, but more importantly I need 66, to beat David Lloyd's 214 against the Indians at the Oval.

At the end we went straight to the team room, where we found a few valuable tins of Guinness. Oh for a pint of Guinness at the Rose and Crown in Ramsbottom. I also wish Steph were here. I think she would be happy.

I was given a huge chocolate cake and a bouquet of flowers by the hotel manager. A lovely gesture, and a very good cake! Later Bernard dressed my septic knees, which my pads had been rubbing all day. Afterwards I was walking around the hotel in shorts and trainers with bandages on both knees. I looked like a schoolboy who had fallen down in the playground. Quite appropriately, John Heaton is here, and he sent me a lovely letter of congratulations. I feel happy, but not satisfied. I haven't finished yet.

I found Scyld Berry sitting in the coffee shop and joined him for a brew. He was surprised to see me alone and quiet. He thought I would be really elated and partying. We watched Rumour Has It, an English singing duo. Against all odds, they weren't bad.

15

Fourth Test, third day
England 611-5 (Gatting 207, Fowler 201)

Sleeping was not easy. I was too tired and my mind was too active – mentally I was still concentrating, and switching off was impossible. A restless night was not what I wanted. Thank goodness I still have my pillow – it is worth its weight in gold.

When the game resumed and I got off the mark, I was applauded. Over here they clap you when you are within reach of your target. It could excite someone with my temperament, but I try to resist it, and in some ways it works for me, making me more controlled and keen not to make errors.

Getting through the 160s and 170s was hard work. The board just didn't seem to move – fortunately Gatt kept it ticking along, although all through our partnership I stayed

90–100 runs ahead of him. Finally I broke out. Yadav tossed a couple up and I went from 182 to 194 in two balls, the second and third shots I had hit in the air. I thought, 'If I hit him over the top he'll split the field up,' so I hit him for six. He didn't, but bowled the same ball again, so I hit it again. But although I had it in my mind to do so, it wasn't something I'd manufactured — again, the right ball had just come along. From there on it was a case of simply picking up the singles. Finally I nudged one down to third man for my 200, and was relieved, thrilled, and felt quite aggressive. It was the best moment in my career. Then a tired-looking defensive shot saw me out 13 runs short of David Lloyd's record. Damn and blast! I shall have to score another double century to get past him!

My record as the highest score by an Englishman in India only lasted a couple of hours. Gatt went from strength to strength, and played bloody well. Thankfully it was not as warm today as it had been yesterday. I was thrilled for him. Both he and I are supposedly lucky to play Test cricket. Now we have records — his is the highest score by an Englishman in India, while I shall always be the first England player to score a double century here.

The hotel kindly produced more flowers and champagne for Gatt and me. Our room looks like a florist's. I went for more Guinness in the team room, and then for a cuddle from the Marks family. Vic had a day off today, so it was good to see him in the evening. I ate with Percy and David Frith. I have never known a bloke with a greater love for cricket facts than Frithy. He took my photograph on top of the stands at the ground, and wants to use the picture on the cover of *Wisden Cricket Monthly*.

Graham Ottway lost out. He backed me to be England's top scorer with the party's bookie, John Thicknesse. It won't be too often that your bet gets 201 and you still lose.

We watched Rumour Has It again and enjoyed it. It is funny how runs can make everything better. Even the food didn't taste too bad.

I am deep-down tired, but I still managed to goggle at anything and everything all night. It is a rest day tomorrow, and I need one. A group are going off to Fisherman's Cove, a resort about an hour away, but I don't fancy it. It could be unpleasant or great, but I don't fancy spending hours on an Indian coach with windows rattling and smells and dust everywhere.

I had another even more complimentary letter from John Heaton. I must admit I feel very proud for my parents, Steph and myself. I also know all my mates will be pleased, and so will Bumble.

16

Rest day

I spent all day pottering around, having a good day doing nothing. I passed a lot of time in the hotel bookshop. I always find bookshops soothing and relaxing, and I love books. I bought novels by Wilbur Smith and P. G. Wodehouse — both new writers to me — the National Geographic magazine and a photography book. I had lunch with the Lambs in the coffee shop again. Papadoms are becoming an obsession.

The trip to Fisherman's Cove was eventful. Frenchy and Spiro returned as heroes after rescuing two girls who had got into difficulties in the strong current.

17

Fourth Test, fourth day
England 652-7; India second innings 240-4 (Azharuddin
103 not out, Amarnath 95)

We slogged 41 in 5 overs. Then Fozzy got going again, and they were 22-3. It looked as if we were going to walk it, but Amarnath and Azharuddin batted very well. We just couldn't bowl at them for a time – they both got after Percy, who was really upset about the way he bowled. Then, just when it looked as if we might really be up against it tomorrow, Fozzy got Amarnath to mis-hook, and Flash caught a blinder out of the sun.

18

Fourth Test, fifth day
India 272 and 412 (Azharuddin 105, Kirmani 75, Foster
5-95); England 652-7 and 35-1 (Fowler 2). England won
by 9 wickets

I dropped Kirmani when they were still 38 behind, a catch which would have won the match there and then. Diving forward at deep cover point, my only reward was a septic elbow.

When we batted I was given out caught behind off Siva. I didn't hit it. It shot through low down out of the rough, and there were noises of bat on pad and bat on floor, but not bat on ball. I was disappointed, but not bothered because we were obviously going to win.

Afterwards we celebrated. Cakes and water flew around the dressing-room, and I dare say that one or two heads were light before the sweat had dried. Then we went back to the hotel. The team room was full of players and wives drinking, laughing and playing conundrum games. We got through eight bottles of champagne at £60 a bottle, and when the press arrived with more the evening was well under way at only 6 p.m. Graham Morris was a late arrival. A while later, ice buckets were being emptied in high-spirited frolics. All harmless, but it does seem to coincide with Morris's presence on these occasions.

I was filled with a quiet calm, which often happens when we win things. The satisfaction of winning provides enough joy and emotion without needing to rave around. I do that at other times.

19

We came back to earth quickly – a 5 a.m. departure for Bangalore, a ridiculous time to have to fly. You should have seen some of the eyes on the bus! It was only a half-hour flight, so we went straight to bed when we got to the hotel. I slept like a log until the afternoon, when believe it or not, we were summoned to a net. I was feeling rather groggy, so I tried to conserve my energy as much as possible. To be honest, the smell of success in the form of alcohol was ever present.

It is a pleasant hotel with a pool literally eight yards from our room. The eyes of the 'loved ones' lit up when they saw the setting. The hotel is a series of blocks, rather like an incredibly luxurious army camp. The only problem was autograph-hunters, using the outside balconies to good effect, banging on your door with cries of, 'Sign, sign.' Then, of course, they didn't even know who you were.

We went to a cocktail party after the team meeting at a hotel called the Winsor Manor, which was very pleasant. I'm still rooming with Percy. Brilliant. The electricity fused at 10.05 p.m., but luckily we were just going to bed anyway.

20

Third one-day international
India 205-6 (Marks 3-35); England 206-7 (Lamb 59 not
out, Fowler 45). England won by 3 wickets

We won the toss and inserted. A rough outfield, with fruit and firecrackers being used by the crowd as friendly gestures! The stadium was absolutely packed. People were sitting in rafters, sitting on top of one another, sitting everywhere.

Skid bowled well, which pleased me a lot. It is difficult touring when you are not in the Test side, and he and Percy have been put into slots as a one-day and a five-day bowler respectively, which neither of them really agrees with. We made things difficult for ourselves when we batted – two run-outs and one or two reckless shots, but Lamby saw us through. Near the end, when it was clear we were going to do it, bottles were thrown on the field, and Gavaskar took his team off. I suspect he knew India were ahead on run rate at that stage – the umpires had their calculators out before they came off. Lamby and Nobby remained on the field, along with loads of bureaucrats directing everyone else to pick up the fruit and bottles. The 'loved ones' were brought over to the players' enclosure from their unstable stand seats when the trouble started. But it didn't get any uglier, although fires were lit in the stands again. It is a good thing that wooden structures have been replaced in international stadiums – the concrete stadiums have less splendour and character, but are certainly safer where riots are concerned.

Eventually it all quietened down and India had to go back on, because the light had not faded enough to make it a nuisance. So we have won the Charmisar Challenge 3-0.

My 45 was OK – I was just unfortunate to be run out. I had an altercation with the wicket-keeper, Viswanath. I told him he was a cheat. I don't mind gamesmanship and professionalism, but both have limits, and he has exceeded even loose limits on every occasion we have encountered him. I'll be polite to him tomorrow, though! A cricketer on the field is an enemy. Off the field he is a fellow cricketer and comrade. It is a funny dichotomy between the two, and not everyone works it out. And even if you do work it out, it may still not be clear all of the time!

We liked the Winsor Manor so much that Percy, the Ellisons, the Cowdreys and I went back there again this evening. The meal was OK, the company good. But somehow I felt drained and was quiet. The events of last week are slowly sinking in and the adrenalin has faded, leaving me feeling worn out.

21

Had a rest day in Bangalore. Some of the intrepid travellers took a trip to Mysore, but as it meant a five-hour round trip on a bus I turned it down. I read and wrote all day, catching up on my diary, among other things. I didn't fancy sun-bathing.

Percy and I presented prizes to the winning team in a national cricket festival. It had been won by a local school. They were incredibly well behaved, all in uniform, and all with uniform haircuts too. Some of the 15-year-olds had beards! Someone gave me an application form for the primary club – the qualification is getting out first ball. I think I deserve it! Also, it is a registered charity and worth supporting.

In the evening we went back to the Winsor Manor again, this time in a large player/press group. The press paid! That produced the wonderful story of Henri and the air-conditioning, which happened last night. The air-conditioning is communal in each block, so you can't control it for individual rooms. Henri wanted it turned off, and asked the manager to do so. It wasn't done. Henri then phoned maintenance and ordered hammer and nails. Then he warned reception of his intentions. No response. So Henri set to work hammering a towel around their outlet. He cracked the whole section of his hotel room wall, showering Frances with plaster and waking up the whole block.

22

I spent the day sitting around the pool and got slightly burnt. Drinking beer, reading *National Geographic*s and chatting, gently enjoying the companionship of my winning colleagues – this really is a relaxed, happy party. Then I went into town and bought a topee for twenty-five rupees. It looks good. And I was given some silk at a huge silk shop.

Then we embarked for Nagpur.

23

Fourth one-day international
England 240-7 (Moxon 70, Fowler 37); India 241-7
(Kapil Dev 54, Gavaskar 52, Agnew 3-38,
Cowans 3-44). India won by 3 wickets

We changed the side to give Froggy, Prince and Spiro a game, and they all took their opportunities, even though we made a bit of a nonsense of it.

Lamby hurt his leg while batting so I went out to run for him. It was amazing that no one got run out. Froggy batted very well, but it was interesting to listen to him when I was out there running for Lamby. He was coming out with the sort of things I would have said twelve months earlier. He was convinced he wasn't scoring fast enough, and felt he should get on with it and swish it around. I said, 'No, you go on picking up your ones and twos.' I could see he would get more runs doing that than someone coming in fresh and trying to smash it. The field was split and he was in charge. But I could have seen myself wanting to do the same thing a year ago, thinking, 'Well, I've got 50 now, I'd better get on with it.' And that is counter-productive. But it takes time to realize it. People have often said to me in the past, 'All you need to do is stay in. You don't need to smash it all over, do you?' I've agreed with them at the time, but it is only now that the message has really clicked in my head.

We flew to Agra and were given an elephant welcome, followed by a superb cocktail party round the pool. Local folk-dancers entertained us, and then got several members of our group, including Moxon and Cowans, to join in, thereby entertaining themselves as well as us.

24

We got up at 5.30 a.m. – this time voluntarily. Percy had organized coffee and toast to start the day. He is a darling. Then it was all aboard the sunrise excursion to the Taj Mahal. Our aim was to see the sunrise illuminate this wonder of the world. On the bus we were subjected to a Kung Fu video starring Bruce Lee. At 6 a.m.! It wasn't a good picture either.

We were presented with garlands when we arrived, but they were soon taken away as an offering at the Taj's inner sanctum. It really is a magnificent structure, but the whole concept is also bewildering – the work of someone obsessed. A truly remarkable sight.

We took photographs, posed and returned to the hotel. I ate a full breakfast, and then soaked in a hot bath. The Taj was not a warm place to be at dawn.

Percy then went to bed. I went back to the Taj Mahal at 10 a.m. on board the press bus. Adrian Murrell was going, and I took the opportunity to sit with him – I am always trying to pick his brains about his art. He is a magnificent photographer, and he is always open and helpful.

The comparison between our jobs is fascinating. One of the things we share is split-second timing; but of course it is not just timing. I have to know what shot to play, and he has to know what shot or part of a shot to capture on film. It makes for some fascinating exchanges of comments and points. Also, I find it invigorating and a privilege to be able to relate to and compare with someone so brilliant in an adjacent field. Besides which, he's a great bloke.

I spent the rest of the day with the press on the other trips, including a visit to a jeweller's. We left in the late afternoon to fly back to Delhi en route for Chandigarh. Oh for a Chinese meal.

.**25**

Did nothing.

26

Early flight — up at 5 a.m. — to Chandigarh. Went to bed again in Chandigarh at 8 a.m. absolutely knackered. When I pulled back the sheets to get into bed, I found three coackroaches. I was too tired to bother, so I killed them and went to sleep anyway.

I am now rooming with Lamby for the first time after three tours. We had been kept apart previously — according to Bernard, the reason is that we are too high-spirited for each other and would be a nuisance. At the moment his leg is still sore and all the press have written him off for tomorrow's game. The thing is, he is not cagey and tells the truth. They expect him to play down the injury, so when he tells them exactly how it is, they draw the conclusion that it is much worse than he is saying. Nevertheless, he is in the twelve, and he is too tough a character to be written off so soon. I think he will play if I know him, being such a robust bundle of energy. Boredom comes easily to him, but his head is screwed on when it matters. His health is not the best at the moment, but he doesn't let it upset him as he bulldozes his way through life.

If all the players knew their limits on and off the field as well

as Legger, the standard would be raised immediately. I cannot
keep up with him in the bar, nor in the little sleep he needs,
and he respects that and does not press me to try. I have a lot
of time for him — a South African who is more like a British
bulldog than 99 per cent of born Britishers.

Robbo got engaged yesterday. We had fielding practice in
the afternoon and someone moaned, 'Nothing to do but
fielding practice.'

'Except get married!' said Legger.

It was like an English day — cool, blustery. The ground had
a good outfield, but any resemblance to England was dispelled
by the sight of the foot-hills of the Himalayas in the distance.
Nevertheless, when I had a net with Adrian Murrell, Graham
Morris and Colin Bateman, it was like being back at
Accrington CC.

We were sitting in Gatt's room when Fozzy ordered some
beer. 'It will only be one minute please,' said the waiter.

'Right,' said Fozzy, 'I'll time you,' and began the countdown.
Thirty seconds, twenty seconds . . . 'Congratulations, it's early'
— by ten seconds.

The meal, however, was not so punctual. In the end it was
too late to eat, so I just went to bed. There are cockroaches in
the bed again, in the bathroom and up the walls, but after
rising at 5 a.m. who cares?

A bad day for Frenchy. He had been promised a game
tomorrow, 'a consolation game' as he put it. Now, after the
defeat in Nagpur, the manager wants to play the strongest
side to prevent them getting a psychological boost before the
fifth Test. So Frenchy has been told he is not playing. That
seems very unfair to me — not that he isn't playing, but
because he had been told that he would.

*

Everyone appears to have huge noses and massive turbans. Bumble would love it here as he would not be out of place.

People – a courting couple we assumed – even knocked on our bedroom door to ask for a photograph and autographs. We were obviously not very pleased, but they weren't in the least embarrassed, and we acquiesced just to get some peace. They can be very persistent.

27

Fifth one-day international
England 121-6, 15 overs (Fowler 17); India 114-5.
England won by 7 runs

There was a storm overnight. Prince watched the lightning for one and a half hours, but I was dead to the world and missed it. I was quite sad to realize I had missed the rain, as I love it!

When we got to the ground there was no chance of play, but we opted to wait in a new concrete dressing-room rather than returning to a cockroach-infested, decrepit hotel room.

No announcements were made to a packed ground. There were puddles everywhere, and the only 'whale' to be seen was Mike Gatting. It didn't look promising, so cards and personal stereos became the order of the day. I stood talking to Adrian Murrell again for quite a while, asking questions like an inquisitive schoolboy. As always he answered all my questions. The more I know of him and his skills, the more I respect and like him. His eyes have a mischievous glint, a deep, hearty laugh issues forth given any reason, but his powerful frame has a gentleness about it.

Finally a limited-over game got under way. The team was changed again. 'By the way, Frenchy, you've got a game,' said Lubo.

'Oh, thanks for telling me,' replied Frenchy. So he did at last get an international appearance, even if it was only a 15-over slog.

Lamby also played. I told him he was mad even if he was 100 per cent fit. If he had injured himself, even in a totally unconnected way, all the press would have jumped down his and the management's throats. As clear-cut as ever, Legger answered as simply as ever, 'If I am fit, I must play.' You can't help admiring his strong will and straightforwardness.

Henri bowled magnificently, and when they needed 10 off the last over, even Sunil Gavaskar couldn't pull it off as Prince bowled a superb last over to save the match. He ended with figures of 1–0–3–1 – fantastic. Why Gatt gets on before him is beyond me – Prince is far and away the superior bowler. Shastri threw it away for them, though. He scored 50-odd, but got run out at the non-striker's end off the penultimate over. 50 in a 14-over slog was pitiful, one more instance of selfish play. He was awarded the 'Man of the Series' title, but he helped us to win the series.

Peter Smith's phone call to his London office took four and a half hours to come through, and he was cut off eight times. Peter Baxter's call to the BBC never came through at all.

30

Kanpur is not one of the high spots of our visit to India. One more Test and then Australia. Hooray.

31

Fifth Test, first day
India 228-3 (Azharuddin 98 not out, Srikkanth 84)

Once again they started playing for themselves. They had a

great foundation with Srikkanth and Azharuddin hammering it around. We dropped Srikkanth four times, including finger-tip ones to Lubo and me in successive balls, which didn't help. But once Srikkanth was out, Azharuddin started playing for his century — he only scored about 10 in the last hour and a half.

Once again Henri bowled very well.

FEBRUARY

1

Fifth Test, second day
India 525-7 (Vengsarkar 137, Azharuddin 122,
Shastri 59)

I woke up with a stiff neck and couldn't field. It feels like a trapped nerve between the shoulder blades. I said that to Bolt, and he just said yes and did nothing. I didn't expect anything else either.

Before play Ellie ran into the boundary fence during fielding practice. It was a mesh of barbed wire, and he cut himself quite nastily.

2

Yesterday I sat and lay around the dressing-room. By tea-time I began to feel worse and I asked to return to the hotel. I got a private car — another Ambassador — and arrived not feeling too well and being quite curt. I went to bed, and by the time the lads returned two hours later I had a temperature of over 102. The doctor diagnosed a virus. Brilliant!

I spent the day in bed sweating it out. By the evening it appeared to have gone as quickly as it came, although I feel weak.

Last night it took me twenty minutes to get through to room service to order a bowl of chicken and sweetcorn soup and a bread roll. During that time I was cut off three times. Cut off phoning room service! You have to pick up the receiver about eight times to get a line once, so you can imagine how difficult long-distance calls are.

Legger went duck-shooting today while I was lying feeling sorry for myself. He was appalled at the dead bodies floating in the river.

The hotel has got a snooker room, which most of the lads and the press are forever scrambling for. The food isn't special and the service is worse, but we keep being told it is a million times better than when the MCC were here in 1981–2.

3

Fifth Test, third day
India 553-8 dec.; England 163-1 (Robinson 84 not out,
Fowler 69)

4

Fifth Test, fourth day
England 373-6 (Robinson 86, Gower 66 not out, Gatting
62)

5

Fifth Test, fifth day
India 553-8 dec. and 97-1 dec. (Azharuddin 54 not out);
England 417 (Gower 78) and 91-0. Match drawn

I batted on the third day and got 69. I should have got millions, the pitch was so slow, but that's the way it goes. Then I was struck down by a recurrence of the virus and had to head back to bed. It was obvious I wasn't having anybody on – I looked bloody awful.

For a time we had a few tremors about saving the follow-on, but Lubo and Henri, who got 49, saw us to safety, which made a draw inevitable and gave us the series.

I wasn't at the ground when the game ended – I was watching it on TV as well as I could, given the standard of the coverage. Gatt got a lump on his head when Lubo dropped the trophy on him, but he didn't seem to care.

Chopper got grit in his eye during our second innings to give Gatt another knock to try and beat Siva for the 'Man of the Series' award. I think Gatt lost out by one point. But we won the series! When the lads got back, German champagne found its way into people's glasses. Even I had a drop. It's not every day you win a series abroad, let alone in this God-forsaken place!

6

Another early flight back to Delhi. I was still not 100 per cent, but I'm sure I felt better than most of the animals who crawled and sloped on to the bus!

8

Two days spent shopping, using up loose rupees for little presents and buying leather jackets. Now it's 'Australia, here we come!'

10

We left Delhi at 4 a.m. and with all the delays we arrived at 9 a.m. yesterday. By the time we arrived I'd had four hours sleep in two days, but I went straight round to see some friends, and I finally went to bed at 5 a.m. this morning. It was just so marvellous to be in a western city again, to be able to walk down the street and not be mobbed, to be able to get a glass of water or milk, or a pint. Especially after being ill at Kanpur, it is such a relief to be somewhere like this. I celebrated by going to a seafood restaurant – seafood in Australia is magnificent, and I like fish much more than meat.

The flight over came via Singapore. We flew upstairs in the bubble of the Jumbo. Sheer luxury – I had a glass of milk for the first time in three and a half months. Some of the lads sampled champagne, and by the time we got to Singapore one or two were well oiled. We were informed that we had a four-hour delay at Singapore airport, so we were collected and taken to the cricket club, which was a lovely place. As soon as we got there we heard the plane had been delayed another four hours, so we had eight hours to kill. We did some shopping, while one or two had a bit more to drink and got well over the top.

13

I love Sydney. You are continually bumping into people you know, and there is so much going on. I spent today at a record studio watching a group finishing an album – all the result of one introduction two or three days ago. I've been spending the time going to gigs. Steph has always said I am a frustrated pop star, and I've really enjoyed the opportunity to get into a different scene for a bit. It is a relief after the intensity of India and seeing the same faces day in, day out.

The West Indies are here too, so I am seeing a bit of them. Malcolm Marshall is a good friend, and I always enjoy spending time with him and some of the others.

15

Sydney Metropolitan XI v. England XI
England 149 (Fowler 23); Sydney Metropolitan XI
145-9. England won by 4 runs

We would have been better off without this. They were only a side selected from Sydney first-grade cricketers. The wicket seamed all over the place, and trying to use this as any sort of practice for playing Australia at Melbourne was farcical.

And of course they were typical Australians – played it very hard, delighted to embarrass the Poms. I was done. I hit the ball to long off. Everyone rushed to the fielder, shouting, 'Good catch,' and so I set off for the pavilion. So he then chucked the ball in and I was run out – it turned out he had in fact dropped the catch. That made my day, that did. Still, at least we stopped them winning.

16

We practised for four hours today, two hours under the lights, which will be used for part of the game tomorrow. I'm not sure how much difference playing under lights makes, but it is a new experience, and I think most people feel a bit tentative about it.

17

First one-day international
England 214-8 (Lamb 53, Fowler 26); Australia 215-3
(Kerr 87 not out, Jones 78 not out). Australia won by
7 wickets

Victoria is celebrating its 150th anniversary, so there was a long, Olympic-style opening ceremony before the game. We walked round the Melbourne ground, getting some choice comments from the cheap seats, then had to endure speeches before play began.

Because of the lights, Lubo batted first when he won the toss so we could bat in daylight. To give us another bowler, Nobby opened with me, and we put on 61 in reasonable time. Lamby then batted well with Gatt, and it looked as if we could get a good score, but we had a collapse, and we just hadn't got enough runs. The silly thing – or the thing I couldn't understand – was that having left out Chopper to play Prince, Prince didn't get a bowl, even though Spiro and Flash to some extent got some hammer.

The Aussies came in afterwards for a chat and a beer. I was glad to see 'Henry' Lawson again. He is an optician and is going to arrange for me to go the University of New South Wales Institute of Soft Contact Lens and Cornea Research Unit to see if they can do anything about my left eye. So far no one has been able to supply a lens to cure the problem, and I don't know when I could find the time to make the transition to playing in glasses, which would be the alternative.

19

Victorian XI v. England XI
England 268-5 (Lamb 95); Victorian XI 264
(Whatmore 99, King 52, Marks 5-42). England won
by 4 runs

Fortunately, I didn't play in this game at Ballarat. The pitch was quick and had variable bounce – lethal. Chopper broke his thumb, and Cow has a bad wrist – certainly badly bruised, possibly broken. With Gatt having hurt his hand at Melbourne, our fourteen are down to eleven. We need games like this like a hole in the head.

21

Victoria 2nd XI v. England XI
England 276 (Downton 111, Moxon 95, Fowler 7);
Victoria 2nd XI 253-4 (Wiener 107, Richardson 60)

Nobby and Froggy both batted well, but it is difficult to gear yourself up for these games. We didn't bowl well, but they never really looked like winning.

22

As I have said, one of the things about being in Australia is that you are always meeting old friends. I spent today with Ian Greener, a friend from Durham University, who now lives in Melbourne and whom I always try and see when we are here.

23

Going out with Ian Greener yesterday has left me in bad odour. There has been some trouble about functions since we arrived in Australia, and yesterday I missed a Lord's Taverners 'do', which most of the lads went to. It was a full day – golf, swimming and a barbecue. I don't play golf. Even though I'm a qualified swimming teacher, I'm not keen on swimming – I think I've been in a pool once so far on the entire trip. And if I can avoid it, I don't eat red meat. So it wasn't my ideal day, and as it was down as an invitation on our itinerary rather than as a function we were expected to attend, I decided to see Ian instead.

But the manager thinks the whole tour is becoming fragmented and that the team spirit, which was so good in India, is breaking down as a result. I don't think so. But if you have been in India for three and a half months, and then have a game every week or so when you get to Australia, what are you supposed to do? Sit in your room cleaning your boots? You are going to go out to restaurants, have a drink and, if you've got nothing to do for a week, stay up late. There are nine of us who have spent a lot of time in Australia playing here, and if you haven't seen someone for two years, the first thing you do when you arrive is to ring them up and arrange to see them. And that has meant that unless something was on the itinerary to start with, people will miss it. In India we were a captive audience for functions. If the manager wanted you, you were always in your room or the team room, so that if he forgot to warn you beforehand he could still say, 'We're leaving for this cocktail party in three hours,' and be sure of a quorum. You would get dressed and be on parade. But over here if he tries to ring people to say, 'We've got a cocktail party tonight, I forgot to tell you,' he can't find anyone. Everyone is out seeing friends.

26

One-day international
India 235-9 (Srikkanth 57); England 149 (Moxon 48,
Fowler 26). India won by 86 runs

We batted like idiots, and against a team we had just beaten 4-1 in one-day matches and beaten in a Test series. We were 100-2, had wickets in hand and were up with the run rate. We should have walked it and instead we committed suicide. A really bad day at the wrong time.

28

New South Wales XI v. England XI
England 111 (Fowler 17); New South Wales 2nd XI
115-4 (Small 44). New South Wales won by 6 wickets

I batted at number three. My first ball I pushed forward and the ball took off and flew straight over my head. The last thing we needed was to play on a horrendous wicket, like this one at Manley, when we are already down to twelve fit men: Prince's wrist has turned out to be broken.

The whole idea of these practice games is wrong anyway. How can you play practice matches when you've been away from home for four months playing cricket? And if you play any sort of cricket in Australia, it is fierce, aggressive and very competitive.

But there are times when you have only got so much mental energy left, and this was one of those games where you couldn't summon it up because it was a pointless exercise, and we all knew it was pointless.

It was one game where I certainly was not going to go in and give it blood and guts for king and country, and end up with a cracked finger knowing that we have at least one more international to play. The logistics of that sort of game are hopeless. I hadn't fancied playing, but I was playing. I wasn't going to get really stuck in, but on the other hand I didn't go out there to just give it away either. But in that situation, unless you do get stuck in, you might as well not bother. So we got rolled over.

Then they batted. Of course they were as keen as mustard to be able to say, 'We beat England,' and they slogged it and they won. And from the press's perspective, it means England played really badly because we've been beaten by a grade side. And one or two go on to conclude that it means that even though we won in India, the state of English cricket is still poor.

MARCH

2

One-day international
Pakistan 213-8 (Mudassar Nazar 77); England 146
(Lamb 81, Fowler 0). Pakistan won by 67 runs

The scoreline looks horrific, but it wasn't quite like that really.
To stand a chance of qualifying for the semi-finals, we had to
win here in Melbourne in 32 overs, and that was what Lubo
decided we should aim for. If we had been trying to win in 49
overs, we would have done it easily. As it was, we might have
won in 32 the way that Lamby played. He was brilliant, but
when he got out we couldn't keep it up and lost wickets in the
hectic attempt to do so – three run-outs, for example.

5

Dispersal day: eight players are going home, six are staying
on in Australia for holidays or other reasons. Legger, Henri
and I are having a week here before going back to India to
play in a double-wicket competition and play two one-day
internationals for the Rest of the World v. Asia.

10

Days at the University of New South Wales have proved
hopeful. I have been equipped with a new type of soft contact
lens, which should solve my problem. That will be a great

relief, because I have been aware of this nagging doubt about my eyesight — and when you are facing Lawson and McDermott, let alone Marshall and Holding, you need good eyes.

12

I heard today that the trip to Calcutta is off, so it was a question of racing around to organize a trip home as fast as I could. Fortunately it was all straightforward.

I was supposed to phone Steph to let her know what the arrangements for Calcutta were, but instead I phoned my mother and said, 'Tell Steph to be at home on Thursday and I'll phone her then.' I shall give her a surprise.

14

I was greeted by the words, 'What are you doing here, you swine?' To say I took Steph by surprise would be an understatement. But her second greeting made up for the first. It is good to be home.

15

Because Calcutta fell through, I am joining the team to go to an exhibition tournament in Sharjah in the United Arab Emirates. Giff is captaining the side, and Tony Brown is manager again, so it is a semi-official side. I've been to Sharjah before, so it won't be a new, exciting experience, but it is a good pay-day. Although not proper international cricket, it's still one of the rewards of it — a nice little perk. So even though it means having to go away again so soon after getting back, it is too rewarding financially to turn down.

17

Our performances in Australia seem to have taken the gloss off our performance in India, which is a pity, to say the least. Partly it is the influence of television – my mum and dad saw more of me playing in those three one-day games in Australia than they did the whole of the India tour. Of course, TV gets very good pictures from Australia and not such good ones from India, but it gave a totally distorted balance to the tour.

And after our achievements in India we went to Australia feeling we were on a loser whatever happened. If we had won the tournament, everyone would have said, 'Well, they played well and won the tournament, that's nice, but it's just an afterthought and it wasn't proper cricket, it was their success in India which mattered.' So we went there on a hiding to nothing. We had two bad days there, and now that seems to have taken the edge off the tour.

But after doing so well on a very tough tour of India, being asked to go to Australia at the fag end of the tour and be expected to maintain the same standards was being asked a lot. After coming back from 1-0 down to win the Test series, and winning the one-days 4-1, we couldn't get any higher, and I think it was impossible to keep it going. It was a combination of little things which built up. Everyone was tired both physically and mentally because we had been away a long time. And as I said, we all knew we were on a loser even if we won the competition, because it was bound to be an anti-climax after the high in India. So if you aren't 100 per cent committed, even if you are 95 per cent committed, you are lost. And that was what happened. It wasn't that the lads didn't care any more – it was just that they had had so much that they couldn't cope. And there is a difference.

I don't think that the different social life in Australia meant that team spirit broke down, but I do think that the practice matches didn't help at all. As I said at Manley, how can you play practice matches against sides like that when you've been away from home for four months? We would have been better off having decent net sessions. I'm sure it would have been better if, rather than holding the group together, they had said, 'Enjoy yourselves, do whatever you want, go and stay with friends or whatever as long as you are mentally ready when you report back. Next Tuesday we are going to have nets, Wednesday we will have a practice amongst ourselves, and Thursday is the international. I don't care what you do in between, I don't even care what you are doing two hours before nets, but you must be attuned and ready for net practice.' That approach would have been far better than having us pitching up twenty minutes before a game at the University of New South Wales and then another one at Manley and not feeling properly motivated.

21

Here in Sharjah I'm rooming with Bruce French. It is a good trip for him, because he hasn't been on the international circuit for very long and — having got married very young and with two kids — he has to look after his money.

He got caught today, though. He always likes his hair very short, and at the end of the trip to India he was about ready for a haircut. But although he didn't come to Australia — he went straight home — he said he hadn't had a chance to get one in England because the septic tank had burst and he had fixed it himself (they live in a converted barn which he is doing up himself). So he decided to go and get one when we arrived here. He came back an hour later and it was so short that it looked as if he should have had 'welcome' tattooed on his head. It was incredibly short, and all sticking up at the back.

'Very smart, Frenchy,' I said, 'how much did that cost you?'

'I don't know.'

'You must know how much.'

'Well, I know how much I paid, but I can't convert it.'

'Go on.'

'Seventy-five.'

'But that's eighteen pounds!'

It had cost him eighteen pounds to have a short back and sides. Poor Frenchy. It is very expensive here, though – half a pint of lager in the restaurant is £3.30.

22

There is a function every night. There was nothing else to do anyway, but they are looking after us really well. At one stage at tonight's really lavish buffet Kim Hughes said, 'It's the best seafood spread I've ever seen.' That is high praise indeed coming from a Western Australian, because the seafood in Perth is gorgeous, but I knew what he meant. It was ridiculous – row after row of tables laden with lobsters, crabs, etc., etc.

The functions are quite good because they give you a chance to talk to the opposition over more than a beer at the end of a day's play. To some degree you stick together at these things – the tendency towards 'security in the group' rather than socializing with people who don't see things the way you do as a player, and who perhaps are going to have a go at you. Players would rather get criticism from one another than from outsiders, and I spent a lot of time talking to Keppler Wessels, Graham Wood, Murray Bennett and Greg Mathews.

23

Henri and I have been consulted by Giff and Tony Brown about team selection – a sign of increasing seniority perhaps.

Except that after we put our views forward they completely ignored them. We'd been adamant after seeing the pitch that Percy had to play – it had turned square when we'd been watching, and against Australia, with all their left-handers, he could be a match-winner.

At one stage Henri came up to me and said, 'Has it crossed your mind, it's crossed mine, that there's only one snag with this selection? If Giff wasn't playing, we'd have a much better-balanced team, but it seems a little sad as he's the captain.' Which is right really. So we have got two left-arm slows, and no off-spinner.

But the whole selection of the party in the first place is shrouded in mystery. It started with people being asked if they were available. I said yes and that was it. But then it seems there was some further selection procedure: for instance, Jonathan Agnew said yes, and he's not here; on the other hand, Rob Bailey, who was never asked, just got this letter saying he had been picked, which was the first he knew about it.

It's all quite strange, neither official nor unofficial. People are getting one-day international sweaters for the game, and I assume they'll be allowed to keep them, so it's like playing for an England side. But it isn't the full England side. Confusing – except I'm here for the dollars.

24

Sharjah Rothmans Trophy, semi-final
England 177-8 (Fowler 26); Australia 178-8.
Australia won by 2 wickets.

Percy didn't play and Swaroop Krishan umpired, and those two facts decided our fate. If Swaroop had come to Sharjah determined to get his own back for us protesting about him in India, he couldn't have made a better job of it. He made some horrendous decisions. Martyn Moxon was given out lbw when it wouldn't have hit another set of stumps, let alone the ones which he was guarding. He was across working it to leg and the ball just clipped the outside of his pads. The bowler shouted 'Aagh,' and Swaroop had his finger up quicker than blinking. Chopper pushed forward with his bat miles away, the ball hit his knees and bounced in the air, Rixon dived across and caught it, and he was given out.

All our fears about the decision to leave out Percy were justified. It turned square, and they had four left-handers. If only we'd had Percy . . . He himself said afterwards that it was the only game in his career in which he could definitely say that if he had played the result would have been different.

We were disappointed, naturally, because apart from anything else not getting to the final cost us money. And it was hot and quite hard work, but nevertheless it was not the same as a proper international. We went into it with the attitude 'We want to win, and if we play well we should win,' but the pressure was lacking. It wasn't a case of 'If we don't do well, our backs are to the wall for the rest of the year.'

25

We've spent more time on a mini-bus than anything else. We are staying in Sharjah, but everything apart from the cricket takes place in Dubai, which is about twelve miles away, and we spend all our time going backwards and forwards along the one road – Suicide Highway or Kamikaze Highway as it is known, because they all just put their foot down and go berserk. Henri, showing the tact and diplomacy which has made him so popular with authority through so much of his career, keeps wanting to know why we aren't staying in Dubai. 'All the functions are there, and as there is so little cricket, wouldn't it have been easier to stay there and just get the bus out to the cricket?' The fact that there is no good answer only makes his repeated question more annoying to those who have to try and answer it.

We went to a store today for a presentation to all four teams. They also offered us the chance to buy things at big discounts. Looking at the prices, we could only conclude that they had put the prices up by 25 per cent before we arrived. To my knowledge, nobody bought anything. It was a bit of a shambles, and we were all sitting there wondering what we were there for. Henri was brilliant. 'What am I doing here?' he kept demanding. He was wandering round, not exactly taking the mickey out of the shopkeepers, but entertaining himself to avoid boredom. I just followed him around listening.

'Hm, I see, it seems a trifle expensive,' he would say, examining something which was totally extortionate.

'We'll make a very good deal for you.'

'Oh? Tell me more.'

But he didn't buy anything.

Derek Pringle, Arkle, Ellie, Dicky Bird and I ended up sitting on settees in the furniture department telling cricket stories. We were trying to get Arkle going because he is brilliant – a very funny man. We started talking about the number of runs people had got in their careers – it started because someone mentioned Dennis Amiss, who has got a phenomenal amount, over 40,000, which is ridiculous. Then someone said, 'How many has Boycott got?' and that was answered. Then I said, 'Arkle, how many have you got?'

'16,526 – and four of them were leg byes.'

In the end we were presented with six dark crystal wine-glasses each. Someone said, 'You can buy these at ASDA,' which just about summed it up really.

26

Sharjah Rothmans Trophy, third place match
Pakistan 175-7 (Javed Miandad 71); England 132
(Fowler 19). Pakistan won by 43 runs.

Percy did play this time, but Pakistan hadn't got a bevy of left-handers. As it was we ended up with Rob Bailey, who was our top scorer, bowling the last overs because the wicket was much more helpful to spinners than to seam bowlers. He batted very well, but he bowls also-ran off-spinners, so that shows what the wicket was like.

28

Last night we got absolutely mobbed. During the official function Clive Butler, who was looking after us, said to Froggy, Derek Pringle, Ellie and me, 'Come on, I'll take you up to the rugby club and we can have a drink.'

When we got there it was absolutely full of squat, muscular, T-shirtless, drunken sailors from HMS *Manchester*. During the day some of the lads had gone on board for a look-round. I hadn't gone and, being a Lancastrian, all the sailors had been asking where I was. Now, at 1 a.m., they'd had a skinful and they'd found me. It was good fun, but it was like holding court. Clive Butler said, 'It's been a quiet night, there have only been two fights!' One bloke kept grabbing me round the neck and kissing the back of my head. 'Hello sailor!' I thought. I wasn't going to argue with him, because he was huge. But he was just legless. They were nutcases – lovely blokes, but absolute nutcases. Not one of them seemed to possess a shirt. They looked like big tattooed bulldogs.

PART TWO

THE COUNTY SEASON

After Sharjah, Graeme had a brief holiday while Lancashire spent a week in La Manga, the Spanish cricket-and-golf complex. He then returned to Old Trafford for pre-season nets and training, attended a civic reception in his honour in Accrington – having originally arrived a week early to find the town hall deserted – and generally got ready for the new season. He was beginning to notice pain and restricted movement in his neck.

The Lancashire club he was returning to was fairly optimistic at the start of the season, as most sports clubs tend to be at that stage in the cycle. Although their championship record was poor, finishing next to bottom to maintain the unenviable record of finishing in the bottom six ten years running, they had won the Benson & Hedges Cup in 1984. John Abrahams, who had captained the side in the absence of Clive Lloyd, had retained the captaincy for the forthcoming season, and with Lloyd returning and a new West Indian fast bowler in Pat Patterson expected to add firepower, they had reason to hope for further progress as young players like Fairbrother, O'Shaughnessy, Watkinson and Folley developed. With Fowler, Allott and the evergreen Jack Simmons to add class and experience, they had the basis of a respectable side, if not one which would be expected to sweep the board, while their team spirit was outstanding, a major factor in their success in limited-over competitions.

It was, however, a less than happy club in other ways. Under the chairmanship of Cedric Rhoades, Old Trafford had been developed into one of the most modern grounds in the country. Rhoades's regime was less successful on the playing side, especially in the championship, and in its handling of the staff. The appointment of Jack Bond, the captain of the very successful side of the late sixties and early seventies, as manager, and the subsequent arrival of the former fast bowler

Peter Lever as coach, had not produced an immediate improvement in results.

Peter Ball

APRIL

23

Ever since India I've had days when my neck has been really sore – a shooting pain which travels down into my arms. And it feels stiff – I can't move it properly and I haven't got full range of movement, which is something of a handicap when you are trying to play cricket. I finally went to see David Markham, a specialist in Manchester. I went back today and got the bad news. It turns out that when I had a car crash in 1978 and I was in hospital with broken legs, I had also broken my neck – or at least damaged it badly. I have two crushed vertebrae on one side, so that I am tilted a little, and the bone is calcifying.

To say I was shattered is an understatement. He was quite reassuring, said it was unlikely to get much worse immediately, and that physiotherapy should help, although eventually he might have to operate. But where that leaves my long-term future, I don't know.

I decided to keep quiet about it, at least for the moment.

26

After a week of practice games we finished up playing a John Player League game among ourselves. I was awarded the 'Green Jacket' as tournament leader for being 2 over par – I scored 34 in 32 overs. I was out in the 36th for 61!

Shauny and Harvey played well, and they needed 4 to win off the last over. We then had Shauny 'run out'. He wasn't really, but we wanted to get Albert in at the non-striking end with 2 to win. Next ball Harvey was caught behind for 49. He had just said a little earlier, 'Better 49 not out than 49 out!' Then Winker came in, slammed Makinson for 4 off the last ball to win the game and walked off proclaiming, 'These bloody batsmen!'

The last five minutes were pure magic. Behind closed doors there was all the excitement and fun of a big occasion – a tribute to the character of the lads who play for Lancashire.

This evening there is a civic reception at Trafford town hall. It seems a strange time to have it – the eve of the first championship match of the season. Hardly ideal preparation.

I had a phone call from the Mayor of Hyndburn – they want to make a presentation to me for scoring 201 in India. It is very touching really, and I shall be proud to be honoured in such a way. Yet somehow I also feel it is all slightly humorous, local councillors being such figures of fun, and especially with all the tales you hear of how local councils operate.

27

Old Trafford
Lancashire v. Sussex, first day
Lancs 236-9 (Jefferies 93 not out, Abrahams 67,
Fowler 10)

We won the toss and batted. It was absolutely freezing and the ball was seaming all over the place. Imran said afterwards it was the most miserable day he had ever spent on a cricket field, it was so cold. It seems strange to be playing in such cold after the winter abroad. I batted in a sleeveless sweater, which is something I very rarely do, but it was still freezing. I lasted for an hour, lbw to Colin Wells, a team-mate in Sharjah four weeks ago. It was so different that it seems a year away. I hope Walt can survive in the morning – Jeffo has never had a first-class century. Albert played a captain's knock.

John Abrahams is known as Albert after Albert Schweitzer, because sometimes he is too good to be true. Butter just wouldn't melt in his mouth and at times he is unselfish to the point of being ridiculous. He is one player in our dressing-room who does not suffer from the 'only-child syndrome'.

His captaincy was marvellous last year. Perhaps because he had periods of struggle, he was a better captain for our team than Clive, because he understood the problems people have. And he really moulded the different characters to pull together. Youthful enthusiasm and a down-to-earth approach were just what the doctor ordered, and the way we all worked so hard for one another was a major factor in us winning the Benson & Hedges Cup. His humour, gentle manner and his ability to cope with just being an average player while being in charge of others with far greater skills are only a few of his talents.

On a personal level I've always considered him a friend, and he has helped me with my game many times. He always listens well, thinks, and then supplies his thoughts. I find he quietly builds my confidence. If he has a fault, he can at times be a bit 'holier than thou', and that rubs some people up the wrong way. A few find his sincerity a bit hard to swallow, but that is a personal thing. It doesn't bother me – I just laugh when he goes too far.

It took him a really long time to establish himself as a regular. He made his début in 1973, but didn't get his cap until 1982, which says something about his character that he stuck it out for so long without becoming bitter or cynical. In the last couple of years he has played some important innings for the team, and he is an outstanding fielder. I've always thought he should try to develop his bowling, because he does spin the ball.

I didn't wake up feeling as fresh as I might have. After the civic reception, which was quite pleasant – I sat between Chairman Cedric Rhoades and 'Mr' Mayor, a woman – Pigs in Space chauffeured Simmo and me home. We called in at the Swan for a pint, then Pigs stayed the night, and I awoke with the feeling I hadn't had too much sleep.

My innings had evidently lasted longer than Goochie's, who was said to be the first batsman out on the day, and therefore in the new season. That gave some of our members the chance to make a few comments. I have nothing against Goochie. I think he is a great batsman and, from what I can gather, a good bloke, but he is becoming my cross to bear. I am getting sick and tired of having his name rammed down my throat. It has been for the last three years, and now that he is available again after his suspension, it is getting worse. People seem to think it is him or me for the place in the England team, and so defend me by criticizing him. I always try to say that this is not the case, and I think I've upset some people by defending his cause and so, as far as they are concerned, not being on their side. But I cannot see him being slandered just because they support Lancashire. For my part I want to play well and score runs. I hope Goochie scores runs too, because I would love to open the innings with him. I don't think it would be 50-0 at lunch if we did.

28

Lancashire v. Sussex, second day
Lancashire 237 (Jefferies 93); Sussex 113-4 (A. Wells 55
not out, Allott 3-22)

It was absolutely freezing again. We started at noon. Jeffo was out in the third over and was obviously disappointed. We all were, because everyone would have liked him to get his century – he is a good bloke. Walt bowled well early on, and got three early wickets, Jeffo getting the other. Then Imran and Alan Wells halted the slide.

It gradually became more overcast and started to drizzle. The sky was Manchester steel-grey, and the clouds were coming from the rain quarter over the ladies' pavilion, known affectionately as 'over Bill's mother's'. Nearly every ground has 'Bill's mother's'. Local knowledge has it that when it comes from there, once you go off you'll struggle to get back on, and so it proved.

Horrible days like this don't endear you to our summer game. Talking to Imran between overs, he said his hands were so cold that he couldn't feel or grip his bat. It was the sort of weather when the ball feels as if it is going to break your fingers when you field it. When the rain set in in earnest and we went off, Shauny organized everyone to pay £1 to buy Trivial Pursuit to play on the coach to away matches – we travel by National Express Coach instead of cars, which is the usual method of transport for most county teams.

I was presented with a cake by two giggling girls for my birthday, which was last week. When we left I went round to some friends to watch a video. I felt incredibly tired – strange, because all I've done is answer about thirty fan letters.

29

No play, rain. Match abandoned as a draw.

We were due to start at 11.30 after an inspection, but it started raining at 11.20. There was an early lunch, and it stopped. Another inspection and we were due to start at 2.30.

At 2.20 it started raining again. The game was finally called off at 3.00.

While we were waiting, the Trivial Pursuit pack arrived and a game was organized – Sussex (Parker, A. Wells, Greig and Reeve) v. Lancs (Shauny, Harvey and Tosh) plus assorted helpers from both teams. One question was: Who sang some song or other in Walt Disney's *Pinocchio*? Shauny said, 'It was that little grasshopper Jiminy Cricket. Was he a grasshopper or was he a cricket?' provoking absolute uproar. Lancs got off to a good start but fell away, and Sussex came through to win a riotous, ribald game in the junior players' dressing-room.

I went off and used our new multi-gym for a while, and had a coffee and hotpot there instead of sitting down to the team lunch. Then I had an indoor net against the bowling machine, which was quite good. If used properly, they can be an extremely useful asset.

When the game was called off the lads embarked for Oxford, where they are having a practice match against the University on the way to Bristol. I stayed behind because my contact lens is still not settling in properly and I have an appointment at the optician's. I also have to see Reebok.

Went out for a drink with Malcolm Taylor and Didge.

30

We finally arrived at Bristol at 1.15 a.m. I spent over two hours at the optician's – inconclusively – three quarters of an hour at Reebok, and then Simmo and I stopped off in Worcester to see Duncan Fearnley. We spent a long time there, picking up a load of gear for the lads while we were about it, and didn't leave Worcester until 11.40. Needless to say, our evening meal was fish and chips, that well-known Simmo diet. The fish-and-chip shop provided a nice example of cultural misunderstanding. We asked for them 'in a bag', the paper folded so there is an opening at one end so that you can eat them easily – a usual thing in Lancashire and Yorkshire chippies. The server wrapped them up completely and then slid the package into a brown paper bag. We laughed, and she stared at us as if we were stupid – we probably were.

Simmo trains on fish and chips – along with tea and cigarettes. He is probably one of the most popular people in cricket. I don't know anybody who dislikes him, and he is one of the nicest people ever to play the game. I know a lot of people who think he is long-winded – I'm one of them – but then I share the same fault. He has been one of the great characters of Lancashire cricket, an outstanding slow bowler in the one-day game and a great asset with the bat. He is completely unprofessional, he is never on time, thinks a net is something to do with fishing, and his diet is something no professional sportsman could imagine. He hates going to bed before midnight, but once in bed hates getting up. He loves to talk about cricket, money and aeroplane timetables. He likes betting on horses, but you can guarantee that if Simmo backs a horse your money is safer in your back pocket.

He runs five or six businesses and spends sixteen hours a day making phone calls looking after them. At the end of the day he probably makes enough profit to pay his phone bill. He rang me in Delhi one night when I was sharing with Percy, with whom he's in business. He didn't know I was sharing with Percy, and after chatting for forty minutes he said, 'Eh, Fow, I'd better go.' So I said, 'What about Percy?' 'Eh, I'd forgot about Percy,' and he then carried on talking to him for another forty minutes.

As I said, he is probably one of the nicest blokes you'll ever meet. You can spend as much time as you want talking about cricket, and he will always help you. He has always helped me. He is a great thinker about the game, but I reckon what happens to him is that he can see so many different points of view that at the end of the day he doesn't always know what he thinks. That can be a good thing sometimes, because he can open up other people's minds by arguing a different point of view, which he loves to do.

He is a phenomenal eater. He will always say, 'No thank you, I don't want any of that, I'm on a diet . . . oh, go on then, just a little piece.' And the little piece becomes four pieces. But he always has a slimline tonic in his dry martini! He smokes like a chimney. He has given up twice, but started again eighteen times. He is what we know as an all-round good egg.

Then we overshot the hotel by ten miles and had to ask directions from a taxi rank. Walt was fairly sleepy when I got to our room, but he gave me the news – we'd beaten Oxford quite comfortably – before we went to sleep. It is our tenth year of rooming together.

MAY

1

Gloucestershire v. Lancashire, first day
Lancashire 318 (Allott 78, Watkinson 57, Jefferies 57,
Stanworth 50 not out, Fowler 30, Lawrence 5-79);
Gloucestershire 2-1

We were put in on a very green wicket and struggled. Syd
Lawrence is being floated as the latest up-and-coming fast
bowler England need. He is a good trier, and he has
undoubtedly improved, but the wicket gave him a lot of help
and I think his figures flattered him. The fall of wickets tell the
story really: 13-1; 22-2; 23-3; 51-4; 88-5; 94-6; 168-7; 196-8;
203-9; 318 all out.

Scyld Berry had phoned early in the day to arrange for
Walt and me to have a meal with him in the evening. He
arrived in time to see Stanny and Walt get personal career
bests. While they were batting Winker said, 'I want Walt to
pass his career best, but I don't want to have to listen to him
afterwards!' Fast bowlers love to talk about their batting
achievements. It has to be said, though, that it was the best I
have ever seen him play.

It was quite an eventful day in every way. Phil Bainbridge,
whom I played with for England Schools, got a fractured
cheekbone trying to catch Aby off his first ball at third slip.
Then when they batted, Walt got Stovold in the first over,
and Jack Russell, coming in as night-watchman, was winged
on the helmet ducking into a ball just short of a length and

had to retire hurt. As well as being green, the wicket had a fair amount of bounce!

Even at its best Bristol is bleak. Every time I've played here it's been cold and wet, and there is never any atmosphere. Even if you filled the ground I don't think you'd get much atmosphere, because it is so flat and open. There's an ugly school at the top and open terraced houses at the bottom, so it never feels closed in, and there is no height anywhere. It is not a little stadium like Mote Park at Maidstone, which is a lovely place to play; what with all the marquees and the big grassy bank at the top, it is a superb ground for the spectators to watch the cricket. But at Bristol you can't even sit in the dressing-room and watch the game. The windows are frosted glass, so you either have to lift them up and peer on your hands and knees or lie on your stomach. Even then you are looking through railings. The alternative is to go on to the top balcony, and it is inevitably freezing up there.

In the event, Scyld missed his meal, because the combined efforts of Walt and Stanny, and Jeffo's career best at the weekend, called for a team meal at the hotel. Mr Dagg, one of our most loyal supporters, gave the captain some money, which paid for the wine, and we had a really enjoyable evening. Walt gave a speech on his career best, and Shauny responded to much laughter. I missed that as I was on the phone to Steph. One of the snags of our life is getting everyday things organized, such as renewing driving licences or car insurance or tax. Or, in this case, producing my documents. They are supposed to be produced in Accrington by tomorrow. There is no way I will be able to. Does this make me a fugitive?

Steph wants a kitten. Apparently it was born in a dustbin, and she has fallen for it. She knows I'm soft, so it looks as if I could be greeted by a barking dog, a scratching cat and the lovely Stephanie when I get home. Still, I suppose a cat is not too bad – what she really wants is a monkey. To save anyone else saying it I will – you would think one would be enough.

And so to bed in yet another hotel on yet another soft bed, which does not do me any good at all.

2

Gloucestershire v. Lancashire, second day
Gloucestershire 189 (Allott 4-44, Jefferies 3-45, Watkin-
son 2-60); Lancashire second innings 126-9 (Fowler 0)

Our first-innings score is looking a very good one. They batted like us, except that they didn't have anyone to get stuck in at the end. Walt and Jeffo used the conditions well. Winker had one of those days – he was either hit for four or they played and missed.

When we batted again I got a nick to Jack Russell. Shauny came in and was vizored first ball. Onky was 1 not out at the time. Shauny came off, sat down for ten minutes and then went off to hospital for a check-up. When he got back he looked at the scoreboard and said, 'Bloody hell. I've been to the hospital, had a check-up and come back, and Al's still only got one.' When Al finally got his second, he doffed his cap. He was out soon afterwards and went straight up to Shauny and asked him in his usual gentle way, 'Are you all right, Shauny?' The response was immediate: 'No, I can't hear a bloody thing.'

3

Gloucestershire v. Lancashire, third day
Lancashire 318 and 165 (Sainsbury 5-44, Lawrence 4-70);
Gloucestershire 189 and 220 (Bainbridge 67, Jefferies 4-64,
Allott 2-25, Simmons 2-53). Lancashire won by 74 runs.

All the injured made fighting recoveries – Shauny ended up as our top scorer in the second innings, and Bainbridge batted well for them. In the end our bowlers won the match with their batting on the first day. So the drag back from Bristol was quite a pleasant one.

CD told Walt and me that Norrie had been trying to check up on what time we had got back in last night. Pete goes to bed early. CD sits in the bar quietly enjoying himself, so Pete asked him what time we came in and went to bed. He would never say, but he said to us, 'Norrie's on me back again. He wants to know what time you came in.' He is a brilliant driver – there was about an inch and a half to spare each side taking the coach in and out of the ground, and he manoeuvred it brilliantly, unlike the second-team driver we used to have, who was useless. He used to get lost every night coming back from grounds.

CD is a very funny man. He loves cricket and has a unique insight into our team because everyone tells him all their grudges. So he gets the earache from everybody, but he also gets all this information on which to base his opinions. I think at times he gets sick of listening to everybody's moans and groans, but he also finds it fascinating. And although he never volunteers an opinion, if you ask him he has quite an astute point of view. And it is good to hear an outsider's views, because they can put things into perspective.

He is a shop steward at his depot and quite militant. He often says, 'I don't know how you blokes put up with all this rubbish.'

4

Lancashire v. Leicestershire, Benson & Hedges Cup
No play, rain

Simmo picked me up as my shiny new sponsored Volvo was waiting for me at the ground. As usual with Simmo we were late, but no one really bothers.

When we left Accrington it was sunny and blustery – not perfect conditions, but OK. Clouds were building up as we got further south along the M66. By the time we were approaching the M63 exit for Old Trafford the sky had blackened, and we arrived at the ground in rain. It was to stay like that all day.

At one stage we actually got our whites on and knocked up in front of the pavilion, going through all the pre-match preliminaries, but we looked like a bunch of men waiting for the rain. It came. I talked to Lubo for a while and did a small circuit in our multi-gym. I also watched Jeffo come and go again with tonsilitis and flu, so he will have spent the day in bed.

In the evening Harvey, Walt, Shauny and I, plus wives, girlfriends, kids and dogs, went to Knutsford for a meal. It was a good night – average to good food – but it is bloody miles away, and I fell asleep on the way home. Steph was driving, so I shall have to wait until tomorrow to drive my shiny new Volvo.

And it is still raining!

5

Lancashire v. Leicestershire, John Player League
Lancashire 127-9 (Fowler 11); Leicestershire 8-1. Rain
stopped play, no result.

Heavy skies and a bitter breeze were the order of the morning until lunchtime. We got started on time – which is now 1.30 instead of 2.00 to fit in with TV coverage – and struggled through our innings. Three overs into their innings it tipped down and that was that.

I was late again; I got there at 12.00. Nothing was said. To be honest, I don't think anyone noticed I was late, but if they did they didn't care! Timing is one of the niggling things at our club. For all-day matches we are supposed to report at 9.30 a.m. For people coming from outside Manchester, particularly from the north like Simmo and me, that means we have to travel through the rush-hour. If it was 9.45, we could leave half an hour later, because the journey would be so much easier. But the annoying thing is we report at 9.30, and then do nothing until 10.10. Even then, 95 per cent of the time there are no decent nets for us to use anyway. So what the point of us arriving at 9.30 is, I don't know.

The theory is to get there at 9.30 and be changed for 9.45. So you get changed for 9.45, and there is nothing to do, so you just sit and have a cup of tea and a biscuit.

6

Lancashire v. Leicestershire, Benson & Hedges Cup
Lancashire 145-9 (Fowler 12); Leicestershire 147-7
(Balderstone 58 not out)

It was cold and miserable, the ball swung all over over the place and batting was a nightmare. Only four people got over 20 — Aby and Winker got 34 apiece, Lubo got 24 and Baldy batted right through their innings for his 58. Shauny bowled well and got 4 for 17, and Jack gave away 5 runs in his 11 overs, but it was the sort of game where the side batting second had the advantage, and they won the toss.

My neck was quite a handicap today, so I told Aby and Pete about it. I've asked them not to spread it around, because I don't want to use it as an excuse, and I don't want all the questions, but I had to tell them because at times I just can't move properly, so I'm going to have to field somewhere where I'm not racing around.

<u>7</u>

A free morning before we travelled to London to play Surrey. We're staying in Kensington – God knows why!

I got up early with Steph (7 a.m.), took Smithy for a walk, cooked breakfast and then messed around all morning. I was too late for lunch at Old Trafford, so I went out to Chorlton and bought two pairs of trousers.

Shauny was no more organized. He was supposed to be having his eyes tested this morning. He didn't go because he said that when he woke up he couldn't see, so there was no point going! Shauny's logic.

On the bus Walt and I played Trivial Pursuit with Shauny and Harvey. We lost. The four of us ended up this evening in a wine bar in Covent Garden. We saw a bouncer beat someone up – a quiet night! Then there was a little horseplay back at the hotel. No damage: shaving foam on their door and solusal through the removed spy-hole.

<u>8</u>

Surrey v. Lancashire, first day
Surrey 341 (Clinton 87, Butcher 81, Jesty 75, Allott
6-71); Lancashire 6-0 (Fowler 2 not out)

Percy won the toss and elected to bat on a slow, docile pitch. Walt bowled tremendously in unhelpful conditions to halt their runaway start – they put on 167 for the first wicket.

Soren Henriksen made his first-class début for us. He got his first first-class wicket, taking a return catch from Trevor Jesty even though he had injured his right shoulder. With his long, loping strides and high action he could be moulded into a useful performer. As you will have guessed from the name, he is a Dane. By TCCB rules he is English, but he can't play for England. But then last week Kevin Curran, who is captain of Zimbabwe, was playing for Gloucestershire against us as an English player because he has an Irish passport. The game has gone mad.

This evening we went to the exiled Lancastrians' dinner. It is one of those things you have to do, and is all very nice in some ways, but personally I don't like being bombarded for over two hours with questions about cricket and my personal life. Still, it's all part of the life – or so they tell me.

9

Surrey v. Lancashire, second day
Lancashire 222 (Fowler 19, Fairbrother 48, Needham
6-42); Surrey second innings 91-3

I scratched my way to 19. Things just aren't working at all. I feel constricted because of my neck at times, and trying to get used to the contact lens is not helping. I've decided to stop using it for the time being and see if that makes any difference.

To cap it all, I felt ill and spent nearly all afternoon asleep on a couch in the dressing-room, emerging only to field when they went in again. Winker had the same problem – it's flu, by the symptoms. Hope that is all, and not legionnaire's disease!

By the close they were 210 on, so our situation is not exactly commanding. The wicket is slow, turning from one end and slightly unpredictable at the other – not a wicket to have to chase a big fourth-innings total on.

I spent the night at Percy's. It was lovely to see them all again – after India I regard the whole family as my friends. He lives right out in Surrey, which is lovely, but a long way from the Oval. In the morning it takes him one hour and ten minutes to get in, which is even longer than it takes me from

Accrington, and I thought that was long enough. We went out for a meal in a pleasant little Italian restaurant in Dorking. He is very philosophical about everything and I spent the time talking to him about my future. I am becoming conscious that I haven't scored any runs yet, and with Gooch available for England I need to. He was just what I needed. Even though I'm playing against him at the moment he still gave me advice. He said, 'If you play 60 to 70 Test matches you've had a helluva good career. You've played 20, so you've got 50 to go. If you reckon you've got another eight or nine years left, that means you've only got to play one match in two, so you don't have to be desperate to play in every Test match there is. So just relax. Don't bat on a short-term basis to be selected for the one-day matches and the first Test. Bat on a long-term basis, work at your technique, don't just try and get runs to secure your place for the next Test, but keep playing, knowing that over the years you will play your Test cricket. You are never going to be a thoroughbred like David Gower, you know that (which I do), but you can still make a hell of a career for yourself if you bat long-term.'

I thought that was sound advice really. I hadn't thought about it that way myself, being impetuous, but he made me think about it, and it isn't a bad way of looking at it. I had been putting a lot of pressure on myself, and I think advising me to bat for each day, not to try to be an international player, but to just play and play and play because I'll be good enough to get runs, and not to bat as if it's a case of 'If I don't get runs today I'll not get picked and that's the end of it', is all good advice.

10

Surrey v. Lancashire, third day
Surrey 341 and 191-7 (Jesty 96); Lancashire 222 and 77
(Fowler 5). Surrey won by 233 runs

As a unit we are not batting very well at the moment; in fact, 'atrociously' is probably a better word. After today's débâcle we had a team meeting to thrash things out. It got quite heated at times, and we were there for an hour slanging and shouting, with the dressing-room attendant coming in and saying, 'When are you lot going, then? I wanna go 'ome!'

As usual when things are not going well, personally and as a team, theories abound. I'm getting offered advice from all and sundry. It isn't what I need. They are all trying to be helpful; but what I really need is to be left alone to work it out, not to have one person saying, 'You're getting square on,' another saying, 'You are opening the face' and a third saying, 'Your backlift isn't straight.' They suggested they could video me, but that's useless – there isn't a video of me when I'm playing well to make a comparison with, and from what I've seen of myself on TV my back lift isn't straight when I am playing well. It looks horrible anyway.

Hubert said much the same thing to me as Percy had when I talked to him about it. He has always maintained that you have to be true to yourself as a batsman. And he said, 'You don't have to prove anything now. You've got your runs in the book, you've done it. Just carry on doing what you do, you don't have to do anything different, you don't have to play like a Test player – you are one. Just carry on playing.' And that is nice to hear when I'm not playing well. I think it makes more sense than all this technical advice, which is often contradictory anyway. If I try and play like an international player, I never score runs. I have to score runs my way and get picked for internationals.

We agreed that we would have ten minutes' fielding practice every day to get the team spirit going again. Shauny wanted everyone to train together first. I opposed that, saying that we should do individual stretching first, because each person knows what he needs; besides, it would be difficult to organize, so we should do our own routines and then get together for fielding.

There was quite a row. Walt and Hubert agreed with me, and in the end I asked Pete Lever, who had been sitting there listening, what he thought: 'Why don't we ask him, he's supposed to be in charge?' And Pete agreed too, but Shauny wouldn't concede. In the end I said, 'You won't take my word for it, you won't take Clive's or Paul's or Pete's. He's been on two tours, Walt's been on two, I've been on three and God knows how many Clive has been on. It seems to me there's a lot of experience there against you, Shauny. Does that indicate anything to you?' But he wasn't happy.

Then Winker said that last year everyone seemed to be pulling together and working for each other and putting everything in because we knew we weren't a great side. 'I knew if I bowled a bad ball, someone was going to dive full length and try and stop it, which was great encouragement. This year it seems to me we are coasting through games, expecting people to surrender for us to win.' I think that was the first time he had ever spoken out in a meeting. And he was absolutely right.

One thing we did agree was that before Benson & Hedges games we should have a team meeting to discuss the opposition and work out our plan and all pull together, which we need to do because we aren't good enough individually to win through. And we said that we would do that tonight on the coach on the way up to Birmingham, because there was nothing else to do on the bus anyway, so we could sit down and talk. And what happened? We played Trivial Pursuit all the way up. Not a word was said about having a team meeting, which is incredible after all the slanging which had gone on in the Oval dressing-room. We got off the bus and nobody even remembered we were supposed to be having a meeting.

*

We are staying at the Cobden Hotel in Birmingham — God knows why, it's a temperance hotel. My mood wasn't helped when I discovered I'd left all my civvy gear in Percy's car. I thought there was something missing when I got on the bus at the Oval, and that was what it was. So I'm without hairbrush, toothbrush and my contact lens — it's just as well I'd already decided not to wear it. And no change of clothes. There are no phones in the rooms, so I had to keep going down to a phone box to keep trying to phone Percy to find out his movements so that he could get the stuff back to me.

Some of the lads went over to the American bar/pick-up joint at the Strathallan Hotel, just opposite us. It isn't the most refined place on the circuit but they wouldn't let me in. I had a pair of smart trousers on, but also a T-shirt and sports top, and I was greeted with, 'No, you can't come in here, you've got no collar on your shirt.' So I went back over to the steak bar next door to the Cobden, had a drink there and then went to the Lychee Garden for a meal.

11

Warwickshire v. Lancashire, Benson & Hedges Cup
Warwickshire 282-4 (Lloyd 137, Kallicharran 37);
Lancashire 219 (O'Shaughnessy 66, Fowler 9). Warwicks
won by 63 runs.

We got to the ground one and three quarters of an hour before the start. God knows why! Perhaps yesterday's team meeting had some bearing.

We fielded first on a bitterly cold day. Long johns are still almost essential equipment. Andy Lloyd played very well for his career best, but our bowling was not up to par early on.

I still can't get going. I hesitated over a drive and gave a return catch to Wall — known as Max or Brick. If I had been in nick, it would have gone for four. I could have cried, but as a senior pro it is best to try and keep cool. So I just went quiet instead. We all batted badly, and lost comfortably. Spirits are not very good.

I went out for a meal with Steve and Jane, Winker and Sue, and Albert and Debbie. Back to the Lychee Garden for another Chinese – it is amazing how often you go back to the same place. A sombre evening was passed.

We then went on to a nightclub, Steve and I borrowing Albert's and Winker's blazers and ties to conform with regulations. We got cheap tickets from the hotel. If I had used my name, we could have probably got in for nothing, but I don't like doing that. You can't scream for privacy one minute and then demand recognition the next. Besides, it would embarrass Steve, Jane and me. I'm also afraid of being told, 'So what?' We didn't stay long. I got back to the hotel in time to watch the end of *10* on TV. I ended up crying, not really at the film, but not at anything else either. I felt better afterwards. Walt wasn't back, and I went to sleep without saying good-night to someone for the first time in ages.

12

Warwickshire v. Lancashire, John Player League
Warwickshire 213-5 (Amiss 53, Humpage 53); Lancashire
190 (Fowler 46). Warwickshire won by 23 runs.

Today we got to the ground one and a half hours before the game, when we had to have our lunch as well as do the pre-match rituals. The logic escapes me.

Clive played today – just seeing him in the dressing-room made me feel better. We fielded first. It was as cold as it had been yesterday. Again I was fielding on the edge and had very little to do. There was one difference, though. Yesterday

Geoff Humpage hit a catch to me at deep square leg. Today he played the same shot, almost identical. His Sunday roast beef stood him in good stead because this time it went for six. I could only root myself and get half a hand on the ball.

Dennis Amiss's 53 took him into the record books as the highest aggregate in the John Player League. He is still a bloody good player. We lost it really in the last 5 overs. They were 151 off 35 overs, 213 off 40.

I opened with Shauny and we put on 76 in good time. I didn't play too badly. I received the identical ball from Brick today, but followed through this time and it went over his head for four. Hubert's little pep talk must have worked. I hit one great shot, a six over extra cover which went a hell of a long way. I must have got everything right. Finally I hit a ball which could have gone anywhere straight to my mate Gladstone. But at least my confidence has gone up a notch or two.

We still lost. Our middle order is not functioning as it should. But if I start to tick over properly, then I'm sure that everyone else will do better; at the moment they are being exposed too early.

Yesterday Harvey and I had a play fight to get rid of our energy and frustration. It was all right until we demolished a pile of autograph bats, and then Pete Lever pulled me off the top of Harvey. It had served its purpose – I think we both felt much better for it.

I discovered that some of the lads turned up at the nightclub after we'd left. They got in free!

All the lads except Simmo, Aby, Walt, Onky and I have been called in for nets tomorrow. I shall go anyway. I hope a net will do me good and, besides, Hubert is going in and he asked me to go. It is probably a classic case of perversity, but if given the choice 99 per cent of the time I will work; if I'm told, I often object.

13

Our nets are not very good.

14

Lancashire v. Yorkshire, Benson & Hedges Cup
No play, rain

Ever since Barry Wood left Derbyshire, there have been stories about him coming back into county cricket. For a time there were suggestions that he would come back to Lancashire. I can't imagine why anyone believed that was possible – I don't think the chairman would allow him through the door, even if Woody said he would play for nothing. Now there are stories going the rounds that Geoff Boycott wants Yorkshire to sign him. That would be interesting: the thought of two such strong, self-opinionated characters as Boycs and Woody in the same dressing-room for any length of time, let alone as opening partners, is mind-boggling.

15

Lancashire 146 (O'Shaughnessy 48, Fowler 29); Yorkshire
144-9. Match reduced to 32 overs a side. Lancashire won
by 2 runs.

I suppose the most astonishing thing was that we got a game in at all. The ground was under water overnight, and it rained hard again early on, but it dried quickly enough for us to have a sort of shorter Sunday match.

Yorkshire gave the worst display of fielding I've seen for ages. From difficult catches to straightforward fielding, they looked bad, but we still only just scraped it in the end. They needed six off the last ball to win. Walt bowled Fergy (Carrick) a length ball on middle stump with the shorter boundary on the leg side. Fergy went inside and hoicked it, and it went one bounce for four. For a moment it looked like a six, and Fergy ran off waving his bat in triumph until he discovered it was four. Walt took a lot of stick afterwards, because it was a terrible ball. The comments were jovial because the ball bounced two feet inside the rope. Had it been a six, the stick would have been serious!

Then we raced on to the coach to head for Worcester.

16

Worcestershire v. Lancashire, Benson & Hedges Cup
Lancashire 258-5 (O'Shaughnessy 90, Abrahams 57,
Fowler 8); Worcestershire 261-4 (Neale 94 not out,
D'Oliveira 47 not out). Worcestershire won by 6 wickets.

It appears that I am getting out to balls that I would normally score off. I was caught behind off Neal Radford, who used to play for us. To make matters worse, I had a boring day in the field, nothing to do at all.

Chris Glass, an old college friend, was on the boundary. I was pleased to see him, and we had a quick drink together, arranging to see more of each other when we come back here for the championship match.

Duncan Fearnley took Clive and me into the committee room afterwards for a drink. I enjoyed the thought of doing that, but at the time somewhere at the back of my mind I couldn't help but feel out of place. Maybe if I was playing better I would have felt more at home.

17

I have been picked to play for the MCC against the Australians at Lord's next week, with Graham Gooch as my opening partner. I'm on trial again, but I feel that they are giving me every opportunity to succeed, which is comforting. I don't think they want me to fail in order to make Test selection easier.

We haven't got a championship match tomorrow, so I shall only have the John Player League match to bat in before then.

19

Old Trafford
Lancashire v. Gloucestershire, John Player League
Lancashire 220-6 (Fairbrother 49 not out, Fowler 35);
Gloucestershire 223-4 (Romaines 65, Davison 57).
Gloucestershire won by 6 wickets.

I was reunited with my clothes at last. David Graveney brought them up – he'd run into Percy somewhere.

21

I travelled down via Legger's house, spending a pleasant afternoon there. Then I followed him to London and all the way to the wrong hotel. Out of habit he went to the Westmoreland, whereas we were actually booked in at the Holiday Inn, Swiss Cottage. After bollocking all the receptionists for not booking us in, he bumped into someone who redirected him to the Holiday Inn.

By this time Andy Peebles had phoned and was on the way round. Legger had arranged to meet some friends at the hotel – the wrong one – so he was leaving messages everywhere. In the end he came out in the evening with Peebles, me and some friends from the record business. We ate in a small restaurant in Camden. At least, I think it was in Camden – I have eaten in some great little restaurants in London, but never remember the names and addresses. I should write them all down, but I never remember to do that either. It was a very pleasant evening, except that I burnt the end of my thumb on a book of matches. Idiot. I didn't say anything, but the blister is proof of the pain.

22

MCC v. Australians, first day
Australians 377-6 (Border 125, O'Donnell 100 not out,
Wessels 60)

'Deadly' Underwood was one of the first people I saw in the morning. I greeted him with 'Good morning, manager.' I'm not sure how pleased he was.

Dressing-rooms in matches like this are fascinating. There is the usual apparently casual air, everyone laughing, joking, trying to appear nonchalant, but underneath very keen to do well, and some obviously nervous, even though nobody knows what purpose this game really serves. I suspect that the selectors use it to scrutinize three or four players, but that's just a guess.

Goochie wasn't nervous, though. He announced he had played in the very same game ten years ago. Now he looked like an established England opening batsman, and that was before he got changed. There must be a lot of pressure on him coming back to reclaim his place after three years in the wilderness, but it wasn't apparent. 'It's a good day for smashing these Aussies about,' he said. 'There's nothing better than making this lot run about.'

Unfortunately, though, we fielded first, in between the odd shower and interruption for bad light. But at least bad light saved me and Goochie from having to face twenty minutes at the end. So Odin came to the rescue. 'Odin' is often heard on cricket fields. He is the god of weather, so when you want it to rain you shout, 'Odin!'

Neil Williams was very nervous, so much so that he couldn't hit the front line with his foot. And if he is going to react to pressure like that in an MCC game, then a Test match now could finish him: it would reduce him to a nervous wreck. I was surprised, because when you talk to Middlesex players they generally rate him above Norman Cowans, but today he didn't look anywhere near the bowler Flash is. Perhaps he is a bloke who looks outstanding when he gets it right, but just couldn't today.

Mark Nicholas, who was captaining the MCC, said to Arnie Sidebottom at the start of play, 'What do you want? Three slips and a gully, or four slips?' Arnie just looked at him in that lugubrious Yorkshire way. 'Who do you think I am – Malcolm Marshall?' I think he was nervous too, in spite of all his experience in sport, but he coped better, and he looked much the better of our two seam bowlers. Not as quick, of course, but he seemed to nip it about a bit. He was a bit unlucky, but he bowled a little on the short side. That might have been nerves, but it is the one criticism I would make of him. He beats the bat too often. If he pitched it a little further up, he'd hit thick edges instead. You don't often see him being drilled back past his feet, but I'd prefer to see that to him being pulled and cut. If it's further up, it means you are giving the ball a chance.

In the evening we had the official dinner welcoming the Australians to England. Both teams went. There was an England player and an Australian on each table. Thankfully I was opposite Graeme Wood, whom I know quite well, and the evening passed quite reasonably for one of these dinners. They tend to get a bit boring sometimes. The outstanding event was the speech by the Australian manager, Bob Merriman, who stood up and slated Henry Blofeld for his reports and comments from Australia. That took everybody by surprise. The Australian lads seemed a bit embarrassed listening to it, and nobody else seemed to know what was going on. He just kept going and going, and by the end I think everybody was feeling a bit awkward.

Afterwards we had a drink and then were glad to get away. I had a chat with A. C. Smith and Phil Sharpe at the dinner. They were both very kind. They said, 'Look, we know how well you can play. All we want is for you to give us some indication that you are getting your form back, some excuse to pick you. Just get a few runs so we can justify picking you.' Then they started talking about Arnie, so it looks as if they are looking at him very seriously.

Frenchy's hair has grown out to a respectable crew cut now. He hasn't had it cut since Sharjah – he said he was getting his money's worth!

23

MCC v. Australians, second day
Australians 377-6 dec. and 39-1; MCC 292-2 dec.
(Lamb 122 not out, Nicholas 115 not out, Fowler 24)

I was caught at mid-on. If I'd been in nick I wouldn't have been caught: either I'd have leaned over it and hit it past him on the floor, or I'd have hit it straight back over his head. Instead you are conscious that you are out of touch, so you try to concentrate extra-hard and be extra-careful; and you end up being too cautious, you hesitate slightly and then you are lost. One thing is for sure. This game does not get any easier, mentally, physically or emotionally. Yet people keep telling me it's only a game!

It was the first time I'd batted with Graham Gooch. Neither of us did that well – he was bowled by Thomson for 15. I did all right until I was out. But I think it was important for me to be given the chance, because the rebels are back. I've always felt I was playing for the 'England Second XI', and it has been a matter of pride, I suppose, that I wanted to be picked when everyone was available. It was also virtually the first time I'd met Goochie, certainly the first time I'd talked to him. Ironic, having spent so much time defending him over the last three years.

Mark Nicholas was really nervous when he came in to bat with me, but he got a very good hundred once he got going. Lamby was his usual self.

In the evening I went out with Andy Peebles, Lamby and Lindsey, and Mark Nicholas. We had a meal and Peebs took us to the Hippodrome, a fascinating place. At one stage we saw this fellow with nothing on but a chain G-string – Lindsey couldn't believe her eyes, and I don't think Lamby could either.

I was taken to the Hippodrome last year by David Bairstow. We were playing in the one-day series against the West Indies, and Bluey said in this very definite voice, 'You're coming out with me tonight.' So I said, 'Yeah, all right, I'll have a drink with you.' And he took me to the Hippodrome. He said, 'The gear you've got, I want to see what happens when you go in this place!', because as we were in London I was all dressed up. But he'd set me up: one of his friends was the bar manager, and it was gay night. So Bluey pushed me in and I got quite a few offers. In spite of what Both thinks, I didn't take any.

24

MCC v. Australians, third day
Australia 377-6 dec. and 222-3 (Welham 81 not out);
MCC 291-2 dec. Match drawn.

It was a bit of a non-event really. They wanted some batting
practice and the weather killed any chance of a declaration
anyway. We were off and on. Goochie had a long bowl – he
bowled quite well, in fact. But it was just a waste of time by
the end, and we were all quite glad to get off and get away,
especially with the Roses game tomorrow – playing against
Arnie instead of with him.

Senior players and the manager will always tell you about
the Roses game, 'This is the one to win.' We all love beating
Yorkshire, but it doesn't give me any more pleasure than
beating anyone else. What I find tragic now is that it has got
to the stage where the first consideration of our committee –
and, I imagine, Yorkshire's committee – is that they don't
want to lose, and that gives the game a negative tinge from
the outset. 'We're not giving these tykes anything' and all that
sort of thing. I don't really agree with that, because we are not
a good enough side to get into a commanding position and
then thrash somebody. We aren't like that. We have to walk
along the tightrope all the time, the thin line between winning
and losing, to even stand a chance of winning. If we are
hedging our bets and trying to make sure we are safe, we will
never get into a position to win, because we aren't good
enough to blast a side out or smash the runs off. We have to
take a gamble, and against Yorkshire we don't do that.

To me it is not our Test match, as it is so often called. To
others it may be. David Hughes absolutely loves beating
Yorkshire – loves it. He hates them, and so does Jack
Simmons. I mean, we all get on with the opposition as
individuals, but because it's Yorkshire . . . I suppose to some

extent I feel that too. I'd hate to lose to them. But I'd rather give myself a chance of losing and winning than take the negative 'We must not lose to them at any cost' approach.

It isn't a Test match, especially for me as an opener. Playing against Surrey or Sussex, or Somerset if Joel Garner is running in, is more of a Test match because that is much more of a challenge than facing Arnie and Graham Stevenson and Paul Jarvis, even though I rate Arnie. It doesn't have the same edge, it isn't as hostile. I don't look at Yorkshire and think, 'It's going to be tough'; I think, 'Do I really need my helmet?' It is that thought rather than 'It's our Test match tomorrow'.

And we do get on with them as individuals. Simmo and Jack Hampshire go on holiday together. I think Arnie is a great bloke, very funny, and so is Bluey. Martyn Moxon and I are very good friends. I've known Neil Hartley for years and years, I've played with Kevin Sharp in Australia, and so it goes on. There's only one bloke in the Yorkshire team who hates me, and that's Graham Stevenson – Moonbeam to his friends. For some reason he absolutely hates me. I've never spent a great deal of time with him off the field, so it must be purely from how he sees me on the field and from brief conversations in pubs. And it is probably built on a total misunderstanding – he probably thinks I hate him. It's one of those things which have built up because we have never taken the time to talk to one another.

I'd been brought up with Yorkshire lads because in schoolboy cricket we always had at least one game against Yorkshire – Under-15, Under-16, Under-19 or Federation matches. And in those years I was always being picked for coaching courses. I got into the England Under-15 side, and from then on I was always there, if never one of the stars. And I found it a completely different world being with Lancashire or Yorkshire lads and being with Millfield public schoolboys. I still do, not that I've anything against public schoolboys – some of my best friends, etc. But at fourteen or fifteen I had a lot more in common with Yorkshire lads than with southern public schoolboys. And on those coaching courses where you go away for four or five days there would be me and Paul Allott, and you could always guarantee there would be three or four people from Yorkshire, all the northern lads would stick together, as would those from the south.

So I've always looked forward to playing against Yorkshire. I've a lot of friends there and I enjoy having a drink with them afterwards. I know no one is going to kill me when they are bowling at me, and it isn't going to be an incredibly demanding game. And that destroys the mythology for me about it being the awesome task that it is portrayed as. Whether people still feel that on the terraces, I don't know. I know they do in the committee room. At least, the impression they give is that if we beat Yorkshire twice they would be quite happy, even if we didn't win another game, because they like taking their friends into the committee room – 'Welcome to my club' – especially when they've just beaten Yorkshire. It's like an old boys' club rather than a business centre.

And since I've been at the club the players, apart from David Lloyd, have generally been friends with them. So although we want to beat them, the real rivalry exists only for people who don't actually participate in the game. All my mates will say, 'Ooh, you're playing Yorkshire next', and I'll say, 'Yes, we'll beat the long chins all right.' Incidentally, I don't know where the nickname comes from; possibly from David Hughes, because he reckons they all walk around sticking their chin out and uttering aggressive, grumpy noises, a bit like Freddie Trueman. I'm not sure about that, but I do know they are all meant to walk with their bottoms sticking out, because it is a well-known fact that all Yorkshiremen have big bums – big bums and long chins, what a combination!

25

Lancashire v. Yorkshire, first day
Yorkshire 205 (N. Hartley 52, Patterson 6-77);
Lancashire 13-2 (Fowler 4)

I was sawn off. A flick down the leg side – I didn't get a touch but Bluey went up for it. I stood there and Shep gave me out. He came up to me in the bar afterwards and said, 'Did I saw you off?'

I just looked at him.

'Well,' he said, 'I wondered, because you didn't walk, and I remembered that you had walked against Gloucestershire.'

So I said I hadn't hit it, and he apologized. But there's nothing you can do. That's the way it goes.

I sometimes think maybe not walking is the best thing. I don't walk in Test matches – nobody does. In fact I did in my first Test, and Bob Willis virtually pinned me to the dressing-room wall when I got back. 'You don't walk at this level,' he said. 'None of those other buggers do, so we don't either.'

In fact there are a lot of good arguments about leaving the decision to the umpire. And you do hear stories about some well-known 'walkers' who won't walk when there's something big riding on it. But I think that on the county circuit, where it is a tight-knit community and you are playing against the same people year in and year out, walking is right, because otherwise it creates so much bad feeling, and most people do walk. Besides, I think it is the right thing to do, although I can't put up as many logical reasons for it as for not walking.

Patto was very quick today and got a career best. It was pretty dark early on – we probably shouldn't have been out there at times – and he was lethal. My neck was bad today, so I couldn't run and bend, and I fielded at gully praying nothing came near me because it was travelling like the clappers. Patto has only just come into the side. He joined us last year on Clive's recommendation. Typically, he made his début in a very important match – against Middlesex in the NatWest quarter-final at Lord's – and he ended up getting smashed all over. That wasn't his fault – he had to bowl the last overs, and at this stage in his career he just hasn't the control. He has no idea where it is going when he lets it go, so he wasn't able to fire it into the blockhole. He shouldn't have been put in that position. I felt sorry for him then, and of course it made it harder for him the next time he played because he had that memory.

He played in the last match against Derbyshire while I was at Lord's, so this was his second championship match of the season and he really bowled quickly. He looked as if he wanted to knock their heads off, and I got the impression that one or two of them didn't fancy it.

The Yorkies must be sick of us and our extra man. Whenever they've got us on the rack, it is always Clive or Michael Holding or Colin Croft who comes to the rescue and pulls us out of the mire. Now they come over here and we let loose Patto at them on a wicket which is not the best, to say the least.

26

Lancashire v. Yorkshire, second day
Lancashire 269 (Fairbrother 128, Folley 69);
Yorkshire 205 and 16-2

When I got to the ground Pete Lever said, 'I've never seen you look so bad.' I was probably a bit white and shaky. I had certainly got a hell of a headache when I woke up.

'Well, I don't do this normally,' I said, 'but getting given out last night was the limit.'

I don't do it normally, and they know I pick my time to have a drink, so they forgive me. I knew I wouldn't have anything to do for most of the day – I just fielded for the last ten minutes – so it was a good day to pick. And I could have played if I'd had to. I had a headache, but I didn't feel ill or unable to coordinate properly. I had a net in the afternoon, did a bit of weight training and beat Ian Folley at squash, so I was all right.

I did have a few, though; Drambuie all night, for some unknown reason. It isn't my usual drink. Steph is away for the weekend, and I was so depressed about another failure that I decided alcohol was the answer. I phoned some friends and said, 'I'm going to have a drink tonight, so if you want to go anywhere you had better come over here, because I'm not driving.' I'd arranged to see them, and so they came over and stayed the night. It was just as well they did, because if they hadn't been there to wake me up I think I would have slept through the day. Around midnight I took Smithy for a walk up on the hill behind our house, fell into a ditch, bruised my knee and ripped my jeans. I haven't been so drunk for ages.

We got a useful lead thanks almost entirely to Harvey and Thatch. Apart from them, Aby was the only one to get into double figures, which says something both about our batting and about the wicket.

I missed a lot of Harvey's knock in the afternoon because I was netting and in the gym, but it was a considerable effort. Once Thatch had gone, there was no one at the other end to stay with him, so he couldn't play a really fluent innings. From the outside, apart from in brief spells, it might not have appeared to be one of his best innings. But from a professional point of view it was. He had to graft and graft. He had to take the attacking shots when the opportunities were there, but he had to make 100 per cent sure that that was the right shot to play at that time. Because if he had made a mistake and got out for 40, there was no one else to get runs. He had to think like that and take the whole weight of the innings on himself. And the wicket made it more difficult. It was a wicket you never felt 'in' on. At no stage could you start hitting it on the up or lean in and guide it, because the consistency of the wicket wouldn't let you. You had to struggle and struggle.

Harvey said at tea that he didn't feel as if he had middled a ball all day. And that is what happens on our wickets. It actually gave me some encouragement to know that he was in and playing well and yet the ball still wasn't hitting the middle of his bat. He thought it was him, but I said, 'No, it's not you. It can't be you. It has got to be the wicket because it is inconsistent. But you've got to keep plugging away because you are middling things better than everybody else. Everybody else is nicking it.'

If I'd been batting with him in the middle, I could have talked him through things like that. Because of the way I play, the score would keep ticking along and he wouldn't have had to worry about runs. But it is difficult to guide someone through an innings when you only see them for twenty minutes every two hours. And that was why it was such a good knock, because he was professional with himself while he was out there. He has a great attitude; he has taught it himself, and it is one which a lot of senior players seem to have forgotten. I've seen others go out and, once they start to struggle a bit, throw it away – or throw caution away. If they get a quick 40, then fine; but if they get out, they come back with a 'Well, what can you expect?', which is a cop-out.

Thatch also did well. He'd gone in as nightwatchman last night and ended up with a career best. He could be quite a reasonable batsman. He is very correct, very sideways on, and technically quite good, especially against seam. So it was his sort of situation. We just said to him, 'Stay in, bat with Neil

Fowler celebrates his double century during the fourth Test against India at Madras, January 1985

Caught and bowled by Sivaramakrishnan, India's eighteen-year-old leg-spinner, in the first innings of the first Test at Bombay, December 1984

Given out l.b.w. in the second innings at Bombay: 'It was the worst decision I have ever had'

Another fierce Indian appeal, this time from Kapil Dev and Kirmani during the second Test at Delhi: 'They have this habit of appealing incredibly well'

With Allan Lamb on an outing to the Taj Mahal
Sitting it out on an elephant

Repairing the wicket at Gauhati: 'The wicket was river-bed silt – low and slow'

Pat Pocock on the boating trip: 'The Calcutta Chief of Police had to contact the police in the neighbouring area to ensure that security and hospitality were maintained'

A suspicious Indian bodyguard, captured by Graeme Fowler's camera

Dressing up for the Christmas snow
In the dressing-room at Gauhati

A thoughtful vice-captain and captain

Best friend, Paul Allott

Paul Downton cools off

Tim Robinson, Phil Edmonds and David Gower look pensive

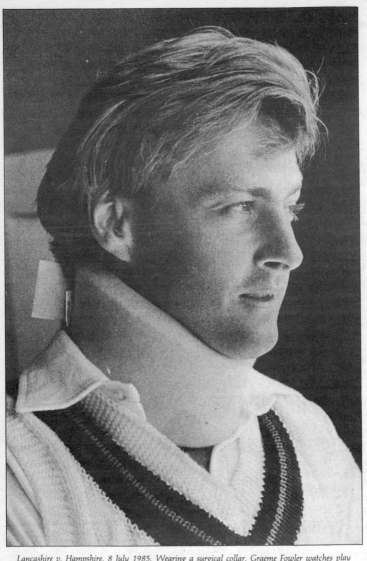

Lancashire v. Hampshire, 8 July 1985. Wearing a surgical collar, Graeme Fowler watches play from the pavilion at Liverpool after injuring his neck in pre-match practice that day

and just help him,' and he did it well. But he isn't the sort to send in when you are needing eight an over; David Makinson is far better equipped for that. Thatch will never go in and tear anybody apart, but he is capable of staying in, and technically he has the equipment to become a reasonable batsman.

At the moment Thatch doesn't know how well he can play, and he is a bit frightened of expressing himself with a bat, which is a bit of a hindrance to him. He won't let himself go; he is restricted all the time and thinks that if he tries a shot and gets out, someone will tell him off and say, 'That's not one of your shots.' But that wasn't a problem today, because all he had to do was support Harvey, and if you look at the rest of the scores so far, it was a considerable effort. He is a better player of seam bowling than of spin, which helped. If you are not fully aware of your potential and your own level of skill, spin bowlers can be a more difficult proposition to assess because you've so much more time to decide. But if you have a level of technical competence, which he has, the shot you play against quick bowlers is dictated for you by the speed of the ball, and he came through that quite well. And if the ball seamed past him, he didn't let it worry him. Possibly he doesn't think about what he is doing, but when it is seaming, that can be an advantage because it means you don't get flustered.

Froggy Moxon and I exchanged condolences and congratulations in the bar. I am in the one-day squad against Australia, which put my mind at rest. I half expected to be in, because I thought they would stand by me. On the other hand, I haven't got any runs, so I wouldn't have been too surprised to be left out. I'm delighted they have stood by me, but of course it puts pressure on too. I'm often thought of as a one-day player, but in fact I do much better in the proper game, and one-day internationals are not a good place in which to be searching for form or playing for your place. Froggy looked out of sorts in the Benson & Hedges match earlier in the season and again this weekend, and he was saying he couldn't bat any more. To me he looks as if he is playing very square on the leg side – the world-class player's syndrome, if you can call it that. It seems with world-class players that anything on the wicket disappears through the leg side. At one stage it affected me, and I started thinking, 'You've got to get further across and get it going over that side.' I believe that has happened to Froggy. He looks at the moment as if he is trying to hit everything through square leg.

Peebs was here doing the match for the radio, so we had an evening out with Clive and one or two of the others – food this time.

27

Yorkshire 205 and 58-4
Lancashire 269. Match abandoned as a draw – rain.

We had them by the short and curlies – they were still 6 behind when the rain set in. And we had got rid of their young batsman Richard Blakey, who had looked as if he fancied it a bit more than some of them. He looked the part and played quite well. He kept it dead simple and looked completely unflustered by anything that was thrown at him.

But there was one instance early on which could have unsettled anyone. I was standing at slip, partly because of my neck, partly because we hadn't many experienced players in the team, and it was dark. Patto was running in and we shouldn't really have been on the field. He slipped – presumably – and this ball came flying through head high at Jim Love. Had it been three inches to the left it would have killed him. Fortunately it missed. It landed two yards in front of Tosh — wicket-keepers don't see beamers until they land for some reason — so he dived, got half a glove on it and it went down to fine leg for a single. So Blakey came up to face. The next ball was a screaming bouncer. It whistled past his nose and he played it really well — weaved inside and let it go through. We reckoned the difference in length was about twenty yards, which says something about Patto's control. But Blakey wasn't flustered by it, whereas I think it is fair to say that one or two of their players didn't fancy it at all.

I suppose his lack of knowledge of what things can be like, his innocence of the game, enabled him to cope with it. I'm sure that is what helped me early on. You would be playing someone and everybody would be going, 'Bloody 'ell, 'e's quick,' where I just thought he was a little bit quick because I wasn't used to it. That ignorance is a great help at times. It is why some people do well when they first go up a grade. They just react, they don't have any preconceived ideas.

If you are a complete novice and don't know what is going on, all you see is the ball and you play that ball, which is perfect. You keep it simple, and when you do that it is easier. It is only when you realize how you can play and you start taking things for granted that you get yourself in trouble. When you are more experienced, you stop playing the ball on its merits because you are weighed down by all these other considerations. You start letting the game dictate the situation, thinking, 'We need a few runs and then we can set them x', and you start looking for the gaps and thinking about accelerating; or you think, 'Well, it's only him bowling, and he shouldn't be able to bowl at me like this'; or you may even come in thinking, 'I've been smashing it in the nets', and before you know where you are you've nicked it or missed it or spooned one up. But Blakey just kept it simple, played straight, and coped very well.

*

Granada were covering the game. At one stage while we were off the field waiting to see what was happening, they zoomed in on our dressing-room. We were watching the TV, so we knew what they were doing and I responded by dropping my trousers and 'mooning'. The chairman was furious. I probably shouldn't have done it, but then should they intrude into our dressing-room?

I am in the squad for the one-days, along with Goochie and Tim Robinson. The papers are suggesting I might bat at number three. I had a chat with David Lloyd about it, and he suggested that Tim and I could open, with Goochie batting three. I'd rather open, but if I had to bat three in order to play I would.

Having said that, if I had my career over again I wouldn't be an opener. I wasn't an opener in the first place. I became one for Lancashire because there was a need for one and I was 'converted' by Jack Bond. For England I got in because there was a gap. There are a few around at the moment: Robbo, Broad, Froggy – even though he isn't having a great time at the moment – as well as Goochie. But when I got in I replaced Derek Randall – he and Chris Tavaré were the openers! But it wasn't my natural position. I opened at times in schoolboy sides, where you put your best players in first, but in the Lancashire second team I batted four. I made my first-team début at six, and the only reason I became an opener was that Jack Bond wanted David Lloyd to go down the order and bowl more, so he needed someone to open with Andrew Kennedy. The two lads available were Iain Cockbain and myself. Iain had batted the whole of the previous season, scoring something like 300 runs at an average of 19. I'd been in and out of the side. I spent the winter in Perth and was going quite well when I came back – I got runs in the pre-season games – so Jack asked, 'Do you want to have a go at opening?'

I said yes. He had me keeping wicket as well so that he could play another batsman. The first game of the season was against Cambridge, and I got 143. I got 41 in the first championship game against Northants, and I carried on from there. And all of a sudden, from being someone who they said was just a slogger, I was an opening batsman, and that was it. But I think the only reason the manager picked me for it was that if I kept wicket it meant he could play another batsman as well, and I move quickly and have a good eye.

I'd sooner bat lower down. But if I'd batted at three or four for Lancashire, I don't think I'd have been playing international cricket, certainly not so early. I was around in the right position at the right time. And, realistically, I couldn't see me breaking into a middle order of Gower, Gatting, Lamb and Botham.

It does irk me, though, that while they quite regularly push middle-order batsmen up to open, they never seem to consider picking opening batsmen to bat down the order. If you are an opener, that's it. I do like opening, but there are times when it is so much easier to bat down the order, and it would be nice to be considered as a batsman rather than as an opener fullstop. If you aren't playing well at one or two, you aren't playing. Whereas if Gatt or Lubo are not playing really well at three, they will shuffle them down to five. And I can't see the logic of doing it in one case and not the other.

I actually batted at six in two Test innings in Pakistan, and I got 50 both times. In Faisalabad I was ill and couldn't open, so Gatt opened and got 70, and I went in six and got 50. So they did it for the next Test in Lahore and I got another 50. But I reverted to opening in the second innings, and it's never been tried again. I think I would find six difficult in a one-day game, not being used to having to go in and work it around like Gatt can. He is a great improviser. But in a Test there is not that much difference – you are either coming in to face the second new ball, or you are in the mire anyway. But the secret is to open the batting and score runs. Then I will be in. That was how I got in in the first place, and I've played 21 Test matches. And as a letter in *Wisden Cricket Monthly* pointed out, I'd scored more runs in my first 20 Tests than a lot of top batsmen, including Goochie.

At the start of the season I still felt under pressure, because I felt I had to score runs to get picked. But Percy's chat has helped. I am only twenty-eight, and there is a lot of batting in front of me. I am not playing well at the moment; but if I don't get picked for these one-day games or for the Test series, it is not the end of the road. It won't mean I'm finished, because I've a lot of cricket left.

We had a bit of a discussion about our wickets, though 'discussion' is perhaps a euphemism. We are not happy with them. Jack Bond said, 'If an uncapped player can get 128, why can't you get any runs?'

We answered, 'All right, have a look at the scores in the game.' And the Yorkshire scores were very similar to ours, except they didn't have anyone who scored a century.

But he insisted that our wickets have got better over the last three years. We said, 'Has it heck? It's worse now than it's ever been.'

'No, it's better.'

'Look, we have to play on it, we should know,' we replied.

So Jack said, 'Well, he got 128, what does he think?'

And Neil said, 'It's worse now than it was last year.'

So there was a big chorus of 'Thank you', and Jack turned and walked out as he always does.

Walt also complained about the balls during the discussion. He said they just seamed too much. We are using Readers balls with great big seams on them, and you can't get near them: they go so far that you end up laughing at the hopelessness of the situation. It is no good for batsmen or bowlers. Walt would nip one back from off stump, it'd go through at the top of pad level and Tosh would end up diving way down the leg side to take a ball which had nipped back from off stump, which is grossly exaggerated movement. If you are playing on a wicket which is deviating and has uncertain bounce, you want the ball to be as near-spherical as possible, but we are playing on bad wickets with balls which have huge seams, so you've got no chance. And because our practice wickets aren't any good you can't sort it out there either. You end up not knowing whether it is you or the wicket.

If you are playing well, it is all right. Neil Fairbrother has been in the same position as me: he hasn't been playing well, although he got a hundred yesterday. Watching him knock up today he was atrocious — he looked as if he had never held a bat before in his life. But mentally he is now 'in nick', so he is all right and not bothered about not knocking up well, whereas three days ago he was really concerned that he wasn't middling everything when he was knocking up. It is all mental, and you know it is all mental, but there is nothing you can do about it, and that is so frustrating. I've always netted a lot anyway, so I can't say more practice is the answer. I like to keep my routine the same. If I'm in good nick and the nets are bad, I won't net. But if you're in poor form, you don't know whether it's you or the net, so you try and ignore it. I like to have a net and practise a lot because there is nothing better than repetition. David Gower hates nets. Gatt can go either way, but Tim Robinson and I are great nets people. Yesterday I spent about three quarters of an hour in the nets, and then had people throwing the ball at me.

But I don't make a point of doing more and more and more and more. Clive said, 'Go and play squash to get your hand–eye coordination going,' so I played two or three games of squash. It does make a difference — it gets you moving and gets the feeling there. And when I had a net after playing squash today, I felt as if I was hitting the ball better. Whether that is psychological or not I don't know, but it might well be down to the squash.

I played Clive today. I enjoy playing him, because he is keen as well, and you get a good sweat on. He hits the ball hard. Before we started we had a really good warm-up and burst one ball. When we started he said, 'We'll play three games, all right?'

This was after four rallies, and they had been something like sixteen-stroke rallies apiece, so we were already half knackered. So I said, 'Yeah, all right.'

I won the first two games, and then he won the third 9–6 and said, 'Do you want another?'

We had been playing quite a time and so I replied, 'No, you said three, we'll call it a day.'

He laughed and said, 'All right,' and we walked back to the dressing-room. When we got there he said, 'He's no stamina, that Fowler! He was 2–1 up and quit, he wouldn't play any more.'

Playing against Clive is like trying to run round a lamp-post. He hits the ball and just stands there; he doesn't move out of the way and you can't get past him. He keeps poking the racket round the back of his legs to hit it. And he is such a funny bloke. He says, 'You're not having a let off that!'

'Come on, Clive . . .'

'No, no, it's not my fault you're not agile enough to get round me.' All that sort of thing.

Because you have so much respect for him, you let him get away with it. But there are times when, if it was in a competition, I could smash the ball and hit him because he just gets in the way. But because it is Clive, and because it isn't a competition, you play round him and end up laughing. There were two occasions today when I could have drilled it right up his backside, which really hurts. One I just refused to hit. I let it bounce twice, then said, 'Listen, if I'd hit that you'd have been dead, so play a let.' And that time he conceded a let.

I used to play a lot of squash, but after I had the operations on my feet I wasn't able to play much – about twice a year at most – and this meant I couldn't play as well as I'm capable of, which frustrated me. But I've now played three games in the last week, so it seems my feet can stand it again. I played Goochie last week – he said, 'Come on, we've nothing else to do,' so we did. It was my first game for ages, and I was useless, so he thrashed me. Yesterday I played Ian Folley and was getting better, and today I beat Clive. If I'd played him last week, he'd have thrashed me.

So as my feet seem OK, I might start to play more. Clive said we should have another game before Thursday. It is only Clive I can have a social game with; everybody else I have to beat. With Clive, because he is so awkward to play against, I just laugh, and because I respect him I can have a social match. But if I played Goochie again, I'd have to beat him. I'd rather not play than have a social game. If I do play, I shall get better. Shauny and Harvey think they are top dogs at squash at the moment, so we'll see. Harvey is very competitive, wants to beat me at things, but hasn't yet found anything he can beat me at, which is quite funny. He plays rugby, so he is quite hard, but I always win our mock fights, which annoys him.

I think squash helps your cricket. I play right-handed, so my backhand is better than my forehand, at least for direction if not for power. It gets a rhythm going and helps your timing and coordination. It makes you watch the ball as well. And as I'm a very wristy batsman, it is quite good for that. I used to play tennis, which is mainly arm action, and a lot of badminton, which is all wrist, but squash demands both.

*

Of course, Woody didn't join Yorkshire after all. He seems to have disappeared – probably up his own orifice. He was picked to play for Bowdon in the Cheshire League. He went out to bat with a cut-off bat – a practice one with the edges trimmed off so that it is only about two inches wide. You use them in the nets to see if you are middling it. Anyway, he went out to bat with this in a League match, got about ten and was bowled – and has not been seen since.

Steph came back from her weekend today and produced further evidence of my state on Saturday night. I had phoned her around 8 p.m., which I remember. She said I sounded very bad-tempered, because I was so depressed about not getting any runs. But I had also phoned her at 1.30 a.m., which I have no recollection of at all. I haven't been that smashed since a Christmas do at Blackburn Northern CC about three years ago, when I found my underpants neatly folded in the chip-pan the following morning. We had the carpet-layers in at the time – we'd only just moved into our house – and when I was trying to find my wallet this voice floated down the stairs: ''Ave yer tried the chip-pan?'

That was in the days when we were together a lot more because I was wintering at home. When we got married, I was a second-team player and Steph was a school-teacher. Now she is lecturing, and I'm an international, and our lives are running on different tracks. It is very difficult when you are away for three or four months at a time. And even in the summer I'm away a lot, obviously. So Steph can either sit at home and wait, which she is much too lively and independent to do, or she has to make her own life, which she has done. So then you get situations like her being away for the weekend when I am at home. But of course I was working for the weekend anyway, so she wouldn't have seen much of me if she had been here. Yet it certainly wasn't what we intended when we got married.

28

A report in the *Daily Mail* this morning said: 'Blakey, whose technically sound 35 was ended by a catch behind the wicket, was one of the reasons why Lancashire manager Jack Bond found so much encouragement in what was virtually a Roses match for learners. Lancashire fielded only five capped players, Yorkshire seven. It shows how many young players have made the grade in county cricket for the two northern counties in the last two years.'

It doesn't show that at all. It just shows how many senior players they've sacked. What gets me is that we've got a youth programme, but they never turn into senior players. We're always playing youths.

29

The England squad for the one-days had nets at Old Trafford, the first of the three games being here tomorrow. If the selectors hoped to gain anything from the nets, they were disappointed. They were awful, so you couldn't tell how anyone was playing.

We are staying at Mottram Hall. We had a dinner this evening to discuss tactics, but there is no sign as to whether I am playing.

30

England v. Australia, first Texaco Trophy match
England 219 (Botham 72, Gooch 57, Fowler 10);
Australia 220-7 (Border 59). Australia won by 3 wickets

I found out I was playing when Tim Robinson came up and wished me good luck. I was delighted to walk down the steps with Goochie, particularly at Old Trafford, where I knew the crowd would be behind me, but I didn't bat for long.

It seems I can stay around, but at the moment as soon as I try and play a shot I get out. I suppose it was a bit wide, but people have always said about me, 'Don't give him any width or he'll hit it,' and it was a ball I would normally have hit for four. And when I saw the replay it looked as if I was trying to burst the ball for some reason. I was trying to hit it too hard, and just nicked it — the third time I've got out that way this season.

We didn't even use up all our overs — Gatt was left high and dry with an over left because no one could stay with him. So we lost. And I didn't get any runs, so I wonder where that leaves me. I think I might get one more game.

JUNE

1

England v. Australia, second Texaco Trophy match
England 231-7 (Gooch 115); Australia 233-6 (Border 85
not out, Wessels 57). Australia won by 4 wickets

Tim Robinson was picked and I was left out for the Edgbaston game. So the blow fell. It wasn't entirely unexpected, but having been picked initially I thought I might have had more than one game, and I am a bit disappointed about that. I hoped I might have had a little longer run, but obviously they wanted someone who is in form and scoring runs, so they picked Tim.

3

England v. Australia, third Texaco Trophy match
Australia 254-5 (Wood 114 not out); England 257–2
(Gooch 117 not out, Gower 102). England won by 8 wickets

Of course I didn't play at Lord's either. I didn't expect to, but it confirms in a way the message of Saturday. As I said when they announced the squad, I wouldn't have been surprised if I had been left out, and I was delighted that the selectors were loyal and stood by me. But, in a way, being left out after one game seems more final than not being in initially would have been. It does say, 'You're dropped; go back to square one and work your way back in.'

Obviously I would have been disappointed if I hadn't been

chosen for the squad, because being left out means not being part of things. I would have understood them not picking me, though, because I could have justified it and it wouldn't have caused me too much consternation. When you're not playing well and you are left out of the England side, in one way the news comes as a release. The pressure and the worry are off.

Yet in other ways the pressure is back on. If you are in the side and playing and also doing reasonably well outside, you seem to maintain a flow. But once you are dropped and you are out of the immediate eleven, it takes a lot to be considered again. I now know that if I had just played averagely well for Lancashire and done quite well for England, I would have stayed in the England side, with them not taking too much notice of what I was doing for Lancashire. And I didn't know that at the start of the season. I thought I had to score a lot of runs to get picked. But now, having been dropped, I think the scores I shall have to get for Lancashire will need to be far better to get me back in than they would have been had I still been playing in the England side.

So, although being dropped takes you out of the pressure of the England games it puts more pressure on you if you want to play for England. Which I do. It puts more pressure on your personal performances for your county, because they come under more scrutiny, and it also increases the pressure you put on yourself.

5

On Monday night I went out with Andy Peebles again, and during the evening I mentioned casually that I would like to see Bruce Springsteen. Yesterday morning I got a phone call at 8 a.m. from Andy saying he had fixed up two tickets for Steph and me to go to see him last night in Newcastle.

It should have been straightforward, but inevitably, the way things are going at the moment, it wasn't. Walt and I drove up to Manchester to pick up my car, which I left at Old Trafford. It wouldn't start. The battery was flat, which seemed ridiculous as it is a brand-new car, with only 1,500 miles on the clock. We bump-started it and I drove up to Accrington. I assumed that that would recharge it, so I stopped off in town to have some lunch. When I got back to the car, cutting it fine because I was supposed to pick Steph up at college, it wouldn't start, so obviously there was a fault somewhere.

I tried to phone Steph, but couldn't get hold of her. I tried to phone my dad, who is a mechanic, and couldn't find him. So I had to take a taxi home, find my dad and phone Steph, and then get a taxi back to the car. In the end Steph had to pick me up and we drove up to Newcastle in her MG. The concert started at 6 p.m. We got there at 6.10, so didn't meet up with Andy and his producer, Geoff Griffin.

The concert, though, was worth it. Steph comes from Newcastle, so she was wondering how many people she would know at the concert. In fact the only person we met was a friend of mine from Durham, Paul Walsh. So we had a drink with him and stayed at her parents overnight.

We had to come back first thing because Steph was teaching and I had to go to the physiotherapist about my neck and shoulder. It is giving me constant pain, and I am restricted in my movement a lot of the time.

8

Essex v. Lancashire, first day
Essex 257-9 (Fletcher 50)

We had a delayed start because of damp patches on the wicket. We picked two spinners and left David Makinson as twelfth man, with Shauny as third seamer – Winker had been dropped. Having done that, we then put them in. By 6 o'clock Shauny had bowled only four overs as third seamer in a game when we had put them in. This seems very strange. Walt was not pleased – understandably. Sometimes our policies leave a lot to be desired.

Walt and I watched the Barry McGuigan fight in the evening. He was brilliant. I don't know how he felt, but we were both knackered by the end. The sighs of relief at the end of each round were enormous.

9

Essex v. Lancashire, John Player League
Lancashire 183-2 (Lloyd 64 not out, O'Shaughnessy 60,
Fowler 30; 28 overs); Essex 91-3 (15 overs). Match
abandoned as a draw

The game was a fiasco by the end. We started late, so the match was restricted to 36 overs a side. Another interruption and it was cut back to 28 overs. Then it came down to them needing 131 off 20 overs. They had got 91 off 15 when there was further rain. It stopped before the close, but Ilford is an out-ground, and they aren't as efficient as they are at the main grounds, and it took them a long time to get the covers off. By then the umpires decided that the 20 overs could not be completed by 6.30, so the game was abandoned with 5,000 people waiting to see an exciting finish. TCCB rules can be infuriating at times.

We had batted well too. Clive, Winker and Soren came down for the game. Clive got 64 not out, Soren got Goochie first ball, which made the Great Dane's day, and Winker had a 500-mile round trip to field one ball!

I was sawn off. Even Pring said so afterwards. To make my day I twisted my ankle during fielding practice.

10

Essex v. Lancashire, second day
Essex 281 (Foster 63, Patterson 4-67) and 50-1; Lancashire
191 (Fowler 24)

In spite of my ankle injury I played quite well. Once again it was one mistake and out. It never rains but it pours. We scraped all the way.

I spent last night at Pring's house in Cambridge. We had a pleasant evening, but the garlic and curry consumed did not endear me to the dressing-room this morning. Of course, everyone wanted to know where I had been and what I had done. Travelling on the bus takes away all your independence and privacy. Because I didn't stay at the hotel, everyone immediately suspects late nights full of booze. Dave Varey, who is a good friend of Derek's, would not come with us for that reason. In my opinion that is quite ridiculous. Self-discipline is the only form of discipline which makes or breaks a player, not the 'naughty boy' treatment you get in junior schools.

Quite simply, if you don't have the sense to go to bed early and sober before a busy day, then you are never going to make it. We all make mistakes, but we all know our capacity and the risks you take in exceeding that capacity, and the good will always come through while the others won't, no matter how many things are said or thought, or crazy rules imposed.

11

Essex v. Lancashire, third day
Essex 281 and 108-9 dec. (Patterson 6-45);
Lancashire 191 and 174-9 (Fowler 12, Gooch 5-46).
Match drawn

Patto was very sharp and took a career best. He looks promising and is quite quick. I hung on to a catch off him at third slip to my pleasure: I quite like gully, but I'm not so happy in the slips and don't catch so many there. But there are times when I can't run because of my neck, and I have to say to Aby, 'Can I stand still today?'

We were set 199 in 51 overs; in the end we hung on for a draw, even though Ian Folley was a bit cavalier in the last over. He hit J. Lever back over his head, and then took a single to leave Patto to hold out for the last two balls. I don't think he had his thinking-cap on, because several times he left Patto, who is not the world's greatest batsman, to fend for three or four balls. It was so unprofessional as to be funny — but only because we didn't lose a wicket. If we had done, the response wouldn't have been humorous. As it was, Norrie put them straight when they came in.

It was good to leave Ilford and the smelly fish-tank dining-tents. God knows what they will smell like by Friday when the week ends.

Then it was back on to the bus for the drag across London in the tail-end of the rush-hour and on down to Bath, armed with a meagre supply of lager, two bottles of Guinness and enough supplies of chocolate and crisps to feed an army. The 'in-flight' movie was *Star Wars*, followed by all the songs from *Grease*, which we had watched on the way down to Ilford.

When a film is on, you can either plug your ears with cotton wool, or blast them with your personal stereo. Otherwise you have no escape. It is like watching a programme in a school class, and there is so much jeering and shouting that it takes all your concentration to follow even the weak stories, which are the usual run of things: *Star Wars*, *Grease*, *Death Wish 2* are about the level — i.e., mainly crap — although recently I've persuaded people to watch tapes of *The Young Ones*. If the plot does escape you, you can always ask

Harvey or Shauny, who have almost certainly seen it already; or, if it is an older film, Yosser or Albert, who are experts on anything bordering on the era of black-and-white cinematography!

I don't like travelling by bus. It's our second year of doing so. It's sponsored by National Express and saves the club about £15,000 in travelling expenses, which is a major argument in its favour. From A to B it's quite comfortable. There are three televisions with the video machine to play the films on. It hasn't got a fridge, but there is the facility to make powdered tea or coffee, although you have got about as much chance of getting a decent cup of tea or coffee as you have of getting peace and quiet on the bus. It's always too weak, too hot, no sugar, and it is guaranteed to spill over the crisps, the cassettes or the Trivial Pursuit board.

The main problem, though, is when you get to the hotel. We're staying at the Old Mill, which is only a couple of miles out of Bath, so that isn't too bad. But last year some of the hotels were thirty-five or forty minutes from the ground, and the bus is then very restrictive. It means you can't make your own way to the ground, you can't disappear at night to go out with friends or even to go to an alternative pub in town instead of being stuck in the hotel bar, because you are struggling to get back to the hotel. On cricketers' wages, taxis have to be used sparingly!

And I hate that restrictiveness, because it means we are all living on top of one another. There is no privacy and no independence. Although I love the rest of the lads and get on really well with them, there are times when I want to be alone. Whether you've had a good day or a bad day doesn't matter. Cricket is such an up-and-down game, and for a team game it is still so individual that someone can have a totally different day from you and be in a very different mood. But when you get on the bus at the end of the day, you are all on top of one another, and there is nowhere to go to get away from people. You can put your personal stereo on, you can put dark glasses on and hide away at the back, but you are still physically in their presence and can't get away from it. Someone will always want to watch a film; someone else will want a tape on; a third will want both turned down so they can listen to their personal stereo. We do have widely different tastes in music, so it's impossible to please everyone, and anyway your own tastes vary according to mood. Then four others will play Trivial Pursuit; and people watching the film or listening to the stereo can't hear because we are all laughing and shouting while playing that.

It doesn't cause major friction, but it doesn't help. And if you do try and opt out and hide at the back, people think you are being strange or funny if you don't want to talk to them. 'What's up with him? Why's he sitting over there?' Which is sad.

Generally, I'd much prefer to travel by car with one or two others sharing the driving, so that you can be independent. Manchester to London and back is fine on the coach, because when you get to London you don't use the car anyway if you are staying in the centre; you rely on tubes and taxis. But even then it puts time on the journey because of the speed the coach travels, and because you have to go back to Old Trafford to pick up your car rather than driving straight home. And although you can relax on the bus, you still know you face a forty-minute drive at the end of it – or at least I do, living in Accrington.

Apart from trips to London, having a car makes life much easier. I'm sure that being able to get away in the evenings is important. If you see the others when you get to the ground in the morning, you start by swapping stories of the previous evening, and the day goes on from there. But when you are reliant on the coach, you are living in each other's pockets all the time except when sleeping. I'm sure it adversely affects the way I am during the day, and at the end of it I still can't get away and relax.

<u>12</u>

Somerset v. Lancashire, first day
Somerset 222-4 (Felton 76)

This is my first-ever visit to Bath. Skid country. We'd been looking forward to it while at Ilford, but I'm not so sure now. We got to the ground to find just what I really don't need in my current run. We were to play on the wicket which had been used for the previous three days. I asked David Constant, who had stood in that match too, how he had marked it then, and he said, 'Poor,' which didn't bode well for our game. They had had a lot of rain, but it seems extraordinary that, because they are an out-ground, they only had enough covers to protect the wicket that was in use.

The state of the wicket quickly became academic as far as I was concerned. The last couple of weeks have been unbelievable. I'd found out about my neck injury. I'd twisted my ankle at Ilford. Now I've got a badly damaged hand. I was in the slips – God knows why, even though I caught Pring there on Sunday – and Felton gave me this chance off Balfour early on. I saw it all the way, so it was nothing to do with Bath's bad reputation as a difficult ground to see the ball on, but it hit me bang on the middle finger of my right hand. I thought I'd broken it. I went off, stuck it in ice and then went to the hospital for an X-ray. I hadn't broken it, but I'd cracked the nail underneath. It might just as well have been, because I couldn't field. And that was me for the day.

Before we went out to field Shauny said, 'Do I have to put my bowling boots on?' In fact he was opening the bowling, so his question summed up the whole situation in our side at the moment. At Ilford we had had several discussions between the senior players and the management about the make-up of our side. And one of the most definite things to come out of it was agreement that one player, Steve O'Shaughnessy, was not physically or mentally strong enough to do the job of third seamer and bat number three. That is not a criticism of him. Number three is one of the most crucial and demanding jobs in the side; third seamer is not quite in the firing line in the same way, but it can be physically more demanding than any other bowler's job if you are operating behind two genuine pace bowlers. Even Botham doesn't combine the two jobs. Yet in the very next game, after we had agreed that Shauny wasn't capable of doing it, he is picked as number three and opening the bowling, giving him even more responsibility. Admittedly they decided to do it because they thought the wicket was going to turn square, and in fact he only bowled four overs, but it was still contradicting everything which had been said a couple of days earlier.

Shauny is very talented. I wish I had his natural ability. He has been unfortunate at Lancashire in having to play at a time when the team is so weak. If he comes in with a good performance, they demand he does it again. If he was playing for a side like Hampshire, doing Tim Tremlett's job, say, he would do it as well if not better than Tim. I think he has more talent than Tim, good a bowler as Tim is. But playing for Lancashire, he is expected to take more responsibility than he is able to handle, particularly at this stage in his career, although he has the ability.

The problem is getting it out of him. To be truthful, he has got a fair cricket brain, although he is not always credited with it. He is always thinking, always trying to work things out. Often his logic might not lead to the same conclusion as everybody else's, but that is not to say he isn't thinking about it. And having thought his argument through, he sticks to it, which I think is admirable.

He speaks before he thinks, and often acts before he has worked out what he is doing. That can be funny – he is a master of spoonerisms and *non sequiturs*. For instance, a woman came into a pub where we were. She had obviously just come back from Majorca or wherever, since she had this beautiful, deep tan, and Shauny asked her 'Are you a sunship worper?'

On the same day a kid asked him for his autograph on a cigarette packet. Shauny said, 'Have you no paper? I'm not signing that pag facket!'

Once a girl rang the dressing-room for him when he wasn't there. He was given the message – she would ring back later, but didn't leave a name. 'Oh.' Pause. 'Was she a blonde?'

On another occasion he was out playing golf with Pete Lever, and Pete, who is a keen bird-watcher said, 'Listen, that's a green woodpecker.'

'Oh.' Pause. 'How can you tell it's green?'

But not working things out can land him in trouble. He has no malice in him, he is a delightful man, but he can see people doing things they aren't supposed to, or he thinks they aren't supposed to, and will take them out of context and do them himself. He will see Walt or me have a late night and think it is OK for him to, but he won't take it in that we do it when we know we have a clear day the following day, and so he might do it at the wrong time. And that sort of thing has often left him in trouble.

He has got a reputation for being a bad boy in our side, which is a complete farce. He is not a bad boy at all, but there are times when everyone needs to be disciplined, and it seems the hierarchy feels the only way to discipline Shauny is to fine him. The press get hold of it and it has given him a bad-boy image. Like all of us he is a little foolish to himself at times, but whereas they can pull me into order in one way, and someone else in another, it seems other methods have failed with Shauny and they have decided the only way they could get to him is to smack his hand.

If he is around, you know it. If he reads a newspaper, he reads the whole thing from cover to cover out loud. If there is anything happening he is there, not just watching but telling everybody about it while it is going on. And he's got one of those voices which carries four hundred yards when he whispers.

He is a lovely bloke, very entertaining, but frustrating at times because everybody can see the talent in him. What they want to do is squeeze it out of him. They've tried so many ways that maybe they should just let him go; wind him up, set him off and say to everybody else, 'Just ignore him, let him carry on in his own way and see if he produces the goods.'

13

Somerset v. Lancashire, second day
Somerset 304-7 dec. Lancashire 153 (Hughes 57,
Folley 38, Fowler 14) and 19-0

We spent a lot of the day in the bus, watching Walt bowling in the first Test at Headingley. He didn't have much more luck than us.

We failed to save the follow-on by 2 runs! We needed 155. I batted at number seven because I couldn't really hold the bat properly. I went in at 85-5 to join Yosser, so we were struggling from the start. It was indeed turning square, but we seemed to have steadied the ship. I finally got a long-hop from Viv which I was going to welly, but it didn't bounce and that was that. But I was sixth out with 27 needed, which looked a doddle. It looked even more so when the seventh wicket added 14, and although Winker and Tosh were then out in successive deliveries to Bird, with Simmo batting at ten and Yosser going strong it looked easy.

But then Simmo had a brain storm. He thought he'd smash Skid over the top to settle things. He worked it out that it was the last ball of the over, so if something went wrong and he was out, Yosser was at the other end facing the next ball, and he would be able to acquire the necessary 2 runs. It didn't work like that. He gave Skid the charge, but missed and was stumped by a mile. And then Yosser hit Joel to third slip, and we had to follow on. Even in the annals of Lancashire cock-ups, it was a pretty gross one.

It had been decided that I should give opening a go in the second innings, but as it was so close to the end of the day they decided another night's rest would give me a chance to recover, so Folley opened again.

I spent the evening with Skid. We went for a drink and on for an evening meal, Italian, and talked about all sorts of things. He is someone whose company I really enjoy; perhaps too much, because I find him impossible to bat against – he always makes me laugh, and I just can't concentrate. I asked David Constant while I was batting whether intimidation could take a humorous form.

'Yes.'

'Well, Vic keeps making me laugh.'

Vic played up to it as usual. He kept saying to David, 'Will you tell the batsman I'm surprised he wanted to come down to my end,' and things like that. He has me giggling all the time. And every time I play against him he stuffs me out of sight.

It is interesting and irritating listening to former players pontificating on TV. I think they forget what pressure is. It is a funny thing, because now I'm out of the Test side I don't feel the pressure either, and I'm beginning to forget what it is like. I think it is like physical pain – it is something you can experience, but can't remember. You can remember thinking, 'Heck, that was painful,' you remember banging your knee and not being able to walk for half an hour, or having an operation, but the pain itself cannot be recalled.

And I think it is the same with pressure. It's only when you've got that horrible feeling in your stomach and you can't sleep and you are nervous. I go very cold and can't sit still. And it is only then that you understand what pressure is. I remember as a very inexperienced player batting against John Shepherd in a John Player game against Kent. I knew all I had to do was get my bat on the ball because there were no circles in those days; and it didn't matter whether it went two feet or thirty-five yards, we would get a run and the senior player would have been down my end and we would have been away.

But as soon as Shep let go of the ball my instinct took over and I took a wild swing at it. I was organized in my mind while he was running up, but as soon as he let go my mind went and I took a huge swing. I think I did that four times. I know I did it two overs running and I almost lost the game. And it would have stuck with me for ever had I lost the game, because it was my inability to cope with the pressure at that time. Fortunately we didn't. I can't remember who was at the other end, but he smashed a couple of fours and we won.

Pressure also varies from person to person. If I'm nervous, I go quiet – which is about the only time I am, to save anyone else saying so. Other people get snappy, abrupt, quick-tempered. Last year when we played in the Benson & Hedges final, I didn't really feel any nerves, perhaps because we were in the middle of a Test series against the West Indies. But it meant I could see the way people around me were reacting, and it was fascinating to sit back and watch what was going on. It was obvious that not only were the people outside the dressing-room not aware of the pressure, but the people inside didn't realize the effect it was having on them and on their interactions with other people.

14

Somerset v. Lancashire, third day
Somerset 304-7; Lancashire 153 and 89 (Fowler 4,
Marks 8-17). Somerset beat Lancashire by an innings
and 62 runs.

I was in for one and a quarter hours for 4 runs. I spent the whole of that time at one end facing Vic. In the end he got me with one which pitched leg stump and hit the top of the off. I looked up at him to say, 'Well bowled,' but he wouldn't look at me. He was too embarrassed – he knew it was a good ball, but he wouldn't look up.

That was the end of my game. I went off, got changed, had some lunch and said I was going round town for the afternoon. It is a very pleasant, picturesque place, and I wanted to get away from cricket for a bit. I bought some earrings for Steph, and a couple of cassettes. When I got back, we were all out for 89. And to my amazement the groundsman was erecting a net around the wicket. Peter Lever had asked him to do that so we could practise on it. So not only are we made to play on bad wickets, we are then forced to practise on them.

If you are out of form – and our scores suggest I'm not the only one who is – there is no way that practising on a bad wicket will get you back in form. It just doesn't work. You are far better off having an indoor net for all its limitations than playing on a bad wicket.

For a batsman in an indoor net, you at least can tell whether your hands and legs are in the right place at the right time. You either middle it or you don't, because wickets in indoor nets don't deviate that much. But if you are on a bad wicket, you don't know if you are playing and missing because of the wicket or because of your own failings; you don't know if you are mistiming it because of the wicket or because you are completely out of form. And it just doesn't help.

Pete Owen, our coach driver, couldn't work it out either. We had to get back to Manchester for a game tomorrow. The one consolation with the early finish — it was over soon after lunch — was that we could have got on the way in good time. Leaving it until towards rush-hour was just going to make the journey that much worse.

I'm always interested to hear what umpires have to say, because they are in a better position than anyone to judge players. I asked Connie what he thought of our young openers — he'd seen us already this season — and we talked about them for a while. Then he said, 'There's one who really looks the part and that's Ian Folley,' which is possibly right. He is very correct, very sideways on and, as I said earlier, could progress. He hasn't found his level yet. At the moment he is a bit stiff. He needs to loosen his arms a bit, but that comes with time. I push like hell now, especially against spinners, even when I'm not playing well.

A lot of it is to do with confidence. If he were a confident lad, he would probably score more freely, and it would then be up to his choice of balls to hit which determined whether he was being too free. But technically he is quite good. The problem is when he has to think about it. When the ball is seaming, like against Yorkshire, not thinking can be an advantage because it means you don't get flustered. But he didn't think at Ilford either, so it can work against you. He will certainly need to think as a slow bowler. I still regard him as a very good swing bowler. I thought he changed too early – he has been bowling spin for just over a season now. I've heard conflicting reports on why he changed, but I've never asked him, so I don't know. But I remember talking to Derek Randall last year and he said, 'Why isn't Folley bowling?'

'Oh, he bowls spin now.'

'Thank God for that! Because he was a bloody good swing bowler. That's one problem less.'

Considering he has changed completely, he has done well. But he is obviously still learning the job. As he has never bowled spin before, I think his fingers get tired. It is a completely different art from swing bowling, and they will get tired until he gets more accustomed to it.

It's an easy thing to say, but I think he falls into the trap of trying to do too many things with it. You can see that from the side, and when I bat against him in the nets I can virtually get him to bowl what I want him to. I've batted against Eddie Hemmings, and when he is under pressure he stops spinning it to try and bowl line and length, and I think that might happen to Ian now and again. But he is improving. How far he will go is difficult to say – whether he will be a bread-and-butter cricketer or improve to the state where he is comparable with David Hughes.

We forget this now, but David Hughes has 610 first-class wickets. Why on earth they told him to stop bowling, I don't know. The story was that he 'lost it', but I don't think so.

I think Yosser has never worked at his game as hard as he should have done. He has performed well over the years, and as long as he is performing well he is happy. If he didn't bowl in a game, he was not the sort of bloke you'd see in the nets trying to keep the rhythm going. He'll turn up in the morning, bowl for five minutes and that will be it. So next time he bowls, if he gets hit about in the first five overs they take him off. And he is someone who needs building up the whole time rather than knocking down. So I think what happened was that he didn't get as much bowling as he should, he didn't make up for it elsewhere, and so his level of performance went down. It just deteriorated gradually. But it was also at a time when they were short of batsmen. He was pushed up the order and did quite well. And there were other slow left-arm options. Bob Arrowsmith bowled well, so they told Yosser he was going to bat and Bob was going to bowl. Then after Bob faded there was David Lloyd, who could bowl slow left-arm. And so, bit by bit, Yosser's bowling took a back seat. And when he was asked to bowl it didn't go well, because you can't just turn it on. It was a combination of events which led him to bowl less and less.

But there have been some great statements made by our club over the years. Yosser was told, 'You're going to bat because Bob Arrowsmith is going to bowl,' and then, 'You're going to bat because David Lloyd is going to bowl.' David Lloyd was told he was only going to play when I was in a Test match. Then there is the latest with Shauny: 'You can't bat three and be first-change bowler,' which is right. But bat three and open the bowling?

15

Lancashire v. Derbyshire, first day
Derbyshire 201 (Wright 75, Makinson 5-60, Simmons
4-55); Lancashire 43-1 (Fowler 21)

That just about sums it up. I was out last ball of the day — a nothing ball, a nothing shot. I just got in my car and came home. I didn't stay and have a drink, I didn't even bother to get changed and have a shower, I just walked straight out of the ground in my whites. I was probably driving out of the gates before several of the Derbyshire players got into the showers.

I probably shouldn't have done it. I should have stayed and had a drink, particularly as David Makinson got a career best, but I didn't want to talk to anybody. I couldn't face it. I didn't want anything to do with cricket, I didn't want to talk to anybody, see anybody, have a drink with anybody. I just wanted to get out of the place. What made it so infuriating was that at last I thought I was getting somewhere. The wicket is awful again, as the scores show, but I'd battled through and I thought, 'Right, I'm "in" now, I'm going to get out of this bad patch.' And there I was 21 not out, with the last over to face off Geoff Miller. I was taking him because David Varey is not too keen as yet on spinners, which is fair enough. He is still inexperienced, but he is obviously an opening batsman because he is a better player against quicker bowlers. Learning to play against spin takes a little more time.

I said, 'Well, I'm quite happy to play Geoff. It doesn't bother me and I'll take him.' And so there I was, last ball of the day. It was a nothing ball, I didn't even have to play it. And I played this half-cock shot, got an edge and first slip dived forward and caught it.

16

Lancashire v. Derbyshire, John Player League
Derbyshire 182-9 (Makinson 4-28); Lancashire 186-3
(Fowler 98 not out). Lancashire won by 7 wickets.

What a relief! It wasn't easy, but I got past 50 for the first time this season, and then the game took over. At one stage we needed more than 9 an over, and I think what happened was that the situation dictated how I had to play instead of me contemplating how I was playing. I was thinking about the game rather than my individual problems, and it began to work. And Aby and I saw us home. We wanted 1 to win and I needed 6 for my hundred, and Michael Holding bowled this really slow delivery. If I'd been playing really well, I'd probably have hit it for six, but as it was I smashed it through the covers for four.

I did feel relieved afterwards. Not so much because I thought I'd suddenly become a bad player, but because it will get people off my back. The lads were relieved afterwards, because if I'm batting well it helps them. It gives them a bit more confidence if they see me scoring runs, and it also helps them because it means they don't get exposed to the new ball; so if I'm ticking over, the team benefits. And I was pleased to win a game for them – I did feel I won the game.

I didn't think I had become a bad player. But people were concerned about it, and even people who are trying to be helpful – as most are – add to the pressure. Even saying 'It'll come right' helps to remind you that it is not right, and I didn't want all the advice I was getting. I wanted to be left to work through it myself.

When I walked off the field on Saturday night, someone shouted, 'You're not fit to play for the second team, Fowler.' This evening you'd have thought I was the best thing ever to happen to Lancashire cricket – standing ovation time, cheers, shouts. It seems they don't see that I was the same player yesterday that I was today. It is almost as if they think that sometimes you are a good player and sometimes you are a bad player, rather than the same player who has good days and bad days, and can't be successful all the time.

The only cloud on the day was the feeling of frustration at getting out on Saturday night. I would love to be batting tomorrow. Having that long innings has made me feel as if my coordination and timing is right again, and I wish I could carry on tomorrow.

I took a bit of stick for my abrupt departure — a few jokes when I got to the ground this morning. But Walt is playing in the Test, so I missed his comments.

17

Lancashire v. Derbyshire, second day
Derbyshire 201 and 5-0; Lancashire 240 (Hughes 68,
Fairbrother 51, Finney 7-61)

The ball was seaming all over the place, and we went from 199-3 to 240 all out. Then it rained.

Talking to the Derbyshire players, they all thought the wicket was terrible too.

18

Lancashire v. Derbyshire, third day
Derbyshire 201 and 251-8 dec. (Wright 95); Lancashire
240 and 215-7 (Fowler 34, Miller 6-110). Lancashire
won by 3 wickets

We won with one ball to spare when Makinson hit their 'Great Dane' for 6. They set us a really tough declaration, given the state of the wicket — 213 in 37 overs. I certainly felt a bit better, although I could have done with batting yesterday. It is still my highest championship score of the season.

We had another post-mortem on the wicket, but it doesn't seem to have had much effect. They say it's the same for both sides, and it was an exciting finish, which is what people want to see.

20

Nets.

21

We are playing Kent tomorrow. Tav came up early and we had a round of golf – one of the funniest ever. He is brilliant. I think it was quite an eye-opener for Geoff, a drinking friend. We met in a pub because the guy Tav was with is a photographer, and of course pressmen like a drink! So Geoff said to me, 'Do you want a drink?'

'Yes, I'll have a pint.'

Then he asked Chris.

'Orange juice, please.'

So Geoff said to me, 'Does he never drink?'

'Occasionally, but not very often.'

'Is he all right?'

'Yes, of course, he is!'

He's a great bloke, bags of fun. If he goes to the pub with you, he isn't going to get ratted with you, he'll drink orange juice. But he'll never stop you having a drink and a bit of fun, but will join in in his own way. And once you accept that, accept his presence and his company for what it is and get on with him, he is a great bloke. And we had a superb afternoon. He beat everybody too. He plays golf like he bats – he has the same foot movement he has when he is batting. But then he whacks it miles. People just don't understand him. He is very set in his ways – almost unbelievably so. He often would like to be different, but he knows he isn't.

He is one of the most organized men I have ever met. If he was in his house or in a dressing-room and was struck blind on the spot, he would know where everything of his was. You open his suitcase and everything is always in the same place, folded in the same way. He is so methodical that it's almost infuriating. He is not given to excess in anything, not in his habits, mannerisms or speech. When he does anything, he does it economically. When he speaks, he is worth listening to, and if he does anything he does it for a reason. I suppose he wastes no energy.

Tav is a great thinker, which goes hand in hand with everything else about him. He has a great talent and you can learn a lot from him. When we had team meetings in Australia and New Zealand, it was always Tav who came up with something which had everyone saying, 'Oh, yes, that's a good point, we hadn't thought of that.' In New Zealand there were three people who used to go out quite regularly – Vic Marks, Chris Tavaré and I. Skid and Tav used to know one another at university. I was the odd one out, I suppose, in upbringing, outlook on life, and personality. Yet we used to have some really good fun together. Chris is a very humorous bloke in a quiet sort of way. He is somebody I can't find fault with really. He has been a victim of circumstance most of the time.

He readily admits that the only reason he played so many Tests was that Bob Willis liked his style of play and could depend on him. Bob preferred to have Tav 64 not out at close of play than to have me getting 100 before lunch and then getting out. That was Bob's idea of an opening batsman, and Tav, batting out of position, supplied what Bob wanted. And Tav has taken the flak for it ever since. Yet I played in a John Player League game at Maidstone where Tav got 100 against Michael Holding, and you have never seen anything like it. He smashed it everywhere. But his methodical approach to life won't let him be rash in anything. Even when he tears a bowler apart, he is methodical in how he goes about it. It is a systematic destruction. I don't know how you define flair, but if Tav has it, it is completely organized. My flair, if I have it, is completely spontaneous. So mine can be out of context; Tav would never be out of context.

I feel protective about him. I don't like people getting at him, because I think he has had a raw deal in the past. I think he has had a bad deal at Kent, is very much misunderstood and has far more talent than people will allow.

It is easy to get at him, because he is not going to smack you on the nose or come back with a volley of abuse. He is completely harmless; he is never going to knock you over and will just accept it, so he is an easy target. If he was slandered in the press, he might think he was getting a raw deal, but he would take it. So it is easy for people to try to criticize him, but I think if they knew him they would find it very difficult to find anything about him to find fault with. I would love to play under him as a captain, or open the batting with him or play in the same side with him. He is a great team man, and that is why he has taken so much stick.

When he was appointed captain of Kent, from what I gather there were two factions – one for Tavaré and the other for Cowdrey. At the time the 'in-betweenies' leaned towards Tav, so he got the job. But when things didn't go to their liking, for whatever reason, the Cowdrey faction must have got at the in-betweenies and persuaded them to lean the other way. So it came to another vote, Tav was out and Cow in. But although he got kicked out, I think Tav's record was pretty good.

I know both lads, and I don't think you can mention them in the same breath as cricketers or captains. If Cow had been called John Ormrod, nobody would have given a toss. I'm certain he wouldn't have toured with England. He is a great lad, a good cricketer, but he is not an England player. And he has yet to prove that he is worthy to take over from Tav. And I think I can make that judgement fairly, because I know and get on with both of them. But Kent is as steeped in its background and its loyalties as our place is.

22

Lancashire v. Kent, first day
Kent 291-7 (Benson 102)

Walter cursed and swore his way through Benson's century. On our wicket it was a magnificent achievement. Once again there was variable bounce, it seamed all over the place and there was some turn too. If we had Middlesex's attack we would be unplayable. It is getting to the stage where a wicket which seams sideways is considered a 'normal' wicket.

The trouble is that both batsmen and bowlers are losing perspective. Not only do you lose your basis for judgement of a wicket, but also there is no way of assessing your own level of performance. So Benson played and missed a bit, and got some edges, and Walt, who has a bowler's view, was frustrated. But from a batsman's point of view it was an outstanding knock.

23

Lancashire v. Kent, John Player League
Kent 142-8; Lancashire 143-6 (Fowler 33). Lancashire
won by 4 wickets

For a John Player League game the wicket was quite impossible. People said to me afterwards, 'You got a bit bogged down out there.' They don't see that we had lost quick wickets, that Kent are a good bowling side, and especially that the wicket was almost impossible to bat on. 33 was probably worth a century on a reasonable wicket, as the Kent score suggests: they got to 72 in their first 26 overs, which is laughable in a Sunday 40-over slog.

But the members don't understand that. I normally field on the far side, because that is usually the longer boundary and

I've got a good arm. Today I felt fit enough to field out, but I wasn't 100 per cent, so I went on the members' side. And as Kent kept on losing wickets, I got chatting to some of them. Tav was batting, and because they had lost early wickets he couldn't smash it around as he would have wanted. Also, he has been having a desperately bad time with the bat. And our crowd don't like him anyway, because they think he is a slow, calculating, methodical, boring player, although he is far from that. So they were all complaining about him. One of the members has got a peculiarly high voice, and he was squeaking, 'You can get these on your own, Graeme,' and all that sort of thing. And instead of humouring them or ignoring them, I spoke seriously to them. So I said, 'Why do you think they are struggling?'

'We're bowling very well,' they replied.

'Why do you think Tav's batting so slowly?'

'We're bowling very well.'

'Why do you think we are bowling well?'

'Because we've got good bowlers.'

So I was getting nowhere, but at that stage I wanted to try and get a point across. 'Why do you think he keeps playing and missing?'

'He's playing down the wrong line!'

'Well, why do you think he's playing down the wrong line all the time? He's a good player, surely?'

But the thought that it might be the wicket never enters their heads. Because it doesn't burst past somebody's nose off a length, they don't notice it. They don't even notice when it shoots along the floor. They giggle and go, 'Eeeeh, he missed that one.' They just don't see that there is only one possible explanation why it is a low-scoring game on a Sunday, even when you've shown them that it is the only possible answer.

Our members come down and watch week in and week out, and they've still no conception of the mechanics of cricket. They never take into consideration that with the ball travelling 50 or 60 m.p.h. you just can't adjust for that sort of deviation, or how it can upset someone's technique and timing. They just don't realize how much a wicket can dominate a game.

But then again, should they have to have the knowledge to understand that we are playing on a rubbish wicket? Old Trafford is potentially one of the best grounds in the world. It is a Test ground and should have perfect facilities. It has the financial resources to have a good wicket, but the priorities are wrong in my opinion. As long as we have sponsors every day and new seating, everything is hunky-dory, it seems. Why should members be expected to adapt their thinking to take in the knowledge that we have the worst Test wickets in the country? And the problems of explaining that apply not only to people who have never played the game but only watched, but also to people who used to play and then stopped. How quickly they forget! But I suppose it is understandable. A batsman who is waiting to go in will ask what is going on out there, and if you can't tell when you are playing, what chance has anybody else? It would help if our members sat behind the bowler's arm instead of at square leg. But then they would have no conception of the pace, so again they still wouldn't know what you are talking about.

I couldn't lay a bat on Eldine Baptiste. He was slanting it across me and I was playing at it and not getting a touch. When I finally middled one I gave myself a round of applause, it had become almost laughable. In one over in particular, he must have gone past the outside of the bat five times out of six. At the end of it Clive came down the wicket. I thought he was going to give me some advice.

'It's not easy,' he announced. *What?* Then he said it wasn't swinging, it was just going straight.

I said, 'You must be joking.'

I should have known what to expect really. Clive believes that batting is an extension of your individual personality and so doesn't go in for technical advice. His mid-wicket conferences have produced some classics. That great telescopic arm shoots out and summons you to go and hear him, and it is almost guaranteed that you will walk away going, 'What?'

In my first season of opening regularly, we played Worcestershire at Old Trafford on a worn wicket. We won the game when we won the toss really. I was batting with Clive. Giff was kicking sods out of the wicket, cursing and sweating like a pig because it was warm and he was scarlet. And he had been coming off, then coming back on, to no result. Anyway, he came on again to bowl into the rough. And I was facing the first ball of his new spell, and as I was about to receive Clive beckoned me down to him. So I thought, 'Oh, change of plan, tactics, he must know something.' He was captain at the time, so I trotted off down the wicket. He looked down at me and said, 'It looks like Giff's going to bowl into the rough. Well, I'm going to kick it, but you're such a short little sod you'll have to use your bat.' And then he turned and went back.

Another time, I can't remember who against, he called me down mid-over. It was getting to a stage where we needed to accelerate. So I went down and asked, 'What?'

'My piles are killing me!' And he turned round and walked back. And I stood in the middle of the wicket completely bewildered. After this second incident – and the two were quite close together – I said to him afterwards, 'What on earth did you do that for?'

'Well, I thought you were looking a bit tense, so I thought I'd break the situation down.'

He certainly did that, because I could not figure out why he would want to tell me halfway through an over that his piles were killing him. I'm less sure about the other occasion. In hindsight I suppose he was right, but at the time it was no use to me whatsoever. In a game against Middlesex, John Emburey was bowling and I couldn't hit it anywhere except straight back at him. I just couldn't. I found it impossible to get inside it and hit it through the off, or to tuck it further round. It just went back to him or to mid-on or mid-off. So I went down and said, 'Look, Hubert, I'm struggling. I can't work it round anywhere. I can't even work a single. What do you reckon I should do?'

And he just looked at me and said, 'Do what you want, but work it out for yourself.'

At the time I was shocked. Had I been batting with David Lloyd, I'd have got a completely different answer. He'd have said, 'Wait a second longer and tuck it further round,' or 'Try and make him pull you on to the front foot and then wait for it on the back foot,' or a technical answer like that. Whether that would have been better for me I don't know, but at the time I was taken aback by Clive's response, and I remember thinking, 'Thanks!'

But subsequently I've found his approach very helpful. When I went on the tour to Australia, I fell into the 'England player syndrome'. I thought I had to bat like an England player, to look the part to please the connoisseurs in the Lord's Long Room, rather than play my natural game. I had a disastrous time. And because I was fairly raw, and no one had seen much of me batting well, everyone was trying to give me advice and get me to do different things. And it was Clive who helped me sort it out, because he said, 'You've got to bat your way. The way you batted for Lancashire was good enough to get you into the England team, and that is the way you should play when you get there. As you get more experienced, there are things you'll want to change, but you do that from the basis of your natural style, not by totally changing your technique.' That made sense. And that is Clive's approach. He doesn't analyse the mechanics of batting for you like David Lloyd; he believes batting is an extension of your person. And what he tries to do is to shape the person, cut off the rough corners, and then hopefully you end up with something you can develop yourself. He believes that if you feel you can hit every ball outside off stump over square leg, then you should do it, because that is you. If you make mistakes and keep getting out, then you have to think about it.

Clive commands respect. I know he has an incredible record, the most successful West Indies captain, but it is more than that. He doesn't work by changing the structure of things, he works by changing the people in the structure. He tries to mould them, to get them round to his way of thinking and put them on the right track. He believes that the best way of having a good ship is to mould the crew, not to change the shipping company.

I don't always agree. What annoys me about Clive – I suppose it does annoy me – is that he is one of the most powerful people in cricket, yet he doesn't overtly use his influence. He always wants to do things quietly, and it just doesn't work – at least not with Lancashire. It might with the West Indies Board, but we should have a far better-organized playing set-up just because he is in our midst, but we haven't, and the reason is that he won't use his power to push for changes.

I had a night with him in Amsterdam once, about two years ago. It was a side of Clive I'd never seen before. Usually you see the shy, retiring side of him, but on that occasion he was the most hilarious man I've ever heard. He just stood up, took the floor, and we all fell about. It was incredible.

Yesterday Walt wore a sun-hat. Today a note appeared saying sun-hats are not allowed, we've got to wear our caps. Walt went out for batting and fielding practice wearing his helmet.

Pete Lever refused to hit him any catches because he said Walt was being stupid and trivial, so Walt stormed off.

If our caps were better quality, we might feel happier about wearing them. But it is the type of silly rule which this club goes in for. The chairman hasn't spoken to me since I dropped my trousers for the TV cameras, and it cost me £100 – he told Pete to fine me. Last year I was fined for going into the committee room wearing a bright green shirt, white leather tie, shiny grey trousers and white shoes. I'd scored 100 that day, yet the chairman wanted me to be fined because of the way I was dressed. A week later I went in wearing a Lancashire blazer and flannels. I got about six runs that day, then smashed it up in the air and was caught – a really irresponsible shot. I was invited into the committee room and they were really pleased to see me because I was 'properly' dressed. I've never been given a rollicking for the way I've performed on the field, only for wearing the wrong shirt or tie. I've even been asked why I'm not wearing my Lancashire tie when I've got an England one on. And that is the reason why the whole discipline at Lancashire is wrong in my opinion. It isn't based on cricket.

24

Lancashire v. Kent, second day
Kent 303; Lancashire 261-8 (Simmons 51, Fowler 0)

It almost did seam sideways. On this wicket you've got no chance.

25

Lancashire v. Kent, third day
Kent 303 and 217-5 dec. (Baptiste 81); Lancashire 261-8
dec. and 234 (Simmons 62 not out, Fowler 18, Johnson
5-78). Kent won by 25 runs

In most circumstances 260 in 59 overs would be a very generous declaration. On our wicket it was beyond us – and they bowled better than us. It was the sort of game where you should have enjoyed the day, because it built up to an exciting finish; in fact, until Walt was out for 20, we were in with a good shout, but then we lost our last two wickets for 3 runs, and they won with 9 balls to spare.

The wicket just spoilt the game for us. We had a long chat about it and about the balls we are using. But the trouble is that nobody at Old Trafford will admit we have a serious problem on our hands. Nobody wants to come to terms with it and rectify it. Aby said to the manager, 'At this stage in my career I shouldn't have to struggle for every run when I'm "in",' but you don't get any understanding or sympathy. I added, 'Because of the way I play, a ball only needs to be six inches out in length and I've got the ability to follow through, play my shots and dictate to the bowler. But these wickets are reducing my level of skill, and making the bowler's level of skill greater. And if that is happening to me, I'm bloody sure it is happening to everybody else. And if Walt pulls a batsman two to three inches outside off-stump and seams it, that's his skill. But if the wicket nullifies that ability, you're taking away his skill as well. You might as well make me bat right-handed.'

Playing on bad wickets destroys you, whether you are a batsman or a bowler. You lose all sense of perspective. As batsmen, we don't know whether we are playing down the wrong line or whether it has seamed. After a spell on this wicket you just can't tell what's happening. You end up middling one, being beaten by one and nicking one, and you just don't know which you were playing correctly and which you weren't. And you can't go into the nets to sort it out, because the nets are rubbish too. So none of the lads are ticking over as batsmen.

And the bowlers have no idea how they are bowling, because it destroys their perspective too. When they get on an average wicket, they think it is a flat one if the ball goes straight through. If a bowler is used to playing on a good wicket, he will know whether he is bowling line and length: if he gets smashed all round the ground he obviously isn't; if he ties batsmen down and bowls tidily, he knows he is bowling quite well. But after a couple of weeks on a bad wicket, he loses all his reference points, because if the ball is deviating, keeping low and stopping, he will forget that the bad ball is going to be hit.

And it is not just us saying this. When I was talking to Tav, he said he couldn't believe how bad our wicket is. The Derbyshire lads agreed. Nobody can. The manager says that should be to our advantage because we have local knowledge. But that argument is wrong. Cricket is a precision game, and playing continually on bad wickets is a vicious circle – or rather a vicious spiral, because you just get worse and worse. If you are used to playing on good wickets – as the Kent team are – when you get on a bad wicket, at least you know it is the ball that is doing something and not you. But if you are used to bad wickets and you get on a good one, you don't know whether you are playing well or not; and if you are used to missing a ball every now and then, when you get a bad ball you haven't the confidence to play the shot you would do normally.

We have been arguing this from both the batsmen's and the bowlers' point of view for weeks. But Jack Bond gives the impression he isn't prepared to listen. It seems he doesn't want to be seen agreeing with us.

We know he can't change the wickets overnight, but we do want him to show some sympathy. He could say, 'This is the legacy we are stuck with, how can we best cope with it? Let's make sure the indoor nets are always available, that they are cleaned and swept and looked after. Let's make sure the outdoor nets are looked after – especially the artificial ones. Let's keep them consistent, and we'll try and ease our way through games because obviously we are going to struggle.' If he responded like that, and gave what encouragement and help he could, then at the end of the day he would have the right to be critical. If we are unprofessional, they would have the right to criticize. But if they don't help along the way and don't provide discipline either, we do become lazy. People say, 'Well, sooner or later I'll get one with my number on it and I'm out,' or, 'Well, I keep seaming it but they keep missing it,' and it becomes an excuse for poor performances and poor work-rates. And this is what the manager goes on about: he thinks our work-rate isn't high enough. But he never does anything to change it. And we have been arguing, arguing, arguing, until we are blue in the face. We said, 'Let's stop using those balls with those big seams, for a start,' because with our wickets you don't need a seam for the ball to deviate. We thought at least we'd made some progress on that. After our protests they said we could play three-day games with a different ball, but would have to keep the Readers ones for one-day games where we could exploit 'local knowledge'.

I said, 'That's ridiculous. Not only are you making it inconsistent from day to day, but you are committing the biggest inconsistency in one-day games, which are supposed to be crowd-pleasing games, by ensuring we get low scores.

'Suppose we bat first in a Benson & Hedges 55-over match, play really well and get 160. I'm certain 160 is easier to get in the second innings against a seaming ball than it is to go in and whack it around at the start. So then you are putting the advantage heavily on the toss as well, and just stacking everything up against skill.'

But there's no progress even on that. The secretary sent us

a note saying that the club has bought all these Readers balls, so we have got to use them.

Aby was not very impressed with our spinners; he complains they don't spin it. I've told him before this season that he should bowl himself more, and I said it again. 'It's no good moaning about people not doing the job, there are times you should bowl. You can bowl, you should bowl more. It's another string to your bow, and it is another option you can give yourself. Because if you get so disappointed or frustrated with our bowlers, you could turn to yourself, and if you can't do it either, then you've no gripes. But you've got to give yourself another option, particularly on our wickets which are low, slow turners anyway.

'Thatch has just started bowling spin, so he will have days when he doesn't bowl that well. Jack doesn't turn it anyway; so it doesn't matter what wicket he bowls on, he is going to bowl to the same level. In fact he is probably worse on a turning wicket. So if the wicket is going to turn, you've got to bowl.'

He agreed. Whether he'll do it remains to be seen.

26

Lancashire v. Warwickshire, first day
Warwickshire 239 (Humpage 75, Dyer 68)

It was another grey day; grey cricket on another Old Trafford crap wicket with poor light cutting short the play.

27

Lancashire v. Warwickshire, second day
Warwickshire 239 and 36-0; Lancashire 207 (Fowler 88,
Ferreira 5-43, Small 4-71)

At last I got past 50, but it was a long, hard grind. Those Readers balls are a nightmare. It swung all over the place and was just made for Anton Ferreira and Gladstone Small. I couldn't say I batted well by any stretch of the imagination, but the infuriating thing was that I was done by Giff only twelve short of a century. But I just feel relieved to have got some runs, however much of a struggle it was.

28

Lancashire v. Warwickshire, third day
Warwickshire 239 and 226-7 dec. (Lloyd 62, Dyer 55);
Lancashire 207 and 165-8 (Fowler 36, Ferreira 5-41).
Match drawn

Basically, they bowled better than we did without Walt. They set us 259 in 60 overs, which was not really on with that wicket, especially the way we're batting at the moment.

29

Sussex v. Lancashire, first day
Sussex 310-6 dec. (Mendis 103, Imran 70, C. M. Wells
69 not out); Lancashire 16-1 (Fowler 7 not out)

Batting after a long trip from Manchester followed by a long day in the field is not fun, but I survived.

30

Sussex v. Lancashire, John Player League
Sussex 234-4 (Imran 80, Green 70); Lancashire 165-7
(Fowler 20). Sussex won by 69 runs

JULY

1

Sussex v. Lancashire, second day
Sussex 310-6 dec. and 193-0 (Mendis 100 not out,
Green 78 not out); Lancashire 173 (Fairbrother 59,
Fowler 23)

For the umpteenth time this season I was dismissed when I was beginning to feel settled. I had done the hard bit on Saturday night and this morning against Imran, and then I got out.

2

Sussex v. Lancashire, third day
Sussex 310-6 dec. and 193-0 dec.; Lancashire 173
and 257 (Simmons 101, Fowler 20).
Sussex won by 73 runs.

The scoreboard doesn't show it, but I probably batted as well in this match as I have done all season. I think the challenge of playing against Imran was what did it. I like batting against him, because I know I can bat against him, which not many can, and I can concentrate on the duel rather than my problems.

Jack hasn't been at his best this season, particularly in the field, but he is still a heck of a good batsman to come in at number seven, and he made them work for it in the end. But we definitely came second.

3

Suffolk v. Lancashire, NatWest Trophy
Lancashire 233-6 (Fairbrother 52 not out, Fowler 41);
Suffolk 133-8. Lancashire won by 100 runs

6

Lancashire v. Hampshire, first day
Lancashire 401-6 dec. (Fairbrother 164 not out,
Fowler 0); Hampshire 22-0

It never rains but it pours. Aigburth is a flat, easy wicket, a batsman's paradise, and I was out first ball to Malcolm. The Hampshire lads said I was a little unlucky to be given out. That is neither help nor consolation, but the more I thought about it the more I thought I was out. And talking to Malcolm in the bar afterwards, he said it was out. End of story.

Harvey played brilliantly and made a career-best score. His best-ever day and my worst: Harvey is a very talented player. He works the game out very well and is still only twenty-one. I think he should be an international player if he carries on making progress, and once he gets in I think he will play very well at that level and be there for a long time.

He is an aggressive little bloke. Though he is quiet and hardly ever drinks, he likes to have a scrap – a friendly fight, not a bar-room brawl. Shauny's mate, he is known as Farbottle, Little Ted and other, unprintable, nicknames.

He has the most extraordinary eating habits in the world. He will eat virtually nothing but steak and chips. He doesn't like this, doesn't like that. He likes Black Forest gâteau, but doesn't like black cherries. He is absolutely pernickety. We put that down to him being an only child, so much so that if he refuses to eat or do anything we all shout 'OCS' – only child syndrome. His mum and dad follow him everywhere he goes. At one stage during the Benson & Hedges Cup Final last year, someone shouted to him on the boundary, 'Neil, does your mum know where you are?,' which caused great mirth in our dressing-room.

He is a little moody and gets a bit stroppy. At the moment he takes things to heart too much, especially if he has had a bad game or if he cannot understand what the plan of attack is for the day. And he can't switch off, which is something you have to do. If he doesn't, he is going to feel like he is fifty-five in about three years' time.

<u>7</u>

Lancashire v. Hampshire, John Player League
Hampshire 235-5; Lancashire 232 (Fowler 5).
Hampshire won by 3 runs

Steve O'Shaughnessy was awarded his county cap today. He should have had it some time ago, but didn't for various reasons. The timing is incredible, though – he's been out of the side for the last couple of championship matches because he is right out of form. The explanation is that it is hoped it will encourage him.

As soon as they heard the news, Harvey and Roger Watson packed all his gear together and threw it into the first-team changing-room. We have made him take a peg between Walt and myself so that we can hit him when he needs it.

I fielded in front of the members once again – not a good place to be when things are going wrong.

Steph spent the day sailing and came down afterwards for a drink with two friends from schooldays, Martin and Karen. Martin's luck has been as bad as mine recently. First his business was broken into and then his car was stolen and a load of his personal gear was nicked. We consoled ourselves by saying things couldn't get worse.

<u>8</u>

Lancashire v. Hampshire, second day
Lancashire 401-6 dec. and 63-5; Hampshire 331-5 dec.

Things can get worse. It was a beautiful day, so I took my E-type. I actually felt quite content with life as I drove through to Liverpool. Then in fielding practice before the game I jumped to attempt a catch and twisted in mid-air with my right hand stretched high. Something snapped in my neck or shoulder region and down I went. The pain was in the right side of my neck. I lay on my back and realized I couldn't lift my head or shoulders, and the pain was so intense that I didn't want to move anyway.

Shauny was twelfth man. I suspect that he had celebrated his cap the previous night, and so the last thing he wanted was to field all day in the sun with a tender head.

'Get up,' he said. 'This is a "do", is this.'

'Broken hand, Fox?' asked Walt.

'No. It's my neck.'

'Oh, shit, Pete, it's his neck,' said Walt, realizing it wasn't a joke. He and Pete Lever knew of my predicament, and so they were aware it could be serious. They were alarmed. Lawrie Brown, the physio, was summoned. He tried to move me, but I had to tell him not to. By now my right arm had gone dead, and the knife was still sticking in my neck.

An ambulance was called. I got Walt to ring Steph and tell her to come over with my parents so that she could drive the E-type home. While we were waiting, people stood around shielding my eyes from the sun and trying to make me laugh, unsuccessfully I'm afraid. Twenty minutes had passed when the ambulance arrived — thank God I wasn't bleeding! They drove on to the field to pick me up. The first thing one of the ambulancemen did was to spot Yosser. 'Hello, David,' he said, 'the last time I saw you I was playing football against you. David Lloyd was playing as well. You kicked me all over the park.' Yosser looked bemused at this information. Meanwhile I was still lying there prostrate. They used a scoop stretcher to lift me. In the process they caught my hair in the stretcher and trapped it for the entire journey, which was not the most comfortable I've ever experienced. But that was nothing to the agony I still felt in my neck.

But at least I knew where I was — the lilting scouse voice and a brief glimpse of the Catholic cathedral through the smoky windows confirmed that. I wanted Pete Lever to come with me, as he knew of my previous neck problems and no one else did. Bob Bennet, one of the committee men, followed in his car to drive us back afterwards. I felt sore, my right arm was still numb, yet I felt embarrassed to be on a stretcher.

At the hospital they took X-ray after X-ray, a surgical collar was fitted and then it was, 'See you later.' It was nothing more than a torn trapezius muscle, but all the other muscles have gone into spasm and my neck is rigid, without any natural curvature, making it very sore.

Peter Lever was nearly as upset as I am. He feels helpless and sorry for me. Neither of us think it can possibly get worse. I hope it doesn't — if I was less obstinate, this could have been the straw which broke the camel's back. At times I just feel totally despondent. Pete has told me to get away from cricket for a week and come back when I'm ready, which I will.

Back at the ground, sympathy was mixed with offers of polo-neck sweaters to cover up the collar. The remarks are funny, but there just isn't a laugh in me. I don't want to talk to the press or have my photograph taken, but I haven't the strength to keep saying no, so I am badgered. One chap even wants me to do an interview for cable TV. I refused, five minutes later he asked again, and again I refused. Then I went out on to the balcony and sat with Peter Ball for twenty minutes. While we were talking a photographer came up and pressed for a photo. Then this TV chap came back and asked if I was sure about not doing the interview. I refused a third time. God!

Finally Steph arrived and we left in the Volvo. My father will drive my beloved E-type home. I telephoned David Markham and will see him in the morning. I hope it is a torn muscle and nothing else, and will be reassured by his diagnosis. He is brilliant, and I am comforted by the fact that I am seeing him. I can neither sit nor lie comfortably, but the pain-killers work. They don't cure the dismay I feel, though. I want to cry, but don't, although I know I should because I would feel better. It never rains but it really pisses down.

I tried to watch the video, but there were too many interruptions. All I want is a silent telephone and peace and quiet; just Steph, Smithy and me, but that seems too much to ask.

9

I was at David Markham's at 8.15 a.m. He confirmed a torn trapezius muscle. He is an excellent doctor, and also very understanding about pressure and about personal success and failure. He prescribed a complete rest away from cricket for two weeks. He is brilliant.

It was the first time he had met Stephanie. Her response was, 'What a lovely man.'

So it is goodbye to the Nightmare Season for two weeks. I told everyone at Liverpool the diagnosis, and arranged to go to Abersoch on Saturday for a week.

11

David Lloyd came by to see me today. He is playing for Accrington in the Lancashire League, where we both started. It is a different game, mainly because the type of wicket you get dictates the nature of play. He was telling me about a game in which the ball was turning square — turning yards, literally — and he ended up bowling with an 8–1 field. And that was eight on the leg side, not the off, for a slow left-armer turning it away from the bat! It was bouncing and turning yards, and this bloke was putting his foot down the wicket and trying to whack everything over square leg. The lad was missing four out of five balls, but because it was turning so much he got away with it. On a good wicket he wouldn't have, because he was being beaten in the air and off the pitch, and he'd have been bowled or Bumble would have found the edge. So eventually David set this 8–1 field, and then the bloke actually went back and cut one for four — but that was only one ball. All the others went over square leg. Talking to him afterwards Bumble said, 'Why did you play that way?'

'I've always played that way.'

It reminded me of playing for Accrington as a kid. They'd say, 'We're up against Russ Cuddin on Saturday. Bloody good player, Russ Cuddin. One of t'finest players in t'league. Hits it really well through extra.' But what they didn't say was that was the only shot he played, and that every ball he got he hit through extra, no matter what you bowled to him.

Trying to talk to club players about first-class cricket is difficult because it is a foreign game to them. It just doesn't occur to them that you don't try and hit an inswinger through the covers because it is playing across the line, and instead you guide it anywhere between straight and mid-wicket. What occurs to them is, 'I've hit it through extra cover all me life, that's me best shot, and that's where it's going.'

For a time it was difficult to talk to my dad about the game. He taught me all the rudiments, taught me how to bat, and I think he found it very difficult to accept I'd outgrown his teaching. He didn't like that for quite a while. Which I suppose is understandable, because he had always offered advice and I took it for a considerable time. He could see what sort of player I was developing into as a kid, and he enjoyed that. And then all of a sudden to have me suddenly come back one day and say, 'No, that's wrong,' must have been hard to accept.

In theory I'm just resting. But sleeping is very difficult – and the phone keeps ringing. Roll on Saturday.

[Graeme did not take his diary to Abersoch. Even there he was unable to escape cricket completely. One day on a virtually deserted beach he was approached by a holidaying Lancastrian wanting to know when he was going to be fit. But his neck recovered slowly, even if his psyche was still scarred, and he reported back to Old Trafford on 22 July, to join in the nets, the team having no match that weekend. In his absence they had lost to Hampshire, lost a remarkable match to Warwickshire, drawn with Glamorgan and been beaten in the second round of the NatWest Trophy by Worcestershire at Old Trafford – Editor]

23

They suggested I should play in the second team tomorrow at Headingley instead of going with the first team to Southport. I was quite happy about that. It will give me a chance to find out if my neck is OK, and to get some practice to try and improve my horrendous form. Also, it is a pleasant idea in other ways. I remember my time in the second eleven with great affection, and if you can put a bit back I think you should. When I was there, both when I was just beginning and when I was a second-team capped player, I always enjoyed having the company of senior players — Barry Wood, David Hughes and Bob Ratcliffe especially — and since I've played Test cricket I am sure that some of the younger lads will be looking forward to having me playing.

24

Yorkshire 2nd XI v. Lancashire 2nd XI, first day
Yorkshire 142 (Jefferies 6-67, Hayhurst 3-27); Lancashire
92-3 (Fowler 24)

From England to Lancashire second team in two months! We fielded first on a wicket which is not fit for first-class cricket. It was very underprepared and did quite a lot. They had quite a strong side, with Blakey and Jim Love both playing, but it was a good wicket for Jeffo and he used it. I think he is a good bowler, a good trier, and hasn't received the encouragement he might have had.

I scratched around for 20. A two-week break is hard to come back from even if you were playing well beforehand, and I certainly wasn't. But the wicket isn't good; it was just like being at Old Trafford except that it flew more.

I drove over to Headingley this morning so that I could have the car to go home tomorrow night and pick up my gear for two weeks on the road with the first team — if required. The lads came over on the bus, also this morning. Whenever possible, they travel on the morning of the first day to save a night's hotel bill. That means some of the lads getting up at 6 a.m. to go in to Old Trafford to pick up the coach for some of the trips. Not the best preparation for playing cricket when you are expected to show your professionalism.

I received a good welcome when I arrived, and I think a lot of them were pleased to see me.

25

Yorkshire 2nd XI v. Lancashire 2nd XI, second day
Yorkshire 142 and 220-7 (Blakey 54); Lancashire 211
(Hartley 7-58)

I came home this evening and picked up my gear. I am going down to London tomorrow to join the lads, but if I hadn't pushed I wouldn't have found out whether they wanted me or not. It is like trying to get information out of MI5, all cloak and dagger.

The second team doesn't seem to run as smoothly as it did when I played. Then it was run by Eddie Slinger, who is now a committee man and a very successful solicitor, and it all seemed very efficient. Whether that was because I was young and didn't know any better, whereas now I'm more aware, I couldn't say, but that is how it seems. Now it is run by Harry Pilling, and some of the lads are not too happy about his leadership. It hasn't seemed too bad for the last two days; but when I said that, they replied it was because I was there, and when a senior player was there his leadership became more reasoned. He didn't want me to see him being totally arbitrary and have me going back to the first team, the coach, the manager and anybody who would listen and say that the second team was being run like a shambles.

I organized the fielding practice before the game, and it turned out that they don't normally have that. Their general complaint is that they receive no guidance, no encouragement, and especially that no reason is ever given for anything. It's 'Do as I say and shut up'. I can see that, because Harry was still playing when I started, and he was then a member of the

210

'If it was good enough for me when I was a kid, it's good enough for you now' school. And I could see him responding to anyone questioning any decision with 'Because I say so'.

That's OK for some people, but it certainly doesn't wash with me. I like to know what is going on, and it is not the way the majority of the lads in the second team expect to be treated either. One minute they are being told they are professional sportsmen and should behave differently and know differently, and in the next breath a decision affecting their career is being made and they aren't given any reason. And that covers the gamut from little things like the time the bus is leaving Old Trafford, to fundamental matters like the batting order and who was bowling when and at which end. Every facet of the game is being decided without explanation.

Harry had a marvellous career. He was probably one of the better players not to play for England, but I don't think he has the ability to pass on information, and teaching is a major function in the second team. He could spot faults in technique very easily, especially if you were a batsman as I was, but he couldn't always help you to put it right. And more fundamentally, I think his knowledge of cricket is a short-term one: he can deal with an immediate situation, but I don't think he has the overall view of what is needed to bring a player along from being a junior professional to being a well-equipped member of the first team. And because of his authoritarian approach, people like Roger Watson, who has played well all season but is cheeky, feel they will never be pushed up for a first-team place.

But in spite of the moans about the leadership, the lads have a good spirit. Possibly they all pull together because they know they are up against it.

We had a classic. The ball flew off a head for four 'head byes' and the umpire signalled dead ball. We explained that it went down as a four – four leg byes. He changed his decision.

26

Yorkshire 2nd XI v. Lancashire 2nd XI, third day
Yorkshire 142 and 238 (Murphy 6-54); Lancashire 211
and 173-3 (Hayhurst 78 not out, Fowler 71). Lancashire
won by 7 wickets

I felt a bit better. I didn't play well by any stretch of the imagination, but I got some runs and felt more in touch than I had in the first innings. And we won early, so I was able to drive to London in good time.

Nicknames, of course, are rife. Tony Murphy is 'The Headless Chicken'; Roger Watson is 'Little Pig' or 'Pigs in Space'; John Stanworth is 'Stick'; Ian Davidson is 'Hippy'; Harry Pilling is 'Harry Dirt'; and the coach John Savage is 'Steptoe'. The worst is Andrew Hayhurst, who by convoluted reasoning is 'Anus'. A. N. Hayhurst became Anurst to Roger Watson, which became Anus, which has also produced 'Big Bot' and other less salubrious variations. When I heard them calling him 'Anus' I said, 'You've got to give him another nickname. He can't go through his career being called "Anus"!' He gets called it in pubs, everywhere. 'Anus, what d'you want to drink?' Not very nice.

He's a thick-set lad, not a bad player, and a good sportsman. He bats like Frank Hayes. He is low down, has a low grip and hits it through extra really well. His hair goes very blond, so I suggested calling him 'Barney Rubble', which suits him in some ways. But no, they'd rather call him 'Arsehole' and things like that, so he is struggling.

Davo played in one of the matches I missed – against Warwickshire – for his first-team début. He was immediately the target for the jokers, John Stanworth ringing him up pretending to be a journalist on his local paper, Norman Shakeshaft, and carrying out an interview with all the lads listening in.

27

Middlesex v. Lancashire, first day
Middlesex 318-4 (Butcher 86, Gatting 74,
Radley 64 not out)

We lost the toss and fielded. The pitch looks really flat. Rain ended things an hour early, by which time I felt very tired as well as bored. Walt bowled 22 overs for 30 runs, which was a magnificent performance on a flat wicket.

Aby said he wants me to bat at number three to protect me. Some protection!

We went to Mr Peakers nightclub in the evening. The manager chose to give us a lecture about safe driving. I'm twenty-eight and he tells me about drinking and driving? His opening line was, 'Don't have an accident.' What a phrase!

28

Middlesex v. Lancashire, John Player League
Lancashire 62-6 (Fowler 21; 10 overs);
Middlesex 65-4 (9.5 overs). Middlesex won by
6 wickets

It poured down, stopping in time for us to have a 10-over slog. A very boring day. I shouldn't have played because it was just too much of a risk in those conditions, but they told me they wanted me to play, which I don't think shows much understanding. As it was, I had to come off two overs from the end of their innings because of my neck. I dived to stop one and it went again. I caught Clive Radley next ball, but I just couldn't move and I had to come off.

I had a meal with Hubert afterwards.

29

Middlesex v. Lancashire, second day
No play, rain

It wasn't called off until after lunch, after we'd spent hours sitting around in school-type dressing-rooms doing nothing. It was fairly obvious that we weren't going to get on in the morning, so my car came in useful, Albert, Harvey and I going shopping in Uxbridge. It would have been impossible if we had only had the bus here. I just bought odds and sods – Walkman batteries, shampoo, shaving cream and razor blades, all those things which no one working a normal existence has to give a second thought about, but which can become a problem to get when you are spending weeks between hotels and cricket grounds.

After play was abandoned for the day, we went into London to Clark Jeans and Casuals and kitted the lads out. In the evening we all looked like Clark Clones.

Tonight was spent at a staunch supporter's house, Mr Dagg. He lives in a beautiful lodge. The main house is used as a business centre. It is a very impressive house and was an impressive evening, in most ways anyway. The butler served Thatch with ginger ale, which turned out to be cooking oil. And he also poured red wine all over my pale blue trousers as well as into my glass, which did not impress me at all. But you just have to pass it off, and I'm resigned to my fate at the moment, whatever it is.

I drove the bus down the drive for a while before handing back to C D – much to everyone's relief.

30

Middlesex v. Lancashire, third day
No play, rain. Match abandoned as a draw

The only activity we had were some exercises to keep ticking over. I did some running and sprints with Winker, Aby and Walt. Tosh didn't do any training at all. Nobody said anything, but he received a silent reprimand. Winker got blisters and Aby felt stiff, so maybe Tosh is not as stupid as people think.

Tosh comes in for a lot of criticism from the hierarchy of the club because they think he drinks too much. He does like a drink, but it is now a case of 'Give a dog a bad name'.

I think he is a good wicket-keeper. He has got a good pair of hands. Keeping seven days a week at Old Trafford is not the easiest thing to do. In fact, it can be a nightmare, because the bounce is so variable, with a particular tendency to keep low, and the pitches vary not only from day to day but sometimes within a day, which doesn't make it at all easy. If you ask the bowlers what he is like, they'll tell you he is a bloody good keeper, and that's good enough for me.

He might not always give himself the best opportunity to succeed, and perhaps he does give people openings to give him stick because he does like a drink, he is a bit lazy, and outwardly he appears very nonchalant and lax. He might be a bit, but I don't believe he is as nonchalant and lax as he gives the impression of being. He is a very genuine lad, a nice soft lad. I've known him since we played for England Schools together, and I have a lot of time for him. He has a great, dry, Brum sense of humour. It surprises me that people don't ask for his opinion more often during the game. He is in about the best position to see what is going on, is very astute and is a quick assessor of the situation.

He hasn't had it easy, because he was promised his cap when he came to Lancashire, and he still hasn't got it. To me that isn't on – if anyone can keep for two and a half seasons in the first team, I think they deserve their cap. They've messed him about in the batting order; he's batted everywhere from three to eleven, I think. If they built him up and encouraged him, which is what he needs, he'd make a very good number eight. A great asset, I believe.

He is a person who mustn't be knocked down. Some people respond to being told they're hopeless, but that doesn't work with Chris. He needs patting on the back and to be told 'Well done' all the time. Keeping wicket is a thankless job, because if you do it well nobody notices, at the end of the day you just walk off – that is all. You very rarely see a wicket-keeper being clapped off first. If he has a bad day – or a below-average day – everybody notices. So you don't gain any glory, just kicks, and it would be nice if a bowler or a senior player came up to him occasionally and said, 'Well done, Tosh, I thought you did great.'

If I had to criticize him, I would say that he doesn't work quite hard enough at his game, and as a result he hasn't realized his potential yet. If he worked harder, he could be a better batsman. I don't really think he could improve much on his keeping, but if he worked at it he might tidy it up a little. He could look a bit more active as a keeper, although that's just his style. But I'll take the bowlers' word for his ability.

The game was called off early, so we got an early start to Leicester. Harvey came in the car with me. It only took us one and a half hours, so we got there mid-afternoon, arriving at a typically faceless, plastic hotel, having left behind a magnificent one. We had a coffee in the room while waiting for the bus to arrive, and then a quorum assembled to pile into my car and go 'shopping in town'. An afternoon feast at McDonald's proved to be the order of the day – Little Ted loves junk food. I bought a silly pink jacket and a couple of belts.

In the evening I didn't want to drive, and there was only one pub in walking distance of the hotel. It smelled of stale sweat and socks, and the carpet was rolled chewing-gum. The lads played pool while Little Ted and I played the fruit machines, which shows how bored I was. I took four pints of Guinness on board, then went back to the hotel.

The Headless Chicken arrived to make his début, Walt has gone off to the Test and Clive is coming in for Patto.

31

Leicestershire v. Lancashire, first day
Leicestershire 327 (Briers 61, Cobb 59, Watkinson 5-109,
Makinson 4-119); Lancashire 17—0

Winker had a blinder — 40 overs with his sore feet and he got 5 wickets. The Headless Chicken bowled well, showing no sign of nerves.

It was cold and damp, and we decided to field. I passed the day chatting to the umpires, Jackie Birkenshaw and David Constant.

AUGUST

1

Leicestershire v. Lancashire, second day
Lancashire 278 (Lloyd 131, Fowler 10)

I am not opening at the moment. The two second-team lads,
David Varey and Mark Chadwick, bat well together, and they
have decided that it protects me at the moment and helps the
rest of the lads psychologically. Supposedly I am also the best
batsman, at least when Hubert isn't playing.

But then I'm told to bat at number three, which doesn't
make sense. Given those criteria, it seems to me the best place
for me to bat would be five or six, which is what Hubert
thinks too. As it is, I end up with the worst of both worlds,
not batting in my usual place, but then being pushed in first
wicket down, which is regarded as the hardest place to bat,
not exactly a rest either mentally or physically. So I start
thinking that being one of England's most successful openers
is not good enough for Lancashire. But trying to work out
our outfit is like trying to decide the course of a rudderless
ship.

The Headless Chicken had a memorable first championship
innings. When he went in it was 231-9, and Hubert still
needed ten for his century. He stuck it out while they added
another 47, Tony accumulating two of them.

It was Winker's birthday, so we organized a kissogram for
him at the Cricketers, the pub next to the ground in Grace
Road. He is a good cricketer, but possibly too much of an all-

rounder for his own good. He has been bowling off-spin some of the time this season, and he can bowl some very good balls; he spins it, and with his height he gets good bounce, which is important for spinners. But inevitably he hasn't got control at the moment, and in limited-over matches, and on other occasions too, they still want him to bowl seam. He says mixing the two doesn't worry him, and I can understand him being reluctant to give up seam because it would mean he probably wouldn't play in the one-day side. And having had a long struggle to get accepted as a good player – he was always the first person to be dropped when things were going wrong – he doesn't want to lose out. I think he is the kind of player you want in a side, because he is always a real trier who puts in a good level of performance, but he has always been undervalued at Old Trafford.

2

Leicestershire v. Lancashire, third day
Leicestershire 327 and 207-3 dec. (Cobb 66 not out,
Whitaker 66 not out); Lancashire 278 and 81-8
(Fowler 13, De Freitas 5-39). Match drawn

We were set 257 in one hour plus 20 overs, which was ridiculous. And then we collapsed anyway.

I really don't feel like playing. I am not fit enough. My head mobility is restricted, and I am apprehensive about damaging it further. I am just passing through the season at the moment. All I really want to do is rest and get fit again.

But at the same time I am torn, because I cannot face the reality that I am not fit. My performances are reflecting my feelings, and I am being a fool to myself by carrying on, yet I don't want to quit because I would feel like a chicken. How very illogical it all is.

3

Worcestershire v. Lancashire, first day
Lancashire 168 (Fowler 0); Worcesterhire 46-2

The nightmare continues. It was cold and the ball seamed all over the place. I was back to opening because we left out Mark Chadwick to bring in Thatch – a spinner for a batsman on a seamer's wicket.

4

Worcestershire v. Lancashire, John Player League
No play, rain

A wet Sunday in Worcester.

5

Worcestershire v. Lancashire, second day
Lancashire 168 and 124-6 (Fowler 4); Worcestershire 264
(Smith 67, Radford 57 not out, Folley 4-39)

Today I got pretty close to saying that's it. I cannot go on like this. I'm not fit. I haven't been fit all season, really; but the trouble is that if I say so, it sounds as if it is an excuse because I am not playing well.

6

Lancashire v. Worcestershire, third day
Lancashire 168 and 165 (Lloyd 50 not out);
Worcestershire 264 and 70-3. Worcestershire won by
7 wickets.

We came second. Before we went out with them needing 70

to win, we had this amazing team talk: 'Come on lads, let's not mess about out there, let's look as if we're really trying.' I thought that was incredible, considering that it was seaming about all over the place.

Decision time. I can't go on any longer, so I've said I'm not fit for Saturday – the Roses match – and made an appointment to see Mr Markham. Then I drove up to Jesmond with Walt to play in an invitation match tomorrow.

8

England XI v. Rest of the World XI
Rest of the World XI 254-6 (Mudassar 67,
Kallicharran 56, Hookes 56, Allott 4-35); England XI
258-6 (Gatting 127 not out, Lamb 60, Fowler 12).
England won by 4 wickets

Henri was completely outrageous. There is a cemetery at one end of the ground, and he kept getting clonked into it. So I kept laughing and saying, 'Eeh, pitch 'em oop, Henri, keep going, son,' and all that sort of thing, and at the end of one over he screamed at me, 'You vindictive little bastard, if you don't keep quiet I'll flatten you.' He was shouting and screaming and I was only fifteen yards away. Greg Chappell, who was batting, couldn't work out what was going on. Afterwards Henri came as close to apologizing as he ever would, turning it into a big joke. I said, 'Greg Chappell was getting embarrassed, you idiot. He didn't know whether you were being serious, or what.'

And he said, 'I was being serious.'

'That just shows how stupid you are for an educated bloke, you big, dozy git,' I replied, and it was all good fun after that.

But Bob Willis, who was there in connection with the sponsors, said to me, 'I'm convinced that Henri thinks he is the best left-arm spinner that ever lived.' Which is a strange thing to say. But you often spot your own faults in other people, and I thought, 'Yeah, and you think you're one of the best fast bowlers that ever lived as well.' Because he doesn't think anybody else can play, nobody at all. On the tour of Pakistan I remember him saying to me that Zaheer couldn't play. I asked, 'How do you reckon that?'

'Well, don't you think you'd score runs playing on these wickets in Pakistan with their umpires?'

And I thought, 'Well, even if he has a point, I've seen Zed get 160 and 110 not out against us in a game. And if you consider his county record . . .' But Bob will say that your county record isn't everything. Which is just as well from his perspective, because his county record is awful.

I don't think I'm Goose's sort of player. He is a funny bloke — three people at once. You meet him one day and he is your best mate, and the next time you meet him he doesn't know you. Whether he is like that with everybody, I don't know. I just get the impression that I'm five foot nine inches, run about like a fairy and dress in bright clothes, and am just not his ideal sort of bloke. I've modelled clothes and for hair salons, and I don't think that fits his image of an England player. I don't quite know what it is, but I feel that he suffers me rather than enjoys my company. When we went to New Zealand I was averaging 55. I was rested for the match before the first Test. Kippy Smith got 150 in that game and I didn't feature in the Test, which reflected Bob Willis's way of playing it. It was always safety first.

He has got his own ideas, his own beliefs, and he is rigid. Yet at times he is completely contradictory. On my first tour he told us not to talk to the press. 'They are all sharks, they'll stuff you soon as look at you,' all that kind of thing. Yet within twelve months of packing up the game it's 'over to

Bob Willis for a few comments'. I'm told that the transition upset a few of the press. It certainly raised a few eyebrows among the players.

Another example of the same thing was his last-minute decision not to join Packer. That was his prerogative, but to then become so outspoken against the people who did just wasn't on in my opinion. And in things like that I get the impression he doesn't really know where he stands. He jumps from one side of the fence to the other.

10

Back in Mr Markham's office at 8.15 a.m. He told me, 'At this stage there is nothing you will do to your neck which will make it worse. Obviously there is still damage there, but you aren't going to make it any worse by the end of the season. The only problem is psychological. You know you've got a bad neck, and because you are tense about it, all the muscles around it, which are protecting it, are going into spasm, and that is why you can't move. If you can tell yourself there's nothing wrong with it and try to relax, you'll be all right.'

I won't say I came out of his office feeling a new man, but it was a huge weight off my shoulders him telling me that, and so I rang Leeds – and ended up feeling totally deflated. Obviously it was too late for me to get over there to play, but I told them what he had said and asked if they wanted me to go over for the Sunday game. And they said no.

'Why not?'

And John Abrahams said, 'We can't keep playing you because you aren't getting any runs.'

'What do you want me to do then?'

'We'd like you to go into the second team and score some

runs.' This was in spite of the fact that the player replacing me in the first team is averaging even less than I am.

So I said, 'You want me to go into the second team and prove that I'm a good player when the people replacing me haven't done that at all?'

'Well, don't look at it that way.'

'How am I supposed to look at it? That seems the logical way to me. I've proved to be the best player for the last three years. I've had a terrible year this year, I admit that, but I'd have thought the best thing to do would be to let me bat five or six, get me going again, and then shove me back up again.'

'Well, we don't really want to do that.'

'All right, I'm in the second team. But why am I not playing tomorrow in the Sunday League?'

And the answer I was given was, 'Because we've already got twelve players here.'

I couldn't believe what I was hearing. I said, 'Pardon?'

'Well, I've already told the lads they are playing.'

'What is that supposed to mean?'

'I've told them. You just go and have a rest.'

And at that I put down the phone, feeling more confused than ever. They didn't want me.

13

Travelled with the second team down to Banstead to play Surrey. Still not sure what is happening. I still feel confused about the whole thing.

14

Surrey 2nd XI v. Lancashire 2nd XI, first day
No play, rain.

15

Surrey 2nd XI v. Lancashire 2nd XI, second day
No play, rain

16

Surrey 2nd XI v. Lancashire 2nd XI, third day
No play, rain

What was I doing in Banstead?

17

As I hadn't got any runs, they couldn't put me back in. In the end there was almost a better side watching Manchester United beat Aston Villa 4–0 than there was playing against Notts this afternoon. Clive, David Hughes, Walt, who had got injured at Lytham in the last match, Shauny, Steve Jefferies, Alan Ormrod and Tosh all went to watch the football.

18

Lancashire v. Nottinghamshire, John Player League
Nottinghamshire 115-5; Lancashire 121-5 (Fowler 6).
Lancashire won by 5 wickets

We won a game restricted by rain to 20 overs a side. As you can see, I played. When I was told I said, 'Hang on, this is ridiculous. You had twelve last week. Why am I being picked this week?'

'Experience, and we know you've got the ability.'

'So you are telling me I'm good enough to come in once a week and smash Hadlee around, but I'm not good enough to come in and play normally against them in a three-day game?'

'Well, Chaddy can't accelerate.'

'What the hell are you picking him for in the first place if he can't accelerate? He's got to learn somehow. How come I'm a better player than him one day a week, to come in and improvise even though I am out of form, yet in a normal game I'm apparently not good enough to play?'

To say I am getting fed up is an understatement; not so much by not playing, although I am not happy about that, but by the way they are handling matters and because they are completely wrong, in my opinion. Clive can't understand why I'm not playing. He thinks I should bat five or six, but when I suggested that, Aby said, 'Well, who should I leave out?'

'That's not my problem,' I replied. 'That's your problem. Your problem is that you have got an international player who is not playing well, and you have got to get him back into form, or give him the opportunity to get back into form. You and I both know there is no point in playing in the second team.'

But the answer is that I am playing in the second team at Peterborough.

19

We had an incredible scene today. When we arrived our TV had disappeared — again! Having a television in the dressing-room has been a constant source of friction. For a long time they said we couldn't have one, because people would watch it while play was in progress. When we demanded to know what was wrong with that, they said, 'Batsmen don't like it.' That didn't make sense: if anyone objected it could be turned off; if no one objected, it could stay on. Some people like to watch it to distract them from the nervousness of waiting to bat. Clive falls asleep; some people listen to head sets and some read papers; others play cards. I couldn't see that TV is any different.

Eventually Jack brought one in. Then the club put it somewhere else. So we got another one. And this morning it had disappeared. And it caused a fearful row because no one would admit to any knowledge of it.

'Where's the telly?'

'It's been taken out.'

'We know that. Why?'

'Because you were watching it on Saturday.'

'What?'

'Because you were watching it.'

'What are you supposed to do with it?'

'We said you could have a telly in this room as long as it wasn't on during the hours of play.'

'So who's taken it out?'

And it took the combined efforts of Walt, Clive, Jack Simmons and myself having a fearful argument with everybody we could find to discover who had taken the TV out. Walt had a go at the chairman. Eventually someone said, 'It was Pete.' So we had a go at Pete. 'Do you think it'll make us a better side if we don't watch telly? Do you think it is going to make people apply themselves if they don't watch telly? There are millions of distractions if people want to be distracted.'

20

The TV saga took a further twist. It turns out that it wasn't Pete's decision at all. He was just carrying the can – or the television. It was John's decision. But he wouldn't stand up and say, 'I took it out because we agreed to something and you haven't stuck to it.' So instead he has made everyone look foolish, because he had everyone running round getting in a lather about it. And that sort of thing can screw up some people's days. It spoilt Simmo's day for one.

Now Aby has finally put his foot down, but put it down in the wrong quarter. So he looks foolish too. But that's the whole emphasis at our club — silly, niggly discipline, like banning sun-hats.

We came to Peterborough without Roger Watson and Gary Speak. It is the contracts meeting on Saturday, and the rest of the lads think their being left out means they will get the bullet. I think Little Pig is quite a good player and could be successful somewhere else.

Jeffo is with us, but he thinks he'll get the bullet too. We've all been told to report at the ground on Saturday morning. 'Bring your own axe,' Jeffo said.

I'm captaining the side and Harry Pilling is going to be twelfth man.

21

Northamptonshire 2nd XI v.
Lancashire 2nd XI, first day
Lancashire 231 (Hayhurst 59, Fowler 20);
Northants 22-1

Anus batted well. I got 20 on a bad second XI wicket. I spent some time talking to Steve Coverdale, whom I used to play against when he played for Yorkshire seconds. He is now the Northants secretary/manager. I asked him how he could combine the two jobs, because I would have thought they were both full time, but he said it wasn't like running a club with a Test match ground, and he had good back-up staff.

Geoff Cook, the Northants captain, never used to think there was a role for a manager. I disagree. I think you need someone who goes to the groundsman four days ahead to sort out the wicket, and who organizes the nets. You need someone who looks at the fixtures and says, 'We're playing Somerset, so we don't want something green and bouncy,' or, 'We're playing Middlesex when there's a Test on. That means they've lost two spinners and possibly an opening bowler, so why don't we make it a result wicket and we'll back ourselves.' I don't think a captain can be expected to look after his unit, and keep his mind fresh for all that that entails, if he has got to do the backroom job as well. But our problem is that we have got too many backroom people, and you can play one off against the other, with the result that you end up either getting exactly what you want, or alternatively getting nothing that you want.

When Jack Bond was appointed manager, it was supposed to simplify the situation, but all it did was complicate it. When Frank Hayes was captain you went to him and said, 'Can I do this?' or 'When are we going?' or 'Why?' And he had to supply the answers, because there was nobody else to go to. But when Jack came, you went to Frank and he said, 'You'd better see the manager.' So you went to Jack and he said, 'What does Frank say?'

And then they took on Pete Lever as first-team coach. That made it even more complicated. You went to see the captain, and he'd refer it to Pete. He'd say something, you'd start doing it, and the manager would then ask, 'Why did you do that?'

'Pete said I could.'

'What's it got to do with him?'

'Well, who am I to ask then?'

So then you ended up asking every one of them and getting different answers.

Now, if I wanted to go into Manchester for something, I'd ask John Savage, the second-team coach, because he is not the strongest. He'd say, 'What does Aby say?'

'Oh, he says it's all right.' But I wouldn't even have bothered asking Aby, because he would just tell me to get on with it.

So if you've got a brain in your head, you can play them all off against one another, and you either get them all arguing, or you can just do what you want. If I just went off without asking anyone, it would be the same. Pete wouldn't know whether I'd asked the manager, and the manager wouldn't know whether I'd asked Pete, because the two of them don't talk to one another. Aby wouldn't know what is going on anyway. So it is just chaos.

And if you are in a situation where there is no discipline, you exploit it. Everyone gets away with things when they can, especially sportsmen, because in the main they are like mischievous lads at school who, if they can take advantage of things, do. Not everyone, but that is generally the sort of characters they are – sharp, alert, the types who manipulate people. And that is where a manager is not a good thing, especially if you've got too many.

I like a strong structure. If there is discipline I'll adhere to it. I don't like chaos.

22

Northamptonshire 2nd XI v.
Lancashire 2nd XI, second day
Lancashire 231 and 58-6 (Fowler 6); Northamptonshire
179 (Jefferies 5-42)

At lunch one of the dinner ladies said, 'Can you come and meet the captain of my club?' I assumed she meant the captain of the club we were playing, so I went along happily, said, 'How do you do?' and made some polite conversation. I think I asked him about the wicket, and it turned out that he was captain of a club up the road. And he said, 'Are you fit now?'

I didn't want to go into long explanations, so I answered, 'Yes, not far off. I'm not so bad.'

And he said, 'You volunteered to come down here to get a bit of practice, did you?'

'Oh, no, I've been dropped.'

And he was so embarrassed he didn't know where to put himself. I said, 'Don't worry, it's all right,' but he was so flustered that in the end I had to excuse myself to get some lunch before we went back out. The woman had thought she would make his day by introducing him to me, but ended up spoiling it for him.

I organized an end-of-season do for this evening – a team meal at McDonald's. Harry didn't come. It was a bizarre sight, all of us sitting there in blazers and ties; we had to have jackets to get into the nightclub we were going on to – while punk rockers and parents with toddlers came in and looked at us open-mouthed, wondering what on earth all these people were doing with red roses on their blazers.

23

Northamptonshire 2nd XI v. Lancashire 2nd XI, third day
Lancashire 231 and 106; Northamptonshire 179 and 148.
Lancashire won by 10 runs.

I can't say that playing on this wicket has done me any good at all. And I wasn't the only one – Shauny got a pair. It was cold too. Jeffo pulled a muscle. Harry stayed in the tea-room and bar in his civvies, while Jeffo stood in the freezing cold. I said to Jeffo, 'Go off.'

'No. I'll stay. Harry's not changed, so he's obviously not bothered. I'd rather stay out here with the lads than sit on my own.'

That sums him up really. Half the blokes would have walked off at the slightest twinge. In fact, in his situation half the overseas players wouldn't even have come to Peterborough. He thinks he is going to get sacked tomorrow, but he wanted to play because he loves the lads.

I don't think the club have treated him right, really. They say he doesn't go into the nets enough, but he is an international player and he doesn't need to be told things like that. He needs to be helped, not bullied. And we haven't got a great record for handling overseas bowlers.

And after that early season blast, Patto hasn't really done it. Thinking back, he was tremendous against the Yorkies. He really ran in and was quick. But apart from that game and against Essex, he hasn't put it in. I hope it isn't the Colin Croft syndrome, he always used to steam in against the Yorkies and looked as if he was going to knock their heads off. Patto seems to think he is a West Indies fast bowler. But he hasn't proved that yet. He certainly could be. I don't know what it is – whether we don't treat people right or whether he is just naturally lazy, but it seems he doesn't want to work at it. If it comes for him, fine; but if not, he shrugs. And after those early performances he seems to have rested on his laurels. During one match I said to him, 'Come on, Patto, put your back into it for four overs, then you're off.'

And he said, 'It's too cold today.'

I thought at the time that didn't sound like somebody who is trying to prove something, more like somebody coasting through.

24

Lancashire v. Somerset, first day
No play, rain

Jeffo did get the bullet. So did Roger Watson and Gary Speak. So did Alan Ormrod. And so did Harry, although it was announced he had 'retired'. It comes to the same thing. He is not happy.

I am back in − if we play − and batting number five! It looks as if they've had a rethink.

Harvey was awarded his county cap, so we celebrated that.

25

Lancashire v. Somerset, John Player League
Match abandoned as a draw

26

Lancashire v. Somerset, second day
Somerset 329-4 dec. (Richards 120, Roebuck 88, Botham
70 not out)

We finally got going after an early lunch. The wicket did a bit, but we just couldn't bowl to Viv and Both. Both and Simmo were going to watch Burnley last night, and Jack found the only way to stop the slaughter: he told Both just past 6.20, 'If you go on any longer we'll never get to Burnley.' Both immediately declared.

27

Lancashire v. Somerset, third day
Somerset 329-4 dec., second innings forfeited;
Lancashire forfeited first innings, second innings 330-4
(Chadwick 132, Hayes 117, Fowler 15). Lancashire won
by 6 wickets.

I did bat at five, but without much success. Viv did me; I got out trying to smash him.

Once it was clear they weren't going to bowl us out, Both seemed to lose interest. He came off about three o'clock with some strain or other – the final Test starts on Thursday. When Somerset came off, Rupert Roebuck said, 'Burnley 1, Somerset nil.'

People don't understand Rupert. The first time I met him was in an England 'B' game, and he was captain. 'B' games are difficult affairs; you are on trial in a way, and since they are usually for up-and-coming players you often don't know your team-mates very well either.

It was pouring down, the light was bad, nobody knew what was going on, people only knew one another vaguely, and we were all sitting around in tense silence. I decided somebody had to say something to break the ice, so I just took the mickey out of Rupert. It was the time of the Falklands, so I asked him if he'd just got his shoes back from having them requisitioned as landing craft. And I got on well with him. I think he is just shy about coming to you, but if you go to him and provoke him he is fine. He has a reputation for being moody and temperamental, but he has never been that way with me at all.

28

India/Pakistan XI v. Rest of the World XI,
Bhopal Disaster match
India/Pakistan 225 (Sadiq 50); Rest of the World 226-8
(Kallicharran 66, Fowler 35). Rest of the World won by
2 wickets

I actually felt in touch for once, probably the best I've batted for weeks. I enjoyed batting with Kalli, who was in real nick and looked exceptional. I gave Pete Lever some stick: he bowled before lunch and then retired to rest his bones.

30

The lads have gone off to play Notts tomorrow and I've been left behind. I can't believe this. I've had one game at five – one *innings* at five – and I'm out again.

An interesting story from the contracts meeting, where they discussed all the players whose contracts were up. Jack Bond and Peter Lever were at the meeting giving their opinions; Harry Pilling and John Savage weren't, but that's by the by. At the end of the meeting the chairman said to Jack and Pete, 'By the way, gentlemen, we'll be discussing your contracts at the end of the season.' If that means they haven't decided whether to keep the manager and coach – and there are one or two mutterings coming from some of the committee – it's ridiculous, because they were taking their advice on the players. That's a bit like getting the captain of a ship to hire the crew and then sacking him.

We're going to New York at the end of the season for a week. It's being fixed up through a contact of Clive's. We'll play a couple of exhibition games.

SEPTEMBER

<u>4</u>

We are in Scarborough for the ASDA challenge – a good party.

<u>5</u>

Nottinghamshire v. Lancashire,
ASDA Challenge semi-final
Nottinghamshire 146-9; Lancashire 147-4 (Lloyd 73 not
out, Fairbrother 51, Fowler 12). Lancashire won by 6 wickets

I had a session with the manager. Whatever my criticisms of him in other areas, he is excellent at sorting out technical problems, and he said to me, 'You never get bowled round your legs, and that is unusual for a left-hander. All your problems are coming outside off stump because the ball is going across you. So move your guard over. Try taking off stump, then you won't be playing across the line.

That actually made sense. I gave it a try. I was caught flicking the ball off my legs, but I shall persevere.

<u>6</u>

Lancashire v. Derbyshire ASDA Challenge final
Lancashire 175-7 (Lloyd 50, Fowler 17, Finney 5-32);
Derbyshire 177-2 (Anderson 75 not out, Roberts 70).
Derbyshire won by 8 wickets.

<u>8</u>

Surrey v. Lancashire, John Player League
Lancashire 160-8 (Fowler 23); Surrey 164-2 (Stewart 74
not out). Surrey won by 8 wickets

<u>9</u>

The manager and coach have been given one-year contracts, so, effectively, they are on probation. It seems strange given the time they've had already, but I think politically they couldn't do anything else. They couldn't sack Jack Bond because it would reflect on Cedric's judgement in employing him. And if they had sacked Pete it would mean that we were back to square one and that the club has made a cock-up in the last three years by taking him on, which would make Jack Bond look a fool. So it was fairly obvious they were going to keep them.

I think John Savage is being moved sideways into schoolboy cricket. He has got an incredible amount of information – who all the lads are, their telephone numbers, all that sort of thing – and he might do that quite well. But it needs ordering; at the moment it is all on bits of paper in his pocket, or in his head.

The only forward step the club has taken this year is in getting rid of Harry. He cannot see why he is being released. He thinks he has been stitched up by the younger players, but if he believes that he is a fool. If I don't have any sway as an international, I'm sure the lads in the second team don't.

Alan Ormrod is taking over as second-team coach, which I'm sure is a good choice. And David Hughes is going to captain the second team, although I wonder whether he shouldn't still be a first-team player.

24

We had the end-of-season party last night. I didn't really fancy it at all. I didn't want to talk to anyone about cricket – I want to forget about cricket for a time – but it was quite fun. Everyone was presented with things. I was given my second-team cap and an electric switch so that I could switch myself back on. Andy Hayhurst got one of those big plastic tie-on bottoms which you strap round your waist; predictable, but quite funny. David Hughes, who is moving into insurance as an outside interest, was given a bowler hat and a false nose – he has a large natural one. Chris Maynard was given a dustbin lid with empty cans of lager tied round it; they reckon he drinks too much, and they call him Grover after the character in *Sesame Street* because they say he is always moaning and never has a good word to say about anybody. The hat was quite effective – it looked like an Australian hat, so he had it on all night.

Shauny was given a goldfish in a goldfish bowl. He was told: 'The reason we've given you this, Shauny, is we want you to watch it all winter. You'll see that no matter how many times it opens its mouth, nothing comes out.' John Stanworth then stuffed Shauny out of sight. He stuck his hand in his bag, got this bit of carrot out, waggled it around and then ate it. Shauny went mad. 'You've eaten me fish! You've eaten me fish! The rotten git, he's eaten me fish!' Of course everybody fell about. But then to cap it all, at the end of the evening just as everyone was leaving, Shauny was in the foyer carrying his fish and this drunken Scot rolled up to him, picked the fish out of the bowl and did eat it. This time Shauny thought, 'Oh, it's another bit of carrot, I'm not falling for that one again.' But in fact the Scotsman had quite calmly picked the fish out of the bowl, eaten it and then cleared off as if nothing had happened, and Shauny was left with this bowl of water. It was unbelievable to watch.

John Stanworth is a great lad. He loves talking, so they are always having him on about boring people. People excuse themselves from his company and leave him all alone. So they bought him a guide to talking to people and a set of candles which won't go out, no matter how many times you blow on them.

25

I haven't really written much about the last three weeks of the season because I was so depressed; if I had done, it would have sounded suicidal. If I could have foreseen events, I would have packed up for the season as soon as I found out what was wrong with my neck. Almost right at the beginning I'd have said, 'Right, I'm going to get my neck sorted out and I'll see you in however long it takes.' But once you embark on it and keep quiet about it, it becomes more and more difficult to open up, particularly if you are not playing well, because it looks as if you are making an excuse.

Talking to Mr Markham, he said a lot of the problem was psychological. If you know one bit of your body is damaged, the other muscles try to protect it, so you go into semi-spasm. Your brain tells your body not to move as a protective measure. And that was what was happening. Some days I couldn't bend down to tie my boots, and I would just have to come off and lie down. I might be batting without problems and then I would do something, not necessarily an excessive movement, that would cause a shooting pain in my neck and down my arms. I couldn't grip the bat properly and I would feel sick at times. So when that happened, I wasn't equipped to do my job.

It was the same with fielding, which was why I ended up some of the time in catching positions. There were days when I just couldn't run and bend down and I had to say to Aby,

'Do you mind if I stand still today?' But sometimes I had to say, 'Can I have a run today?' because I had to run around to keep myself loose; otherwise I would have stiffened up completely. It got to the stage where John didn't know whether I was having him on or whether I was serious: one day I would feel all right, the next I'd be dreadful; sometimes I'd feel both within the same day. I'd feel dreadful in the morning, well in the afternoon and then dreadful again after tea. It was a funny situation because sometimes I couldn't even say where the pain was. I just felt rigid.

Of course, this made it difficult, for them as well as for me. But after Liverpool, when it was clear that I had a serious problem, I didn't think they helped me. I thought playing me in the 10-over slog at Uxbridge, when they knew I wasn't quite fit, and then putting me in at three just showed no understanding. And it was then that I got to the stage where I thought, 'They know how injured I am, but they don't take it into consideration.' I felt that if I fell in a heap, the only person who would pick me up was me. Even though they said they would take my injury into consideration, when it came down to it they didn't. When I tried to tell them how bad it was, they acted as if they thought it was just an excuse because I wasn't playing well. So eventually I just called a halt.

I don't think they reckoned I should have gone and played at Jesmond and then been unavailable for the Roses match. And when I then called in fit, I suppose they wondered whether I was messing about or not. But things just went from bad to worse, and I got more and more fed up because I didn't think they handled things right at all.

Nor was the atmosphere in the club very good. There were rows right through the season, from the early arguments about the balls and the wickets, which went on for ages, right down to the end-of-season fracas about the television. That had been another ongoing dispute. And then, to cap it all,

New York was a shambles, and Walt and I came home early. The promoter, Bert Smith, had made all these promises. But by the time we flew out there, nothing had materialized. We had been promised a good hotel, but when we got there we were stuck out by the airport, miles from the city centre with no money, because that hadn't arrived, despite all the assurances. Naturally, the lads wanted some spokesmen. Clive had organized it – or put us in touch with Smith in the first place – and obviously Clive was the big lure, but he wouldn't respond. Simmo is Clive's big mate, but he is too nice a fellow to put his foot down and say anything. The manager came with us, but as a holiday, not in his capacity as manager. So it ended up being me and Walter. We got hold of him and said, 'Right, Bert Smith. We want a change of hotel now. And if you don't deliver what you promised us four weeks ago by tomorrow, we're going home.'

So he promised – again – and we did change hotels. The new one was at least in the centre, although it wasn't a five-star hotel by any means. But next day there was still no money, just more promises. So we had a meeting, Walt and I saying, 'Right, that's it, are we going?'

And Shauny came out with this incredible statement. He said, 'Bert's been trying. He just hasn't managed to do it for us yet. Let's give him another day.'

'Bloody hell, Shauny,' I said. 'He's had six weeks to organize this. We haven't been given anything. Things don't look like they are going to get any better. We've given him three deadlines and he hasn't met any of them. He's come late to meetings; and there's still no sign of anything coming. The only reason you want to stay is because it is New York. You are going to get ripped off by this bloke. You've asked us to speak for you and this is it. So please yourself.'

And they all backed down. When it came to the crunch they all backed down. So Walt and I came home on our own. I just felt very, very disappointed with the rest of the lads.

That was almost the last straw. I just wanted to get away and forget about cricket – I wasn't even interested in seeing the lads and saying goodbye, I just wanted to come back to Accrington and lick my wounds.

Another thing that happened while we were in New York was the announcement that Aby had been sacked as captain. You may sympathize, but the job, which was a very difficult one because of the season we were having, had got on top of him. There were too many forces trying to manipulate him. Advice came from all over the place and criticism from even greater areas, and poor Albert was left in the middle, a puppet with stretched strings. With Pete and Jack pulling in opposite directions a lot of the time, he didn't know where he was, and I don't think he stuck out for his own beliefs enough.

And he also probably didn't get as much support from us as he should have. When a senior player standing thirty yards from the wicket bellows, 'Oh no!' at a field or bowling change, it undermines the captain. And I contributed to his problems. An England player who had suddenly failed, complained of a bad neck all the time and was permanently depressed couldn't have helped.

But then I didn't feel he helped me. It was he who batted me at three when I requested to go in five or six, and it was he who dropped me from the side. And I feel I've lost sight of him as a friend.

Instead they have appointed Clive Lloyd, with Jack as vice-captain. We've had a youth policy for four years and we end up with a 41-year-old captain and 45-year-old vice-captain. That sounds like a confession of failure to me. It certainly doesn't look like a policy for the future. But I'm sure it wasn't Jack Bond's choice, or Pete Lever's. I suppose the argument is that Clive is only going to play half the games because he and Patto can't play together, and so they want Simmo as captain when Clive's away. But in that case it would have been better making Simmo captain. And if that's not the reason, then they should have picked a younger vice-captain to prepare him to take over. I don't understand it.

Simmo hasn't got the job in the past because of the way he is. He turns up at 9.45 or 10 a.m.; he doesn't have a net; he's always on the telephone. Nevertheless, he goes on the field and does his job – usually – although I think his age is beginning to show. But they wouldn't give him the job because they must have said, 'Can you imagine Simmo being captain and coming in at quarter to ten? Nobody'd bloody bother,' and all that business. Of course people would bother, because the atmosphere would be better immediately. Instead, there is only dissatisfaction, the result of all their trivial rules about getting people in unnecessarily early and banning TV and worrying about dressing in blazers. All the emphasis is wrong at Old Trafford.

But the time has passed now for Simmo to be captain. He has become so relaxed that he doesn't make the same effort as he used to. Where he used to be five minutes late, he is now fifteen or thirty minutes late. And if you do that for a time without anyone saying anything, you'll go on doing it.

This season Jack has not really been with us on the field. He's been doing his autobiography. He is heavily involved in other businesses, ranging from finding professionals for league clubs, selling little suitcases and bags with 'Simmons' printed on them, to trying to organize a massive indoor cricket and bowling centre. Most of his time was spent buried in scrapbooks and talking into a machine. He would often come back from the telephone in his vest and slippers, or put down his tape machine, pad up and go out to bat, and then as soon as he was out he would go straight back to the tape machine or telephone.

He has been a magnificent servant for Lancashire. In the

time I've been there I've seen him deteriorate physically. He has always been overweight, and perhaps because of that everyone adopts the attitude of 'Oh, that's Jack' and just lets it go, which is fine. But I don't want to see him make himself look foolish. He could always run round the boundary in his own fashion and pick the ball up, and he had a great arm. But over the last two or three years he has been getting slower over the ground, he can't turn and his arm is not so good. So for whatever reason – age, injury or weight – his fielding has deteriorated, and not only in the outfield. We now have to put him in the circle or in a catching position. But this season, out of ten chances off Mike Watkinson he has dropped nine. He has always been regarded as one of the best slip fielders in the country, so it is rather sad to see his performance drop like that.

Nor can he run quick singles any more, though he is still a fine asset with the bat. His bowling is probably the most accurate slow bowling in the country, and I cannot understand why he has not played a single one-day international in his career. I'm sure there are many people who have played for England who have not had the ability or the figures in one-day cricket to match Jack's.

But he is now forty-five, and I don't want to see him make a fool of himself when he is fielding or batting for Lancashire. He has been such a marvellous character that people have always laughed with him, and I would hate to see him get into a situation where, instead, people are laughing at him. But being the sort of bloke he is, I don't think he will ever retire. They will have to shoot him to stop him playing.

26

I went to David Markham today to see where we go from here. He said again that some of the problem was psychological, although obviously my neck injury is real enough. He is sending me to physiotherapy to try to get the calcification broken down, so I hope that will sort things out.

30

Today I went to see Phil Racle, a Manchester physiotherapist. He gave me a lot of neck-cracking manipulation and I'm having a course of various kinds of physiotherapy – traction, manipulation, etc. which I hope will work. My neck certainly felt looser after he had finished.

OCTOBER

2

There is no escape. I was mowing the lawn this morning, wearing my head-set, quite happy. This car drove by, stopped at the top, turned round, drove down again, slowly turned at the bottom and drove back up, stopping outside the house. This little kid jumped out, ran up and said, 'Can I have your autograph?' Mowing the lawn!

8

I have had a few invitations to speak at dinners this winter – local clubs, cricket societies, league dinners, that sort of thing. I suppose it's one way of passing the winter. I did the first one at Milnrow tonight. I think it was quite successful – I'd picked David Lloyd's brains about it beforehand. But as it was Mark Chadwick's old club, I told a story about him. At the end this bloke got up and said, 'I'd like to thank Graeme for coming along and taking the mickey out of one of the best players we've ever had!'

23

I heard on the news that Peter Roebuck has been made captain of Somerset. I've always thought he writes well, but this could be interesting.

28

I have been going to Phil Racle for a month now, and I can't say that I've noticed any real improvement. In fact it feels as if my neck is getting weaker. I can't sit in a chair or lie down in any one position comfortably. I am permanently in some pain and it is really getting to me.

The thing is that after my physiotherapy it seems easier for a time. When I get in the car to drive home, it seems to have done some good and I feel looser; but two days later I just feel as stiff as ever, and the discomfort is more constant. It is just making me permanently bad-tempered and fed up.

30

A year ago we set out for India. It seems like a decade. I cannot believe what has happened in that time. But it seems a fitting place to end the diary – at least until next season, when I hope the nightmare is behind me.

I am still going for physiotherapy, and that will obviously continue for a time. I can't say that I feel unqualified optimism about it, but we will have to wait and see.

PART THREE

THE ROAD BACK

Graeme's problems were a long way from being solved. He had an eventful winter, earning his living supply-teaching, modelling and speaking at the occasional cricket dinner. In between times he spent two weeks in the Cayman Islands and two more in hospital, and finally, as the new season arrived, separated from his wife.

Peter Ball

APRIL

1

As the previous entry in the diary suggests, I wasn't very happy when winter set in. I'd ended the season with a sigh of relief. All I wanted to do was pack my bags and get out. I had no interest in farewell parties, saying goodbye to the lads or even thinking about cricket. Of course it kept intruding, but I felt as though I had spent the last months of the season waiting for a nightmare to end; and now I had finally woken up, I didn't want any part of it. I just wanted to clear off and get my body and my head straight.

That proved a longer exercise than I expected. My neck didn't seem to be responding to the treatment; I was in fairly constant pain – or at least discomfort – and it was getting to me mentally. Things which I would normally have found funny, I couldn't. And I preferred this introversion anyway, because my relationship with Steph was not being helped by the pain I was in.

In November I started doing supply-teaching at my old school, which used to be Accrington Grammar School and is now Moorhead Comprehensive. I started doing that because one day my cousin's wife Val, who teaches domestic science there, came round with her heels covered in mud. I asked, 'What the heck have you been doing?'

'I've been refereeing a couple of football matches.'

Of course I asked why, and she explained that the PE teacher had had a knee operation. So I said, 'I could do that,' because I am a qualified PE teacher. The next day I had a

252

phone call from the headmistress asking me if I wanted to do some supply-teaching. I was going to the Cayman Islands towards the end of the month on a cricket tour, so I said I'd go until then. Obviously having lost my Test place and with no tour fee to get, our finances were considerably reduced.

I was therefore glad to go in. Apart from the money, I enjoy kids. On the Wednesday of the second week I was teaching the third- or fourth-years gymnastics — I forget which. We were doing different kinds of rolls — forward roll, backward roll, etc. — and one or two static balances. Then I got them to combine the two, and as an example did a backward roll into a handstand. And as I did the backward roll, pushing my neck down on to my chest, I pulled something again. I didn't let on to the class, but at the end of the day I was in absolute agony. I went home and all the muscles in the back of my neck were in spasm. By then I had had enough. I rang Mr Markham and said, 'I've got them again.'

He said, 'You had better come in,' and I went into hospital that night. I was on traction for a week. To complicate matters further, Steph and I were meant to be flying to the Cayman Islands with this Invitation XI run by Freddie Trueman. I desperately wanted to go because it was a chance for Steph and me to have a holiday together, and they let me out on the Saturday night so that I could fly out on the Sunday. They said, 'When you get back, get in touch with Mr Markham and he will have you back in and we'll really sort it out.' So we went off to the Cayman Islands, me wearing a collar on the plane because I was still uncomfortable. There was Frank Hayes, Brian Close, Jack Hampshire, Farokh Engineer, Robin Hobbs, Butch White, Chris Old, Trevor Bailey, Colin Milburn and Roger Freeland from British Airways in the party, as well as Freddie Trueman. I played in the first game and scored 50, which they said was the first 50 ever scored in the Cayman

Islands — another first. But as you would expect, my neck went again. It was so weak that all the muscles went into spasm and pulled the spinal column out of alignment. I just had to lie on the floor and try to relax as much as possible to get the muscles to relax — which they didn't always. Therefore I couldn't play in the last two games.

We arrived home on a Wednesday, the last week of November. On the Thursday I rang Mr Markham again. He took me into hospital on the Friday, and operated on the Saturday — a manipulative operation. He also put some cortisone into the damaged muscles. When I woke up, I wasn't sore at all. It was an uncanny feeling, as if someone had put some ball bearings in my neck. My head swivelled freely, and I had no pain, no discomfort, no restriction. Where I had very restricted movement before, I now had complete freedom. My first thought was, 'I'm waiting for the anaesthetic to wear off.' But it wore off and there was still no pain. It was as if somebody had turned a switch. Suddenly I felt physically whole again and the relief was enormous. I felt completely happy. It was absolutely brilliant.

So I went home. Mr Markham told me I had to strengthen the muscles, but otherwise to carry on as normal. I felt like a new person. Immediately he had finished the operation, I got the strength back in my hands. I hadn't realized I had lost the strength in my arms, and my hands in particular, until I went back to a job I'd been doing in the house before the visits to hospital. I'd been putting some pine planks on a bedroom wall, and when I went back to finish it off there was just no comparison. I had so much more strength in my hands that I could stick the wood in together and put it on the wall extremely easily. I had always had strong hands for my size, and that made me realize how much I had lost when I was not fit.

I felt completely changed — no pain, I was so much happier,

my sense of humour had returned. I became optimistic again. But then at Christmas we went up to Steph's parents at Newcastle. I didn't really want to go. Having spent so many Christmases away from home, and not having seen my own parents at Christmas for so many years in consequence, I really wanted to stay in Accrington. But Steph was determined that she wanted to go home. Things weren't really right between us; we weren't getting on, so I gave in and we went to Newcastle.

It was a disaster. We fell out. Neither of us enjoyed it and we both accused the other of making it the worst Christmas we'd ever had. I said to myself, 'This is the last time I'm coming up here!' Then, to cap it all, I was sitting watching television on Boxing Day when the muscles on my neck went into spasm again. That was the last straw. I felt absolutely devastated. I thought I had finally cured it after eight months of messing about, and now it had started again.

We went back to Accrington for New Year, and then I returned to see Mr Markham again. He said that the operation had been a success and the damaged joint was perfectly O K, but where I had torn the muscles there was quite a bit of scar tissue, and they weren't as strong as they could be. So he put some more cortisone in, and since then I've been perfect. And I had quite a good second half of the winter in most ways.

Immediately after the operation, in the first week of December, I went into Manchester to have lunch with the editor of the *Manchester Evening News*, Mike Unger. I was talking to him about the possibility of doing some work during the rest of the winter, but it turned out I couldn't because I wasn't a member of the NUJ, and he was having a few hassles with them at the time. Also at the lunch was Pamela Holt, who owns a fashion agency. Pamela asked me if I had ever done any modelling. I said I'd done a bit – a double-page spread for the *Manchester Evening News*, some work for a hair salon in Australia, some promotional work and a few other bits and pieces.

She said, 'That's a fair amount. Do you want to work for me?'

'Yes,' I replied.

So she said she wanted me to let her have a composite card – a pic on the front, three on the back and all my details (height, weight, eye colour, shoe size, inside leg and waist measurement, etc.) – which was going to cost around £120. I was a bit doubtful. I thought, 'Here we go, I'm going to shell out for this and never hear anything more about it,' because you tend to get these sorts of things suggested and never hear anything from the person again. But she seemed genuine, so I went along with it. And the first week of January she phoned and said, 'I've a job for you starting on Monday. Allied Carpets in Blackpool. Be there at 9 a.m.'

They wanted still photographs for the middle of a TV commercial for their January sale. I did a full eight hours, so I got my money back on the comp card straightaway. And after that I did quite a bit of modelling – books and catalogues, Dolphin Showers, Goldberg's department store in Scotland, which took me to Portugal for a week. And with a bit more supply-teaching and some dinners, that tided me over the winter and sent me back to cricket in a positive frame of mind.

22

We had a meeting yesterday and it was decided that there may be some games in which neither Jack nor Clive will play, and that I shall captain the side if that happens. Quite a leap for someone who couldn't get into the team at the end of last season! I suppose that, having just ditched Aby, they couldn't then give it to him, and Walt and I are the next senior players, so it came down to me. I've always said I wouldn't fancy being captain, but I'm actually quite pleased by the thought.

There was the press lunch today, and the manager evidently told the press that they will see a 'new Graeme Fowler' this season. I do feel in good nick. I was also told that Peter May had said at the Centenary dinner a couple of weeks ago that I hadn't been forgotten, which is encouraging.

26

Sussex v. Lancashire, first day
Lancashire 331-4 (Fowler 180, Fairbrother 84)

I should have got more than 180, but I was shattered by tea-time. I haven't got my match or mental fitness back yet. Nevertheless, it wasn't a bad start, especially as I was told twenty minutes before tossing up that I was captaining the side. I was nervous anyway, because I felt I was under pressure and being scrutinized. I'd played well in the nets and in the practice games, I'd trained hard and my neck felt perfect, and I was confident. But I know there are people around who are sceptical and are thinking, 'This is the game. You've done it in the nets, but this is where it really counts.' I felt that people were watching me and saying, 'He's playing for his place. He only got 400 runs last year. He's lost it, he doesn't care,' and I think this has answered it.

It wasn't as testing as it might have been. Imran isn't back yet, and Pigott wasn't selected for some reason, so despite losing the toss and being put in — the Hove wicket looked green — we coped OK, although Mendis lost out. Their lads reckon Adrian Jones can be quite lively; but in April, when bowlers are still feeling stiff joints and it is a bit cold, he was quite tasty when you are 80 not out.

It was wonderful being able to put myself in the right place at the right time just when I wanted to. It made me realize how restricted I was last year. I couldn't coordinate then as I wanted to. I didn't have the mental image of what my body wanted to do or of what I was trying to do. But now my neck has been sorted out, things seem to have fallen into place again. I feel as if I'm straight after being all bent and twisted. I can close my eyes, stand in front of the mirror and open them again to find my shoulders level, my neck level and my head straight instead of tilted.

That correction has helped me to get my hands in the right place at the right time and coordinate again. It was marvellous to bat and feel that I was in complete command of myself and that all I had to worry about was watching the ball. And the pressure to prove my ability again was compounded by being made captain – from the second team to captaining the side without playing a game. So I think that made me really concentrate. I went out thinking, 'This is it. It's now or never.' Thank heavens it is now.

27

Sussex v. Lancashire, second day
Lancashire 431-4 dec. (Abrahams 73 not out,
O'Shaughnessy 50 not out); Sussex 157-9

My first day in the field as captain. I enjoyed it, the only problem being bad light, which stopped us bowling them out in the day. Everything went right: Aby and Shauny scored at over a run a minute, so we were able to give ourselves a long time to bowl them out, and Walt and Patto both looked a lot more hostile than their bowlers.

Captaining Walt is easy. He knows exactly how he bowls: he bowls in the same way every day, wants the same field every day and gets his wickets in the same fashion every day. Occasionally someone might try to hook him and he surprises them and gets a wicket that way, but the vast majority are lbw, caught by the wicket-keeper or slips, or bowled. So he is easy to look after.

28

Sussex v. Lancashire, third day
Lancashire 431-4 dec. and 23-1 (Fowler 0); Sussex 160
(Allott 5-32) and 293 (Parker 78, Watkinson 5-90).
Lancashire won by 9 wickets.

What a good way to start a season, although we also won our first game last year. Perhaps we should play all our games in April, since we obviously cope with the cold better than the others.

I actually thought I made a contribution in helping Mike Watkinson get his wickets, which was really satisfying. He is playing as a 'speamer' as Tosh christened it — bowling seam or off-spin as the occasion dictates. Today he did it with his off-spin. Inevitably, because he is not bowling the stuff the whole time, and hasn't been bowling that style all that long anyway, his control isn't all it might be. But the thing about his off-spin is that all of a sudden he will get bounce from nowhere, and that is the important thing — not spin, but bounce. He gets his wickets in the right areas for an off-spinner, leg slip and bat and pad. Today he had licence to bowl. He kept getting square-cut for four, but I was able to say, 'It doesn't matter, we've got runs to play with and time. Even if they pass our total, we've got time to get the runs, so don't worry, just relax.' And he bowled well once he realized that it didn't matter if he went for eight an over, as long as he was taking a wicket every five overs.

I suppose my duck was inevitable, but it didn't matter.

I moved in with Steve O'Shaughnessy today. Ever since Christmas I have felt that communications between Steph and me had broken down. It had got to the stage where I didn't know whether I was right or wrong. I lost all point of reference, I couldn't tell whether I was being stupid or sensible, whether it was all my fault or none of my fault, all Steph's fault or none of Steph's fault. I just couldn't work it out. And it has been really upsetting me. I've found it very difficult to concentrate on anything.

Our relationship had become very superficial. We never spent any time together. It was all very matter-of-fact, quick conversations – 'What are you doing?' 'OK, see you later' – and leaving messages on the kitchen table for one another, or eating a meal and then rushing off with friends.

We have had problems since 1983, and I've tried and tried – in my own mind anyway – since it first blew up. We have discussed splitting up before on occasions, and I don't think either of us really wanted it. But we have been talking about it more and more, and all the time the lack of communication has been building up. And I just felt that I could no longer carry on this way. Something had to be done, because all I want to do now is concentrate on my cricket. And that is what I am going to do.

INDEX

FOR THE BEST IN PAPERBACKS, LOOK FOR THE

In every corner of the world, on every subject under the sun, Penguin represents quality and variety – the very best in publishing today.

For complete information about books available from Penguin – including Pelicans, Puffins, Peregrines and Penguin Classics – and how to order them, write to us at the appropriate address below. Please note that for copyright reasons the selection of books varies from country to country.

In the United Kingdom: Please write to *Dept E.P., Penguin Books Ltd, Harmondsworth, Middlesex, UB7 0DA*

If you have any difficulty in obtaining a title, please send your order with the correct money, plus ten per cent for postage and packaging, to *PO Box No 11, West Drayton, Middlesex*

In the United States: Please write to *Dept BA, Penguin, 299 Murray Hill Parkway, East Rutherford, New Jersey 07073*

In Canada: Please write to *Penguin Books Canada Ltd, 2801 John Street, Markham, Ontario L3R 1B4*

In Australia: Please write to the *Marketing Department, Penguin Books Australia Ltd, P.O. Box 257, Ringwood, Victoria 3134*

In New Zealand: Please write to the *Marketing Department, Penguin Books (NZ) Ltd, Private Bag, Takapuna, Auckland 9*

In India: Please write to *Penguin Overseas Ltd, 706 Eros Apartments, 56 Nehru Place, New Delhi, 110019*

In Holland: Please write to *Penguin Books Nederland B.V., Postbus 195, NL–1380AD Weesp, Netherlands*

In Germany: Please write to *Penguin Books Ltd, Friedrichstrasse 10–12, D–6000 Frankfurt Main 1, Federal Republic of Germany*

In Spain: Please write to *Longman Penguin España, Calle San Nicolas 15, E–28013 Madrid, Spain*

In France: Please write to *Penguin Books Ltd, 39 Rue de Montmorency, F-75003, Paris, France*

In Japan: Please write to *Longman Penguin Japan Co Ltd, Yamaguchi Building, 2–12–9 Kanda Jimbocho, Chiyoda-Ku, Tokyo 101, Japan*

Relative Strangers Maureen Rissik

Angie Wyatt has three enviable assets: money, beauty and a tenacious instinct for survival. She is a woman fighting for success in a complex world of ambition and corruption. '*Relative Strangers* is a wonderful, intelligently written novel – a pleasure to read' – Susan Isaacs, author of *Compromising Positions*

O-Zone Paul Theroux

It's New Year in paranoid, computer-rich New York, and a group of Owners has jet-rotored out to party in O-Zone, the radioactive wasteland where the people do not officially exist. 'Extremely exciting . . . as ferocious and as well-written as *The Mosquito Coast*, and that's saying something' – *The Times*

Time/Steps Charlotte Vale Allen

Beatrice Crane was the little girl from Toronto with magic feet and driving talent. She was going to be a star. It was more important to her than her family, than friendship or other people's rules . . . more important, even than love.

Blood Red Rose Maxwell Grant

China 1926. As Communist opposition to the oppressive Nationalist army grows, this vast and ancient country draws nearer to the brink of a devastating civil war. As Kate Richmond is drawn into the struggle, her destiny becomes irrevocably entwined with the passions of a divided China and her ideals and her love are tested to the utmost.

Cry Freedom John Briley

Written by award-winning scriptwriter John Briley, this is the book of Richard Attenborough's powerful new film of the same name. Beginning with Donald Woods's first encounter with Steve Biko, it follows their friendship, their political activism and their determination to fight minority rule to Steve Biko's death and Woods's dramatic escape. It is both a thrilling adventure and a bold political statement.

A SELECTION OF LIGHT READING

Imitations of Immortality   E. O. Parrott

A dazzling and witty selection of imitative verse and prose as immortal as the writers and the works they seek to parody. 'Immensely funny' – *The Times Educational Supplement*. 'The richest literary plum-pie ever confected . . . One will return to it again and again' – Arthur Marshall

How to be a Brit   George Mikes

This George Mikes omnibus contains *How to be an Alien*, *How to be Inimitable* and *How to be Decadent*, three volumes of invaluable research for those not lucky enough to have been born British and who would like to make up for this deficiency. Even the born and bred Brit can learn a thing or two from the insights George Mikes offers here.

Odd Noises from the Barn   George Courtauld

The hilarious trials and tribulations that George Courtauld underwent when he became a midwife on his wife's stud farm and found he didn't even know the difference between a mare and stallion. 'A cross between James Herriot and *Carry On Up the Haystack*' – *Daily Express*

The Franglais Lieutenant's Woman   Miles Kington

To save you having to plough through the classic works of literature, Miles Kington has abbreviated them and translated them into Franglais so that you can become acquainted with Thomas Hardy, Jane Austen, John Betjeman and many, many more in this rich and expressive language.

Goodbye Soldier   Spike Milligan

This final – for the time being – volume of Spike's war memoirs has our hero inflicting entertainment on the troops stationed in Europe, falling in love with a beautiful ballerina, and, finally, demobbed and back in civvies heading for home. 'Desperately funny, vivid, vulgar' – *Sunday Times*. 'He's a very funny writer' – *The Times Educational Supplement*

BIOGRAPHY AND AUTOBIOGRAPHY IN PENGUIN

Jackdaw Cake Norman Lewis

...om Carmarthen to Cuba, from Enfield to Algeria, Norman Lewis ...illiantly recounts his transformation from stammering schoolboy to the ...n Auberon Waugh called 'the greatest travel writer alive, if not the ...reatest since Marco Polo'.

Catherine Maureen Dunbar

Catherine is the tragic story of a young woman who died of anorexia nervosa. Told by her mother, it includes extracts from Catherine's diary and conveys both the physical and psychological traumas suffered by anorexics.

Isak Dinesen, the Life of Karen Blixen Judith Thurman

Myth-spinner and storyteller famous far beyond her native Denmark, Karen Blixen lived much of the Gothic strangeness of her tales. This remarkable biography paints Karen Blixen in all her sybiline beauty and magnetism, conveying the delight and terror she inspired, and the pain she suffered.

The Silent Twins Marjorie Wallace

June and Jennifer Gibbons are twenty-three year old identical twins, who from childhood have been locked together in a strange secret bondage which made them reject the outside world. *The Silent Twins* is a real-life psychological thriller about the most fundamental question – what makes a separate, individual human being?

Backcloth Dirk Bogarde

The final volume of Dirk Bogarde's autobiography is not about his acting years but about Dirk Bogarde the man and the people and events that have shaped his life and character. All are remembered with affection, nostalgia and characteristic perception and eloquence.

FOR THE BEST IN PAPERBACKS, LOOK FOR THE

PENGUIN BESTSELLERS

Illusions   Charlotte Vale Allen

Leigh and Daniel have been drawn together by their urgent needs, fin
a brief respite from their pain in each other's arms. Then romantic l
turns to savage obsession. 'She is a truly important writer' – Bette Da

Snakes and Ladders   Dirk Bogarde

The second volume of Dirk Bogarde's outstanding biography, *Snakes and Ladders* is rich in detail, incident and character by an actor whose many talents include a rare gift for writing. 'Vivid, acute, sensitive, intelligent and amusing' – *Sunday Express*

Wideacre   Philippa Gregory

Beatrice Lacey is one of the most passionate and compelling heroines ever created. There burns in Beatrice one overwhelming obsession – to possess Wideacre, her family's ancestral home, and to achieve her aim she will risk everything: reputation, incest, even murder.

A Dark and Distant Shore   Reay Tannahill

'An absorbing saga spanning a century of love affairs, hatred and high points of Victorian history' – *Daily Express* 'Enthralling . . . a marvellous blend of *Gone with the Wind* and *The Thorn Birds*. You will enjoy every page' – *Daily Mirror*

Runaway   Lucy Irvine

Not a sequel, but the story of Lucy Irvine's life *before* she became a castaway. Witty, courageous and sensational, it is a story you won't forget. 'A searing account . . . raw and unflinching honesty' – *Daily Express* 'A genuine and courageous work of autobiography' – *Today*

PENGUIN BESTSELLERS

Goodbye Soldier Spike Milligan

The final volume of his war memoirs in which we find Spike in Italy, in the movies and in love with a beautiful ballerina. 'Desperately funny, vivid, vulgar' – *Sunday Times*

A Dark-Adapted Eye Barbara Vine

Writing as Barbara Vine, Ruth Rendell has created a labyrinthine journey into the heart of the Hillyard family, living in the respectable middle-class countryside after the Second World War. 'Barbara Vine has the kind of near-Victorian narrative drive that compels a reader to go on turning the pages' – Julian Symons in the *Sunday Times*

Rainbow Drive Roderick Thorp

If Mike Gallagher (acting head of the Homicide Squad, Los Angeles Police Department) hadn't been enjoying himself in the bed of a married German movie producer, he wouldn't have heard the footsteps and seen the Police Department helicopter . . . 'Quite exceptional . . . powerful, gripping and impressive' – *Time Out*

Memoirs of an Invisible Man H. F. Saint

'Part thriller, part comedy, part science fiction . . . a compelling, often frightening novel. H. F. Saint makes the bizarre condition of his hero believable' – *Listener*

Pale Kings and Princes Robert B. Parker

Eric Valdez, a reporter on the *Central Argus* has been killed in Wheaton. His chief, Kingsley, suspects he was involved in the local pastime – cocaine smuggling. But, knowing Valdez's penchant for the ladies, it could be sexual jealousy. Spenser is about to find out. 'The thinking man's private eye' – *The Times*

Pearls Celia Brayfield

The Bourton sisters were beautiful. They were rich. They were famous. They were powerful. Then one morning they wake up to find a priceless pearl hidden under their pillows. Why? . . . 'Readers will devour it' – *Independent*

Cat Chaser   Elmore Leonard

'*Cat Chaser* really moves' – *The New York Times Book Review* 'Elmore Leonard gets so much mileage out of his plot that just when you think on is cruising to a stop, it picks up speed for a few more twists and turn' – *Washington Post*

The Mosquito Coast   Paul Theroux

Detesting twentieth century America, Allie Fox takes his family to live in the Honduran jungle. 'Imagine the Swiss Family Robinson gone mad, and you will have some idea of what is in store . . . Theroux's best novel yet' – *Sunday Times*

Skallagrigg   William Horwood

This new book from the author of *Duncton Wood* unites Arthur, a little boy abandoned many years ago in a grim hospital in northern England, with Esther, a radiantly intelligent young girl who is suffering from cerebral palsy, and with Daniel, an American computer-games genius. 'Some of the passages would wring tears of recognition, not pity' – Yvonne Nolan in the *Observer*

The Second Rumpole Omnibus   John Mortimer

'Rumpole is worthy to join the great gallery of English oddballs ranging from Pickwick to Sherlock Holmes, Jeeves and Bertie Wooster' – *Sunday Times* 'Rumpole has been an inspired stroke of good fortune for us all' – Lynda Lee-Potter in the *Daily Mail*

The Lion's Cage   John Clive

As the Allies advance across Europe, the likes of Joe Porter are making a killing of another kind. His destiny becomes woven with that of Lissette, whose passionate love for a German officer spells peril for Porter and herself – and the battle for survival begins.

Is That It? Bob Geldof with Paul Vallely

The autobiography of one of today's most controversial figures. 'He has become a folk hero whom politicians cannot afford to ignore. And he has shown that simple moral outrage can be a force for good' – *Daily Telegraph*. 'It's terrific . . . everyone over thirteen should read it' – *Standard*

Niccolò Rising Dorothy Dunnett

The first of a new series of historical novels by the author of the world-famous *Lymond* series. Adventure, high romance and the dangerous glitter of fifteenth-century Europe abound in this magnificent story of the House of Charetty and the disarming, mysterious genius who exploits all its members.

The World, the Flesh and the Devil Reay Tannahill

'A bewitching blend of history and passion. A MUST' – *Daily Mail*. A superb novel in a great tradition. 'Excellent' – *The Times*

Perfume: The Story of a Murderer Patrick Süskind

It was after his first murder that Grenouille knew he was a genius. He was to become the greatest perfumer of all time, for he possessed the power to distil the very essence of love itself. 'Witty, stylish and ferociously absorbing . . . menace conveyed with all the power of the writer's elegant unease' – *Observer*

The Old Devils Kingsley Amis

Winner of the 1986 Booker Prize
'Vintage Kingsley Amis, 50 per cent pure alcohol with splashes of sad savagery' – *The Times*. The highly comic novel about Alun Weaver and his wife's return to their Celtic roots. 'Crackling with marvellous Taff comedy . . . this is probably Mr Amis's best book since *Lucky Jim*' – *Guardian*

Only a Game? Eamon Dunphy
Edited by Peter Ball

'The best and most authentic memoir by a professional footballer about
sport that I have yet read' – Brian Glanville

The 1973–4 season that began so well for Republic of Ireland internatio[nal]
Eamon Dunphy, at Second Division Millwall ended in disillusionment.

This is his diary, written during those critical months, recording events fr[om]
the dressing-room. Never before have the joy and anguish of professio[nal]
football been so lucidly voiced.

'Eamon has put into words,' writes ex-Liverpool and Plymouth Argyle player,
Brian Hall, 'the intimate feelings when you suddenly realize ... that all the
years of sweating, working and developing relationships with everyone at the
club will now be evaluated in simple cash terms.'